THE UNIVERSAL CATECHISM READER

THE UNIVERSAL CATECHISM READER

Reflections & Responses

Mary C. Boys, S.N.J.M.
Francis J. Buckley, S.J.
Lisa Sowle Cahill
Lawrence S. Cunningham
Avery Dulles, S.J.
Peter E. Fink, S.J.
Monika K. Hellwig
David Hollenbach, S.J.
Elizabeth A. Johnson, C.S.J.
Raymond A. Lucker
Berard L. Marthaler, O.F.M.Conv.
William J. O'Malley, S.J.
David N. Power, O.M.I.
William C. Spohn, S.J.
John H. Wright, S.J.

Edited by Thomas J. Reese, S.J.

HarperSanFrancisco
A Division of HarperCollins*Publishers*

FIRST EDITION

Library of Congress Cataloging-in-Publication Data

The Universal catechism reader : reflections & responses / edited by
    Thomas J. Reese.—1st ed.
        p. cm.
    Includes bibliographical references and index.
    ISBN 0-06-066839-3
    1. Catholic Church.   Commisio ad Catechismum Redigendum pro
Ecclesia Universali.   Catechism for the universal church.
Provisional text—Controversial literature.   2. Catholic Church—
Catechisms.   3. Catechetics—Catholic Church.   I. Reese, Thomas
J., 1945–
BX1968.U66   1990
238'.2—dc20   89-46465
                                                                            CIP

---

90   91   92   93   94   VICKS   10   9   8   7   6   5   4   3   2   1

Contents

Acknowledgments

I am exceedingly grateful to the authors for the fine work they did under very tight deadlines. Their willingness to drop other projects and work on the catechism shows their love for the church and the seriousness with which they take the universal catechism. Not only did they examine the catechism from the perspective of their various specialties, but their suggestions and comments on each others' papers contributed to the refinement and clarification of ideas beyond what any individual author could have done.

Thanks also are due to my agent, John Breslin, S.J., and to the editors at HarperSanFrancisco who had the faith and wisdom to commit themselves to this project before the papers were written, in fact before the universal catechism was released. Their work in getting the book through production with speed, accuracy, and style is much appreciated.

I am also grateful to James L. Connor, S.J., director of the Woodstock Theological Center, for the encouragement he gave to this project from its beginning as a memo in November 1988. Finally, this project could not have been done without the generosity of contributors to the Woodstock Theological Center. In particular, we are grateful to an anonymous foundation and to thirty-five U.S. bishops who contributed to financing this project. We also express thanks to our other faithful friends and benefactors, especially to the Maryland and New York provinces of the Society of Jesus and the Woodstock Jesuit Community.

Although many generously contributed to the success of this project, the editor and authors are solely responsible for the words they have written.

Thomas J. Reese, S.J.
Woodstock Theological Center
Georgetown University

THE UNIVERSAL CATECHISM READER

Introduction

Thomas J. Reese, S.J.
Woodstock Theological Center, Georgetown University

The catechism fails to reflect contemporary developments in Scripture, history, liturgy, doctrine, catechetics, and moral theology.

In my opinion, the document needs to be totally rewritten.

The *Catechism for the Universal Church* is the most important document distributed in the Catholic church since the Second Vatican Council.[1] The universal catechism, which is to serve as a "point of reference" for national and local catechisms, will determine how the faith is passed on to those who will live their lives in the twenty-first century.

Religious education, both for adults and children, has always been an important ministry of the Christian community. If the faith is not passed on, it will die. If the faith is taught in a distorted way, Christians will live warped lives. As a result, religious education is a concern of the entire Christian community: students, parents, catechists, priests, religious, theologians, bishops, and Vatican officials.

After the Second Vatican Council, religious educators revised their methods and texts to reflect the reforms and teachings of the council. Incorporated into texts and courses were the fruits of contemporary Scripture scholarship, ecumenism, liturgical renewal, and a greater awareness of history and the development of doctrine. These changes did not come without controversy. The improvements were opposed by conservatives who wanted their children taught in the same way as they had been taught. Religious education also became a battleground for issues left unresolved by the council.

Most people welcomed the new approaches after the changes were explained to them. Most would also agree that mistakes were made in the trial-and-error period following the council. Teachers needed better training, and attention needed to be given to content as well as methodology. Few Catholics, however, wanted to return to the old and simple days of the *Baltimore Catechism*, the text that was in common use in the United States before the council. But these few were often vocal and active.

The first postconciliar attempt to give direction to religious education was through the *General Catechetical Directory*, issued by the Vatican in 1971.[2] After a long and extensive consultative process, the American bishops developed the highly successful *National Catechetical Directory* in 1977.[3] These documents guided religious educators and publishers in developing texts and courses.

Universal Catechism Requested

Some people were still not satisfied and wanted more specific directions from the hierarchy. In the 1970s Cardinals Silvio Oddi and Joseph Ratzinger of the Vatican curia advocated a universal catechism. In 1985 Cardinal Bernard Law of Boston called for a catechism for the universal church at the synod of bishops meeting in Rome. He argued that the world was becoming a global village and therefore a universal catechism was necessary and desirable. The synod agreed and adopted his recommendation. The synod report stated:

> Very many have expressed the desire that a catechism or compendium of all Catholic doctrine regarding both faith and morals be composed, that it might be, as it were, a point of reference for the catechisms or compendiums that are prepared in the various regions. The presentation of doctrine must be biblical and liturgical. It must be sound doctrine suited to the present life of Christians.[4]

On July 10, 1986, Pope John Paul II appointed a papal commission of twelve prelates, half from the Roman curia and half from around the world, to prepare a universal catechism. The Commission for the Preparation of a Catechism for the Universal Church is chaired by Cardinal Joseph Ratzinger, prefect of the Congregation for the Doctrine of the Faith. The two American members of the commission are Cardinal Law and Cardinal William W. Baum, then prefect of the Congregation for Seminaries and Educational Institutes.[5]

The catechism commission appointed an editorial committee of seven bishops (including Archbishop William J. Levada of Portland, Oregon) to do the actual work of writing the catechism after consulting with around forty experts.[6] The actual texts were written in English, French, and Spanish with additional translations into Italian and German. There is no Latin version. The work of the commission was coordinated by the staff of the Vatican Congregation for the Doctrine of the Faith.

The papal commission met in 1986 and determined that the catechism should be directed to bishops and others responsible for writing catechetical works. It would be organized into three parts explicating the Apostles' Creed, the seven sacraments, and the Ten Commandments. Later an epilogue was added on the Lord's Prayer. The commission also decided that "the Catechism should offer an organic and synthetic presentation which is as concise and complete as possible, of the essential and fundamental elements of Catholic doctrine on faith and morals in the light of the Second Vatican Council and in connection with the preceding Tradition of the Church. It is to draw abundantly from the sources of Scripture, Church Fathers, the liturgy, and the Church's Magisterium."[7]

Following these instructions, the editorial committee drew up an outline (schema) for the catechism that was reviewed by the commission in May 1987. In December 1987 a first draft (called "Advance Draft") was completed and circulated to some forty consultors. At a meeting in May 1988 the papal commission critiqued the draft and gave many suggestions to the writing committee which then had to recast the whole text.

A second draft (called the "Draft") was discussed by the commission in February 1989. The papal commission gave approval in principle to the draft but also suggested several changes to be made before its distribution to all the bishops of the world.

This "Provisional Text" (also called "Revised Draft") was sent with a cover letter dated November 3, 1989, to all the episcopal conferences in the world for distribution to all the bishops. The bishops were asked to respond to the draft before the end of May 1990. The 434-page, single-spaced, typeset document did not arrive in the United States until the middle of December, which meant that the American bishops had only five months to respond to the text. During this five-month period, there was no scheduled meeting of the National Conference of Catholic Bishops (NCCB). As a result, it was impossible for the conference as a whole to respond to the catechism.

The catechism was labeled "Sub Secreto" (under secrecy) with no explanation given for interpreting this phrase. Some bishops thought it meant that they could not show the text to anyone. Not until the end of February was this clarified when Archbishop Pio Laghi, the Vatican pronuncio, told CNS (Catholic News Service) that the secrecy protocol was meant to avoid wide distribution of the draft, not to prevent bishops from consulting with theologians and catechetical advisers. When a draft gets widely distributed, he said, it tends to get treated by some as if it were an official document and not just a draft. This interpretation is consistent with Cardinal Ratzinger's statement to the 1987 synod promising a consultation "of all the bishops of the episcopal conferences and, through them, of the catechetical institutes, theology departments and of other institutes expert in this area."[8] But the confusion over "sub secreto" left some bishops with only three months for consultation.

The bishops were asked to give their overall impression of the draft. Does it respond to the desires of the 1985 Extraordinary Synod? Is it an organic and synthetic presentation of the essentials of Catholic doctrine? They were asked whether each section of the catechism (creed, sacraments, Ten Commandments, epilogue) treated Catholic teaching in a synthetic, organic, and complete way.

In addition, the "Explanatory Note" that came with the catechism indicated that "only those recommendations (*modi*) will be taken into consideration which offer an alternative text for the revision." These instructions created a dilemma for those bishops who believed that the draft was totally inadequate. To send in some specific recommendations on language might be wrongly interpreted as an endorsement of the rest of the catechism. To abstain from sending in alternative texts could leave to the draft's supporters the task of modifying it. To send in numerous detailed recommendations would be a waste of time if the draft is ultimately rejected.

In January 1990 the president of the NCCB, Archbishop Daniel E. Pilarczyk of Cincinnati, created an ad hoc committee to review the catechism. Appointed to the ad hoc committee were chairs of six conference committees: Bishop Joseph P. Delaney of Fort Worth, Texas, chair of the Committee on the Liturgy; Bishop John R. Keating of Arlington, Virginia, chair of the Committee on Canonical Affairs; Archbishop Oscar Lipscomb of Mobile, Alabama, chair of the Committee on Doctrine; Archbishop Francis B. Schulte of New Orleans, chair of the Committee on Education; Archbishop J. Francis Stafford of Denver, chair of the Committee on Ecumenical and Interreligious Affairs; and Archbishop John F. Whealon of Hartford, Connecticut, chair of the Committee on Pastoral Research and Practices. Archbishop Lipscomb was appointed chair of the ad hoc committee, and the committee was served by the staffs that serve the various conference committees.

The conference staff circulated the universal catechism to about thirty experts in various fields of theology, catechetics, and canon law. The responses from the experts were overwhelmingly negative. The ad hoc committee then prepared a report on the catechism that was presented to the fifty-member NCCB administrative committee in March. The administrative committee received the fifty-one-page report only twenty-four hours before discussing it and had little time during its meeting to debate the report. As a result, the committee did not vote to endorse the report.[9] Instead, the administrative committee authorized its transmittal to the U.S. bishops and to the Vatican as a report of the ad hoc committee.

Woodstock Catechism Project

In order to assist in the consultation, the Woodstock Theological Center recruited fifteen scholars with expertise in Scripture, liturgy, doctrine, catechetics, and moral theology to analyze the catechism from their particular areas of expertise. The Woodstock Center is a research institute established in 1974 at Georgetown University to examine theological issues facing the church and contemporary society. Although our research was shared with the bishops, the project remained independent of episcopal control. Each scholar wrote a paper that was discussed at a symposium in late January 1990.[10] The papers, revised in light of the discussions at the symposium, make up this collection (throughout this book, reference to the catechism will be by paragraph number not page number). Some of the authors also gave a workshop on the catechism at the spring 1990 meeting of the Catholic Theological Society of America in San Francisco.

The collection is divided into five parts. Part 1 is a general overview of the catechism, part 2 is an examination of the creedal section of the catechism, part 3 looks at the treatment of the seven sacraments, part 4 examines the exposition of the Ten Commandments and the Lord's Prayer, and part 5 discusses how the catechism might be used.

Many of the authors of these articles are leading figures in American Catholic theology and catechetics. The first article is by Berard L. Marthaler, O.F.M.Conv., editor of *The Living Light*, an interdisciplinary review of Christian education. He is professor of religion and religious education at the Catholic University of America and author of *Catechetics in Context: Notes and Commentary on the General Catechetical Directory* (1973). He also wrote *The Creed* (1987), a commentary on the Apostles' Creed and the Nicene-Constantinople Creed. Father Marthaler examines the universal catechism to see how well it reflects the teachings of Vatican II and the church's catechetical traditions.

The second article is by Lawrence S. Cunningham, professor of theology at the University of Notre Dame. He is author of several books, including *The Catholic Heritage* (1983) and *The Catholic Faith: An Introduc-*

tion (1987). He focuses on the structure of the catechism and on what we can learn from the long tradition of catechesis in the church.

Next is an article by Mary C. Boys, S.N.J.M., associate professor of theology and religious education at Boston College. A widely recognized expert on the use of Scripture in catechetics, she is author of *Biblical Interpretation in Religious Education* (1980) and *Educating in Faith: Maps and Visions* (1989). Her article examines the important issue of the use of Scripture in the universal catechism.

After these introductory articles come three papers examining the treatment of doctrinal issues in the section of the catechism dealing with the Apostles' Creed. John H. Wright, S.J., professor of theology, Jesuit School of Theology, Berkeley, discusses how God, especially the Father and the Holy Spirit, is treated in the draft catechism. Father Wright is a past president of the Catholic Theological Society of America and is working on a book on God's providence.

Next is an article on how Christ is explained in the catechism by Elizabeth A. Johnson, C.S.J., professor of theology at the Catholic University of America. She is author of *Consider Jesus: Waves of Renewal in Christology* (1990) and articles on Jesus and Mary in *Thomist, Theological Studies,* and *Journal of Ecumenical Studies.*

The last article on the creedal section of the catechism deals with how the church is described, written by Avery Dulles, S.J., Laurence J. McGinley Professor of Religion and Society at Fordham University and an associate fellow of the Woodstock Theological Center. Father Dulles is professor emeritus of theology at the Catholic University of America and a past president of the Catholic Theological Society of America. He is author of *Models of the Church* (1974), *Models of Revelation* (1983), *The Catholicity of the Church* (1985), and many articles.

The next section of the catechism, and therefore of our collection, deals with liturgy and the seven sacraments. Discussing the treatment of the liturgy is Peter E. Fink, S.J., of Weston School of Theology, Cambridge. He is author of *Eucharistic Liturgies: Studies in American Pastoral Liturgies* (1969) and editor of the *New Dictionary of Sacramental Worship* (1990).

Following Father Fink's article is one on the sacraments by David N. Power, O.M.I., professor of systematic theology and liturgy at the Catholic University of America. He is a member of the editorial board of *Concilium* and co-editor of its volumes on the liturgy since 1970. He has written several books, including *Ministers of Christ and His Church* (1969), *Unsearchable Riches: The Symbolic Nature of Liturgy* (1984), *Gifts that Differ:*

Lay Ministries Established and Unestablished (1985), and *The Sacrifice We Offer* (1987).

The Lord's Prayer, dealt with by the catechism in an epilogue, is treated next by Monika K. Hellwig, professor of theology at Georgetown University and a member of the board of directors of the Woodstock Theological Center. She has written *Christian Creeds: A Faith to Live By* (1973), *Understanding Catholicism* (1981), *What Are the Theologians Saying?* (1970), and *Jesus the Compassion of God* (1983). For three years she was also the author of "The Word," a column on the Sunday liturgical readings, in *America*.

The moral section of the universal catechism is based on the Ten Commandments. An overview of the catechism's moral theology is given by William C. Spohn, S.J., professor of moral theology at the Jesuit School of Theology, Berkeley. He is author of *What Are They Saying about Scripture and Ethics?* (1984) and articles on moral theology in *Theological Studies* and other journals. He is a visiting fellow at the Woodstock Theological Center.

Examining the catechism's view of social ethics is David Hollenbach, S.J., professor of moral theology at Weston School of Theology and an associate fellow of the Woodstock Theological Center. Father Hollenbach has written *Justice, Peace, and Human Rights: American Catholic Social Ethics in a Pluralistic World* (1988), *Nuclear Ethics: A Christian Moral Argument* (1983), *Claims in Conflict: Retrieving and Renewing the Catholic Human Rights Tradition* (1979), and many articles. He was a consultant to the NCCB committee that drafted the pastoral letter on economic justice.

Looking at the treatment of sex and family in the catechism is Lisa Sowle Cahill, mother of four children and professor of moral theology at Boston College. She is author of *Between the Sexes: Foundations for a Christian Ethics of Sexuality* (1985), *Religion and Artificial Reproduction* (1988) and articles in *Theological Studies* and other journals. She was elected vice president of the Catholic Theological Society of America in 1990 and will become president in 1992.

The last three articles in our collection bring not only a theological perspective but also the experiences of practitioners in religious education. Francis J. Buckley, S.J., professor of theology and religious education at the University of San Francisco, is a past president of the College Theology Society and was a theological adviser to the U.S. bishops at the 1977 synod of catechesis. He is author of *Children and God* (1970), *Deepening Christian Life* (1987), and of several widely used catechetical series: *On Our Way* (1966–70), *New Life* (1971–74), *Lord of Life* (1978–81), *God with Us* (1982–84), *Familia de Dios* (1990). He worked with the American bishops on their pastoral letter, "To Teach as Jesus Did," and the *National Catecheti-*

cal Directory. Father Buckley discusses how the structure, style, and content of the catechism will affect religious education.

William J. O'Malley, S.J., teaches theology and English at Fordham Preparatory, Bronx, New York. He is also an actor, a director, and an author of numerous works on teenagers and religion. His writings appear frequently in *America*. His article discusses the universal catechism from the perspective of one who has taught high school students for twenty-eight years.

Finally, the collection closes with an article by the Most Rev. Raymond A. Lucker, bishop of New Ulm, Minnesota. He is author of *My Experience: Reflections on Pastoring* (1988). He was director of the bishops' conference department of education, 1968–71. He is widely respected by his brother bishops and was elected by the U.S. bishops to represent them at the 1977 synod of bishops, which dealt with catechetics. He stresses the need for consultation in developing such an important document and describes how beneficial was the wide consultation that preceded the American bishops' writing of their pastoral letter, "To Teach as Jesus Did," and the *National Catechetical Directory.*

Personal Reflections

No attempt was made to force a consensus position among the scholars who participated in the project. Each was left free to articulate his or her views on the catechism after having heard the comments of the other participants. Nor would it be proper for me to pretend to speak for all the participants. As a result, the reflections that follow are my own and do not necessarily represent the views of all the authors.

After reading the papers and listening to the discussions, I found at least seven significant issues that came up repeatedly during our consideration of the catechism.

First, is a catechism for the universal church necessary? The writers of local catechisms have available to them the same resources available to those who wrote the universal catechism: the Scriptures, the documents of Vatican II, the *General Catechetical Directory*, the teachings of the church and theologians through the ages. Will not a universal catechism short-circuit the study and meditation that should be done by authors of local catechetical works? Likewise, we must ask, is a catechism for the universal church possible? The prologue to the draft indicates that it does not attempt adaptations demanded by inculturation of the Christian faith which, it says, is the responsibility of local catechisms. But can any statement of the Christian faith stand outside history and culture? Does not

the draft itself reflect a particular culture and a particular school of theological thought?

Second, the four-part structure of the catechism came under heavy
criticism for compartmentalizing faith from life and worship. The catechism is divided into four parts: an exposition of the Apostles' Creed, the
seven sacraments, and the Ten Commandments with an epilogue on the
Lord's Prayer. This structure easily falls into the trap of presenting Christianity as a series of doctrines one must believe, a set of commandments
one must follow, and sacraments one must receive without any explanation of how what one believes affects how one lives and celebrates.
Liturgy and action need to be seen as a response to faith.

For example, one learns about God and then wades through pages
and pages before anything is said about how this knowledge might affect
one's life or how one worships. One learns that God is creator, but how
that affects one's actions (for example by being concerned about the environment) and one's celebration of creation is not explained.

Third, the catechism fails to distinguish what is essential from what
is less important in its teaching. Everything, from angels to the Trinity, is
presented without consideration of what theologians call the hierarchy of
truths. No distinction is made between infallible teaching and theological
opinions. Ignoring these distinctions confuses the faithful when something they thought was essential is later placed in doubt or changed.
Would it not be better to have a shorter statement of the essentials of the
faith?

Fourth, the universal catechism is seriously deficient in its use of
Scripture. Although it speaks of the need of considering literary form and
historical context of the Scriptures, it in fact uses Scripture in a proof-text
fashion. Texts are cited to bolster doctrinal teachings without respect to
context or literary form. As Archbishop John F. Whealon told the Hartford Courant, the catechism overlooks fifty years of biblical scholarship.
Anyone who learns the faith from such a catechism will be confused
when confronted with the results of contemporary Scripture studies. Nor
does the catechism give sufficient attention to the public ministry of Jesus
or his parables.

Fifth, the catechism has numerous quotations from the Second Vatican Council, but these quotes are selective and sometimes mistranslated.
For example, the council fathers had a long debate about the relationship
of the church of Jesus Christ and the Roman Catholic church. They ultimately said that the church of Jesus Christ "subsists" in the Catholic
church. The catechism changes "subsists" to "exists," in contradiction to
Abbott and Flannery, the two English translations of the documents of

Vatican II. The ecumenical and outward-looking thrust of the council is downplayed.

Sixth, the catechism lacks an appreciation of history and the development of doctrine. The sacraments are presented as if they were always celebrated in the manner they are today. And St. Paul and the Gospel writers are presented as if their theologies are not only identical but also the same as the theology expressed at Nicaea and Trent.

Seventh, in the United States at least, the sexist language of the text is unacceptable. One can no longer speak of "man" in search of God without upsetting significant numbers in the American church. Nor will Catholic feminists approve of language that speaks of the sexes being equal but complementary. One section of the catechism speaks of God choosing the "weak" and then goes on to list several women from the Hebrew Scriptures, including Judith. As Elizabeth Johnson notes in her article, one can say many things about Judith, but anyone who charms her way unarmed into an enemy general's tent and then cuts his head off is not weak.

In the discussion of the various parts of the catechism, many other problems arose. The catechism devotes only a couple of inadequate paragraphs to the relationship of science to religion and pages to the angels. The treatment of Jesus reflects a Christology that stresses his divinity so much that his humanity is almost lost. Little attention is given to his public ministry.

The treatment of the liturgy was a complete surprise to the scholars. The catechism describes the liturgy from an Eastern perspective, so much so that Peter Fink says it sounds like it was written in Constantinople rather than in Rome. Most Catholics brought up in the Western tradition will find this section very confusing. When the catechism goes on to treat the seven sacraments, it reverts to the Council of Trent's theology rather than the more participatory emphasis of Vatican II. The catechism even goes so far as to say that the Eucharist is not a meal.

The section on the Ten Commandments is praised for including much of the church's recent teaching on peace, social justice, and human rights. Sometimes the teachings were shoehorned in at strange points. For example, the treatment of human rights comes under the seventh commandment.

The Ten Commandments are treated in the catechism without any consideration of their historical and literary context, namely, the covenant between God and the Hebrew people he had liberated from bondage in Egypt. Scripture in fact plays a small role in the moral teaching of the catechism. When Scripture is cited, it is used in a fundamentalistic proof-text fashion. And the natural law is presented as a deductive system with unchanging absolutes that gives moral answers independent of context and motivation. The overall impression is that of a legalistic morality based on obedience.

In brief, the catechism fails to reflect contemporary developments in Scripture, history, liturgy, doctrine, catechetics, and moral theology. It is as if the last thirty years of scholarship in the church never happened. Official approval of this text, in my opinion, would be more than a setback, it would be a disaster.

The cover letter from Cardinal Ratzinger, chair of the catechism commission, asks bishops for specific amendments and suggestions. This presumes that the draft is fundamentally correct in content and methodology. On the contrary, in my opinion, the document needs to be totally rewritten. It cannot be saved by amendments that only tinker with the text. If this were a draft submitted to an ecumenical council, it would deserve an overwhelming *"non placet"* from the bishops. It is questionable whether a universal catechism is needed at all and whether the papal commission can write one that fulfills the criteria of being faithful to Vatican II and useful for the church.

Bishops and Others Respond

As the catechism gained wider distribution, others besides the Woodstock scholars commented on it. Few had much good to say about the catechism. One exception was Rev. Peter Stravinskas of St. John's University who told *Our Sunday Visitor* that he thought the first draft was well done. "It's an intensely scriptural document, uses Patristic sources, quotations from the present Holy Father," he said, it "has a wonderful reliance on the liturgy as a source of teaching the faith, and also of various saints."

On the other hand, Russell Shaw in *The National Catholic Register* called it a "bad first draft." He wrote, "From any point of view—liberal, conservative, whatever—criticism of this document is warranted."[11]

"The project should be abandoned," Rev. Richard McBrien of the University of Notre Dame told *The Philadelphia Inquirer.* "It's going to have to be pretty thoroughly revised," commented Germain Grisez, professor of theology at Mount Saint Mary's College, to the same paper. Professor Grisez, a member of the Vatican International Theological Commission, thought the revisions would take five or six more years. When the draft is ready, he said, the pope should give up his international travels for three years and give the catechism his full attention because "he's going to have to answer to Our Lord for every sentence in it."[12]

Nicholas Lash, professor of divinity in the University of Cambridge, was very critical of the catechism in an article in *The Tablet*. He called on the bishops "to reject the text in its present form, even as a basis for discussion."[13]

The most important response was that of the NCCB Ad Hoc Committee on the Catechism for the Universal Church. The members of the committee have been described as "doctrinal conservatives."[14] Yet, while phrased in polite episcopal language, the committee report was a devastating critique of the draft catechism. It noted many of the problems mentioned by the essays in this volume. The committee had consulted about thirty scholars and had received advanced copies of the essays in this volume. In the report, the committee called for a second round of consultations on a new draft.[15]

The pope's original deadline for the final version of the catechism was sometime in October 1990 during the synod of bishops, which would also be the twenty-fifth anniversary of the closing of the Second Vatican Council. This optimistic schedule had presumed that the first draft would be released in December 1989. It was also hoped that few amendments or criticisms would be sent by the bishops to the Pontifical Commission for the Preparation of a Catechism for the Universal Church meeting in September 1990 to review the amendments. Because of the criticisms directed at the first draft it is likely that the final draft will take years to complete.

PART 1

AN OVERVIEW OF THE CATECHISM

The Catechism Seen as a Whole

Berard L. Marthaler, O. F. M.Conv.
The Catholic University of America

The present draft of the catechism does not recognize aggiornamento *as an issue.*

It is not necessary to compile a new catechism if it does no more than expound traditional doctrine.

The immediate impetus for the *Catechism for the Universal Church* is well known. When the synod of bishops met in 1985 to evaluate the results of the Second Vatican Council, it recommended that "a catechism or compendium of all Catholic doctrine regarding both faith and morals be composed, that it might be, as it were, a point of reference for the catechisms or compendiums that are prepared in the various regions."

It is no longer a question whether a *Catechism for the Universal Church* is necessary or desirable. The recent distribution of a provisional text makes its ultimate appearance all but certain. The challenge now is to insure that the document, which is likely to shape the thought and attitudes of Catholics for generations to come, is the best we can make it. In the end, history will judge whether one catechism can serve the needs of a church that is truly catholic.

The English version of the provisional text is obviously the work of many hands, uneven in style, repetitious in places, and with some noticeable lacunae. Before the catechism appears in final form, a good deal of editorial work must be done to make the language more inclusive and readable. Biblical scholars, church historians, specialists in liturgical studies, and theologians with various specializations need to analyze its presentation of doctrine. They must insure that it is accurate, clear, faithful to Catholic teaching and practice on specific points, and that it truly represents the breadth and depth of Catholic thought.

The prologue to the provisional text states that the catechism is planned as a whole and "must therefore be read as a unity" (0021). The critique that follows, taking its cue from this directive, looks at the provisional text as a unit. It surveys the catechism's chief sources and makes some generalizations about how well it serves the catechetical ministry in our time.

In evaluating the provisional text I rely chiefly on criteria that are suggested by the catechism itself: How faithful is it to the spirit and documents of Vatican II? How does it fit in with the church's long catechetical tradition? How do the "condensed formulae" that appear throughout relate to the text and purpose of the catechism? Finally, I add a word on inculturation and a suggestion for the improvement of the text.

Vatican II

The prologue makes a conscious effort to link the catechism to the council. It cites the "renewed attention" that the catechetical activity of the church has attracted "under the impulse of the Second Vatican Council." By way of examples it points to the *General Catechetical Directory* (1971), the sessions of the synod of bishops on evangelization (1974) and catechesis (1977), and the corresponding apostolic exhortations *Evangelii Nuntiandi* (1975) and *Catechesi Tradendae* (1979). It recalls that Pope Paul VI regarded the documents of Vatican II as *"the great catechism of modern times,"* and states that "this present catechism draws its inspiration from these texts" (0009–10, emphasis in text).

The catechism is not, strictly speaking, "the catechism of Vatican II" in the sense that the Council of Trent "lies at the origin of the Roman Catechism" (0008). In its final session Trent decreed than an official catechism of the Catholic church should be published under the aegis of the Holy See. Vatican II was lukewarm to the notion of a single catechism for the universal church. Instead it mandated the compilation of a directory that "should deal with the fundamental principles of [catechetical] instruction, its arrangement, and the composition of books on the subject" (*Christus Dominus*, no. 44).

In the catechism's prologue Cardinal Joseph Ratzinger describes the catechism as an "organic and synthetic exposition of the essential and fundamental topics of catholic doctrine concerning faith and morals, in the light of the Second Vatican Council and in continuity with the preceding Tradition of the Church" (0017). From the way it uses the sources and addresses questions, the catechism obviously is intended to blend the new wine of Vatican II with the old wine of tradition.

The provisional text makes frequent reference to conciliar documents. The "Introduction" uses the "Declaration on Non-Christian Religions" (*Nostra Aetate*), the "Dogmatic Constitution on Divine Revelation" (*Dei Verbum*), and the "Dogmatic Constitution on the Church" (*Lumen Gentium*) in describing the human quest for God (chap. 1), the nature of revelation (chap. 2), and the response of faith (chap. 3). Nonetheless, these are overshadowed by the many quotations and references to Vatican I in chapter 3.

Part 1 on the creed, entitled "The Profession of Christian Faith," is subdivided into three sections (Father, Son, and Holy Spirit) and is the longest segment of the text. The first section, "I believe in God the Father," is replete with biblical and patristic quotations and citations. It contains dozens of references to Denzinger-Schönmetzer's collection of official church documents and to the works of St. Thomas. It seems to draw more on the *Roman Catechism*, Pope Paul VI's "Credo of the People of God," and the series of catechetical instructions that Pope John Paul II gave in his public audiences in 1986 than from the documents of Vatican II. The few quotations from the "Pastoral Constitution on the Church in the Modern World" (*Gaudium et Spes*) are used as proof texts, as are the passing references to *Lumen Gentium*.

Much the same can be said about the documentation in the longer second section, "I believe in God the Son," with two notable differences. First, there are several quotations and citations that link the life and work of Christ to liturgical documents (but a surprising absence of citations to the "Constitution on the Sacred Liturgy," *Sacrosanctum Concilium*). Second, the commentary on the creedal phrase "*incarnatus est de Spiritu Sancto ex Maria Virgine*" (1320–47) frequently refers to Vatican II's reaffirmation of the special place of Mary in Catholic tradition (*Lumen Gentium*, chap. 8, and *Sacrosanctum Concilium*).

One has to read well into the third section of part 1, "I believe in God the Holy Spirit," before the influence of Vatican II becomes apparent. The catechism again cites Pope Paul VI to the effect that *Lumen Gentium* has become "the great catechetical text on the Church" (1613), and the text begins to show greater reliance on the conciliar documents. The paragraphs explaining the mystery of the church, the "notes" of the church, and the communion of saints draw their substance from *Lumen Gentium*, supported with references to *Gaudium et Spes* and the "Decree on the Church's Missionary Activity" (*Ad Gentes*). The "Decree on Ecumenism"

(*Unitatis Redintegratio*) is quoted several times concerning the unity and oneness of the church; it is also cited concerning holiness and catholicity. One does not find, however, any reference to the "Decree on the Eastern Catholic Churches" (*Orientalium Ecclesiarum*).

The influence of Vatican II is more obvious in part 2, which explains how the church celebrates its faith in liturgy and sacraments, than in any other section of the catechism. The "Decree on Ecumenism" is cited on baptism and Eucharist; the "Decree on the Ministry and Life of Priests" (*Presbyterium Ordinis*) on ministerial priesthood. Isolated references to the decrees on religious life and the training of priests (*Perfectae Caritatis*, no. 2, and *Optatam Totius*, no. 10) are named in support of the esteem for virginity that "the Church has always shown" (2824).

Despite the many references to the conciliar documents in the section on the sacraments, the influence of Vatican II remains superficial. Avery Dulles notes in the pages that follow that the catechism, unlike the council, does not make the church its central theme. As a result, the ecclesial and paschal foundations of the sacraments, staked out in the "Constitution on the Sacred Liturgy" (*Sacrosanctum Concilium*), do not provide a grounding for the liturgy and sacraments. In the ancient tradition that Vatican II tried to retrieve and in the Eastern tradition to which the catechism makes frequent mention, sacramental catechesis is integral to the rites and symbols of celebration. But because the catechism slights the church as a community of believers, what does it mean to speak of "sacraments of initiation"? One can only agree with David Power's critique (later in this collection) that the catechism has missed an opportunity to model its presentation of the sacraments on the introductions (*praenotanda*) in the revised rites. The citations of the 1983 *Code of Canon Law* regarding sacramental discipline are not enough.

Part 3 is also subdivided into two sections: the first outlines principles of the moral life of Christians under the heading "The Law of Christ," and the second addresses specific issues, linking them to the Ten Commandments. The Vatican II documents most frequently cited in the first section of part 3 are *Gaudium et Spes* and *Dignitatis Humanae* ("Declaration on Religious Liberty"). These two documents inspired not only the letter but the spirit of much that is in these paragraphs. Since the "moral responsibility of Christians is not only concerned with personal faithfulness" but also with "the mission of the Church" (3009), it is not surprising that the catechism cites *Lumen Gentium* and *Ad Gentes*. It is in this context that the "Decree on the Apostolate of the Laity" (*Apostolicam Actuositatem*) is quoted to the effect that Christians are to witness to moral values and apply them "to the problems of our times" (3157–58).

There are relatively few citations of Vatican II documents in the section dealing with the commandments. The chapter on the first commandment has a subheading on liturgical prayer that references *Sacrosanctum Concilium* (3343–48) several times, and it is quoted again about the observance of Sunday in the chapter on the third commandment. The first mention of the "Declaration on Christian Education" in the catechism appears in the chapter on the fourth commandment, in paragraphs dealing with parental respect and responsibility (3475, 3480–81).

But in this chapter and throughout the section on the Ten Commandments, the conciliar document most often cited is the "Pastoral Constitution on Church in the Modern World" (*Gaudium et Spes*). Its influence is especially notable in the chapters that deal with contemporary issues, such as the chapter on the fifth commandment, where issues regarding the rights and dignity of the human person are addressed, and in the chapter on the seventh and tenth commandments, where these same issues are dealt with in the broader context of the solidarity of peoples, economic and social justice, and the quest for world peace. The chapter on the eighth commandment that explains "the duty to live in the truth" twice refers to the "Decree on Social Communications" when considering the responsibility of mass media (3782–83).

In part 3 the many cross-references to other parts of the catechism may partly explain the fewer citations of conciliar documents. These cross-references are not integral to the text itself and were probably added later by the editor (see 0021). Part 3 refers to several postconciliar documents: *Humanae Vitae* of Pope Paul VI; Pope John Paul II's encyclicals on work (*Laborem Exercens*), social justice (*Sollicitudo Rei Socialis*), and women (*Mulieris Dignitatem*). The document most commonly referred to, however, is the apostolic exhortation *Familiaris Consortio*.

The epilogue, a reflection on prayer in general and the Lord's Prayer in particular, takes its inspiration from the Sermon on the Mount. Frequent citations to the church fathers show a decided influence of the Eastern tradition, but the epilogue contains no reference to the documents of Vatican II.

Although the provisional text of the catechism makes frequent reference to the documents of Vatican II, the citations usually are used as proof texts. The catechism does not come to grips with the fact that *aggiornamento* (reform) represented a paradigm shift in the way that the church deals with modernity. In his opening address to the council, Pope John XXIII made it clear that it was not necessary to convene an ecumenical council to discuss "one article or the other of the fundamental doctrine of the Church." Pope John challenged the council fathers to take

> a step forward toward a doctrinal penetration and formation of consciousness in faithful and perfect conformity to the authentic doctrine, which, however, should be studied and expounded through the methods of research and through the literary forms of modern thought. The substance of the ancient doctrine of the deposit of faith is one thing, and the way in which it is presented is another.[1]

Just as a council was not necessary simply to reaffirm long-held fundamental doctrines of the church, a new catechism will not be very useful if it does no more than repeat traditional formulas. The provisional text is a partial success in isolated places like the section on the commandments where mention is made of contemporary social issues. Just as it is selective in quoting the documents of Vatican II, the catechism is selective about the postconciliar documents that it uses. There are frequent references, for example, to *Familiaris Consortio,* but one looks in vain to the paragraphs under the heading "How Is Scripture to Be Interpreted?" (0275–83) for a reference to the 1964 *Instruction of the Biblical Commission on the Historical Truths of the Gospels.* Instead one finds an allusion to "literary forms" that could have been written any time after Pope Leo XIII's encyclical *Providentissimus Deus* (1893) and a reminder that "ancient tradition" distinguished the literal, allegorical, moral, and anagogical senses of Scripture.

Vatican II's agenda was at its roots a search for a symbiosis of Christianity and modernity (see *Gaudium et Spes,* no. 11). The present draft of the catechism, however, does not recognize *aggiornamento* as an issue and offers little guidance for coming to grips with the social, psychological, moral, and religious changes described in the "Pastoral Constitution on the Church in the Modern World." Unless it is quoting this constitution, the catechism hardly even acknowledges the changes.

General Catechetical Directory

A specific and important aspect of the relationship of the catechism to Vatican II is the catechism's position vis-à-vis the *General Catechetical Directory.* The apostolic exhortation *Catechesi Tradendae,* promulgated by Pope John Paul II after the 1977 synod of bishops, directed that all who take on "the heavy task" of preparing catechisms should "take their inspiration as closely as possible from the *General Catechetical Directory,* which remains the standard of reference" (no. 50). The directory, "published in accord with the directive in the Decree on the Bishops' Pastoral

Office in the Church, n. 44," is very much a document of the council in spirit and content.² The directory was intended to provide

> the basic principles of pastoral theology—these principles have been taken from the Magisterium of the church, and in a special way from the Second General Vatican Council—by which pastoral action in the ministry of the word can be more fittingly directed and governed. . . . The errors which are not infrequently noted in catechetics today can be avoided only if one starts with the correct way of understanding the nature and purposes of catechetics and also the truths which are to be taught by it, with due account being taken of those to whom catechesis is directed and the conditions in which they live. (Foreword)

The directory provides a theoretical framework as well as practical guidelines for the church's catechetical mission. It identifies catechesis as a form of ministry of the word. Catechesis is distinguished from evangelization, liturgical preaching, and systematic theology, but "in the concrete reality of pastoral ministry, they are closely bound together" (no. 17). In this framework the *Catechism for the Universal Church* as a "compendium of the whole of Catholic doctrine, both of faith and morals" seems to fit better under theology than catechesis.

In its present form the catechism seems to have taken on the task that the directory says is proper to sacred theology, namely, "ordering the truths of faith according to an organic plan." It incorporates the same "norms or criteria" that the directory outlines for "the discovery and exposition" of the content of catechesis (no. 36)—the trinitarian and christocentric focus, its organic unity, and the analogy of faith. (It must be noted, however, that the directory is more explicit regarding the "hierarchy of truths.")

The directory adds, however, that "it is not possible" to deduce from these norms an order to follow in catechesis. In selecting a pedagogical method, one can "begin with God and proceed to Christ, or do the reverse," according to the circumstances of the learners (no. 46). It is impossible to compile a catechism (or any work) without a definite structure and order. One needs to be reassured, however, that the catechism allows the kind of flexibility that the directory finds necessary for effective and sound catechesis. For example, is the high Christology in part 1 of the catechism normative? Can catechetical texts, because of particular circumstances, begin with the human and proceed to the divine? In any case, a clear statement on the relation of the two documents would provide a better understanding of the purpose and parameters of the *Catechism for the Universal Church*.

The Church's Catechetical Tradition

A broader question asks how faithful the catechism is to the church's ancient catechetical tradition. The opening paragraphs of the prologue situate the catechism in the context of the church's mission to proclaim the gospel and to instruct the faithful in the teachings of the Lord. Quoting at length from *Catechesi Tradendae* (nos. 1, 2), the catechism describes catechesis as "the whole of the efforts within the Church to make disciples, to help people believe that Jesus is the Son of God . . . and to educate and instruct them in this life and thus build up the Body of Christ."

The prologue holds up the *Roman Catechism*, commissioned by the Council of Trent, as the exemplar for a *Catechism for the Universal Church*. The Tridentine catechism is praised for having "given rise in the Church to a remarkable programme of catechesis," and it is credited with inspiring the publication of numerous catechisms, "thanks to the work of holy bishops and theologians such as St. Peter Canisius, St. Charles Borromeo, St. Toribio of Mogrovejo, and St. Robert Bellarmine" (0008). It also cites the names of Martin Luther and John Calvin in a conscious effort to situate the catechism in "the great tradition" of sixteenth-century catechisms both of the Catholic and Protestant Reformations (0011).

It should be remembered, however, that the church's catechetical tradition is a good deal older than the printed catechism. There are in fact two catechetical traditions. Before infant baptism became the universal practice in the church, Christians were initiated into the community step by step in the catechumenate. This early tradition of practical catechesis makes instruction an integral part of the catechumenate. This tradition is described in Hippolytus of Rome's *Apostolic Tradition* of the third century and the *Peregrinatio Egeriae* of the fourth (also see Lawrence Cunningham's article in this collection). This tradition is represented by the prebaptismal instructions attributed to Cyril of Jerusalem and the mystagogical homilies of Augustine, Ambrose, John Chrysostom, and other fourth-century writers. These homilies were intended to nourish the lifelong conversion of the faithful by explaining the creed and sacraments in the context of liturgical celebration.

The second tradition is the catechetical sourcebook, such as Gregory of Nyssa's *Great Catechism* and St. Augustine's *Enchiridion*. It is ironic (or perhaps simply illustrative of a superficial use of patristic sources) that the universal catechism does no more than cite an occasional text from these latter two works. One would have expected the authors and editors of the catechism, men obviously steeped in the writings of the church fathers, to make an effort to link the *Catechism for the Universal Church* to the catechetical tradition and practices of the early church. Gregory composed the *Great Catechism* (A.D. 385) for an audience very similar to that intended by the universal catechism (0018), namely, "presiding ministers" who "have need of a system in their instruction."[3] Similarly, Augustine, as a favor to a certain Laurentius, wrote his *Enchiridion* to be a sourcebook of Christian doctrine.

> You are anxious that I should write a sort of handbook for you . . . containing answers to the questions you put, viz.: what ought to be man's chief end in life; what he ought, in view of the various heresies, chiefly to avoid; to what extent religion is supported by reason; . . . what is the starting point, what is the goal, of religion; what is the sum of the whole body of doctrine; what is the sure and proper foundation of the catholic faith.[4]

Augustine's *Enchiridion* shaped to a large extent the catechetical tradition of the Latin West and is a link to the practice of Christian antiquity long after the catechumenate fell into disuse. It presents an exposition of the creed, the seven petitions of the Lord's Prayer, and a very brief reflection on the twofold commandment of love of God and neighbor. In his *Retractationes* (2.63) Augustine describes the *Enchiridion* as a treatise on faith, hope, and charity. St. Thomas Aquinas referred to it when he wrote, "Three things are necessary for salvation, knowledge of what is to be believed; knowledge of what must be hoped for; and knowledge of what must be done. The first is taught in the creed which acquaints us with the articles of faith; the second, in the Lord's Prayer; and the third in the Law."[5] St. Thomas incorporates an explanation of the seven sacraments in his exposition of the creed under the phrase "communion of saints, the forgiveness of sins." It should be noted, moreover, that his series of sermon-conferences explaining the Apostles' Creed, Lord's Prayer, and Hail Mary, and the commandments was more in the tradition of instructions given by Cyril of Jerusalem than in that of the *Great Catechism* of Gregory of Nyssa and *Enchiridion* of St. Augustine.

The sixteenth century developed its own twofold tradition. In the Church of England the *Book of Common Prayer* made an effort to situate catechesis in a liturgical context, but for the most part catechetical instruction was divorced entirely from the sacraments of initiation. The prologue states that the plan of the universal catechism "is based on the great tradition of the catechisms both of the protestant Reformation (M. Luther, J. Calvin), and of the Catholic Reformation of the sixteenth century" (0011). Luther produced a *Large Catechism* (*Deutsche Catechismus*) and a *Small Catechism* (*Enchiridion*). (The universal catechism surprisingly makes no mention of the *Heidelberg Catechism*.) Similarly, Peter Canisius, Robert Bellarmine, and Toribio of Mogrovejo, who first produced large catechisms, found it necessary to produce abridged versions for practical use.

In suggesting that the *Roman Catechism* of the Council of Trent is the paradigm for the catechism, the prologue clearly situates it in the tradition of the great or large catechisms that are in fact theological compendiums. The prologue, however, does not advert to the significant differences in the organization of these texts.

The Tridentine catechism, "structured around four 'pillars': the Apostles' Creed, the sacraments, the commandments and the 'Our Father'" (0011), is something of a departure from medieval catechesis based on St. Augustine's threefold division. The organization of the *Roman Catechism*, inspired perhaps by St. Thomas, represents a reaction against Luther and Calvin. Because of his law-gospel theology, Luther ordered his catechisms under the headings commandments, creed, Lord's Prayer, and sacraments. Calvin structured the *Geneva Catechism* of 1545 (which belongs more properly to the category of "small catechisms") according to four parts of divine worship: faith, the Law (service and obedience), prayer (invocation of which the Lord's Prayer is the model), and the sacraments. Calvin's reformed ecclesiology is reflected in the way he divides the creed into four parts, Father, Son, Spirit, and church, with the sacraments treated at the end.

Sixteenth-century cognoscenti easily understood the implicit theology in the ordering of the Tridentine catechism, but is it as clear to Catholics in the twentieth? Does a slavish adoption of the structure of the *Roman Catechism* make it appear as if the *Catechism for the Universal Church* represents an attempt to pour new wine into old wine skins? It must be asked, therefore, whether a better structure, still faithful to the catechetical tradition of the church, might have been found for the catechism. The Second Vatican Council returned to the sources of patristic theology, and the provisional text of the catechism itself seems intent on retrieving their words and spirit. Might not a return to Augustine's categories of faith, hope, and love provide a structure that could be adapted to a fresh statement of the faith we profess, the faith we celebrate, the faith we live (0012–14)? As it is, by relegating the Lord's Prayer, an integral part of the catechesis on prayer in the sixteenth-century catechisms, to an epilogue, the catechism makes it look like an afterthought.

Condensed Formulas

There is some indication that its authors would like the new catechism to serve a dual purpose: first, it is to serve as a "compendium of all Catholic doctrine regarding both faith and morals," and second, it is to be a bridge to the smaller, popular texts that are used in practical catechesis. In describing how the *Catechism for the Universal Church* should be used, the prologue points out that "at the end of each section covering a particular theme, a series of brief texts sum up in condensed formulae the essential teaching. These 'In Brief' texts are provided as suggestions to local catechists for comprehensive, memorable formulae" (0025).

These "condensed formulae" must be evaluated from an editorial standpoint as well as from the standpoint of their purpose and substance in the context of the catechism as a whole. In the final appraisal, they are likely to be the most controversial element in the catechism's provisional text.

The first point that needs to be clarified is whether these formulas are intended to sum up "the essential teaching" *in the preceding paragraphs of the catechism* or whether they are summaries of "the essential teaching" *of the Christian message.* The two are not contradictory, but they are different questions. The first raises an issue of editorial judgment; the second raises issues of substance.[6] These questions surface because assertions made in the summaries are at best tangential to the preceding text.

Two examples in the introduction illustrate the point: One "In Brief" paragraph (0149) contains a quotation from *Gaudium et Spes* (no. 36) that does not appear in the earlier text; another (0294) introduces a quotation from Hugh of St. Victor not cited in what had gone before. It also quotes the well-known aphorism of St. Jerome, "to be ignorant of the Scriptures is to be ignorant of Christ," that is cited in *Dei Verbum*, but not in the body of the catechism text. As in the latter case, at times the "condensed formulae" represent an attempt not so much to summarize as to remedy deficiencies and highlight certain points omitted from the text itself.

In some places it must be asked whether the "In Brief" formulas are adequate summaries of the catechism text. The six formulas at the end of the first article on revelation (0228–33), for example, single out the covenant made with Noah but do not mention the revelation to Moses, the prophets, and Israel as a nation (0218–20).

The second point that needs to be clarified is the purpose of these "In Brief" texts. According to the prologue, they are to "provide suggestions to local catechists for comprehensive, memorable formulae" (0025). Does the catechism establish, as the Tridentine catechism did for many people, a "rule of faith" governing not only the content but the manner of speaking about the faith? The *General Catechetical Directory* speaks both of dogmatic formulas and prayer formulas (no. 73). The catechism makes no such distinction, and in paragraph 1010 blurs it by lumping the ancient baptismal creeds together with "the professions of faith" of the councils of Toledo XI (675), Lateran IV (1215), Lyons II (1274), and Trent (1564). The latter are theological statements hammered out in the crucible of controversy. The former, drawing heavily on New Testament language and having their origin in the liturgy, are of a different character—more like doxologies than tests of orthodoxy.

Also in need of clarification is a third point: Who are these "local catechists" and how are they to arrive at "comprehensive, memorable formulae"? Are they bishops, pastors, writers of catechisms, publishers of catechetical materials, the catechist in the field, the teacher in the classroom? It is debatable to assert, as the provisional text does, that "communion in the faith is not possible without a common language of faith, setting the standard for all and uniting all in the same confession of faith" (1001). (This reasoning echoes *Veterum Sapientiae*, the last gasp of the Latinists before the vernacular made its entrance into the liturgy and theological manuals.) But granted for the sake of argument that the catechism does not overstate the case, how can the matter be left to local catechists or even regional and national conferences of bishops?

A fourth point that needs clarification is the relationship of the "In Brief" summaries to the proposed glossary. The purpose of the glossary is "to permit easy access to the key-words of the catechism and to propose a basic lexicon for catechesis" (0025). Unless it is the intention of the authors to provide a list of official definitions or a basic vocabulary for "Catholic-speak," it is difficult to imagine how bishops and authors of catechetical materials will use the lexicon. And what criteria will be used?

The two-page sample glossary provides definitions for words beginning with *a*, from "absolution" to "auxiliary bishop." The last term, by the way, was not in the body of the catechism itself. Liturgical terms like *anamnesis* and the books of the Bible were not listed (at least, Acts of the Apostles, Amos, and Apocalypse are not described among the examples). On the other hand, if all the terms that Catholics commonly use are included in the lexicon, another volume might be called for. (*The Catholic Word Book* published by the Knights of Columbus runs to forty-four pages of six-point type!)

Finally, the "In brief" statements risk taking on a life of their own. The *Catechism for the Universal Church* (and, it is hoped, every catechism) "is planned as an organic exposition of the whole of the christian faith" (0021). Removed from their original context of the catechism, the summary statements lose any nuance and are in danger of being misunderstood and misused. It is not unthinkable, and in fact it is very likely, that church censors and self-appointed inquisitors will use them as a checklist to evaluate the doctrinal soundness of catechetical texts.[7]

The chief criticism of the *Baltimore Catechism* and similar works in that genre was that they never presented the Christian message so that it excited the imagination and moved the heart. Even after reading the four hundred-plus questions and answers, the ordinary believer did not understand how the faith we profess, celebrate, and live came together as an organic whole. The Nicene-Constantinopolitan Creed and, to a lesser extent, the Apostles' Creed, present the mystery of salvation in "comprehensive, memorable formulae" that maintain the organic unity of the message. It may be (as one could infer from the catechism) that the traditional creeds no longer express the church's "essential teaching" adequately, but despite whatever shortcomings they are said to have, the ancient creeds present the Christian message as an organic, living whole in a way that a compilation of summary statements of the kind found in the provisional text of the catechism can never do.

Inculturation

In his opening address to the Second Vatican Council, Pope John XXIII explained that it was not necessary to convene an ecumenical council to discuss "one article or the other of the fundamental doctrine of the Church." Controversies over the church's stance on particular issues may be symptomatic, but the problem facing the church today is broader and deeper than challenges to specific doctrines and moral teachings. Similarly, it is not necessary to compile a new catechism if it does no more than expound traditional doctrine. The catechism gives well-deserved attention to social issues and the traditions of the Eastern Catholic churches, but that hardly justifies the amount of time and energy being expended on the project, especially when it is all but silent on inculturation, a major issue—perhaps the major issue—of the day.

The prologue states that it is not the catechism's function "to supply the adaptations demanded by the 'enculturation' of the christian faith." It implies that inculturation is extrinsic to catechesis and leaves the matter of "catechetical methods" to "those who instruct the faithful" (0020).

Catechesis is of its very nature a process of inculturation, and inculturation in turn goes to the heart of the church's mission to proclaim the Gospel and make disciples among all nations.[8]

Pope John Paul II has addressed the issue of faith and culture on many occasions. In *Catechesi Tradendae* (no. 53) he stated, "The term acculturation or inculturation may be a neologism, but it expresses very well one fact of the great mystery of the incarnation. We can say of catechesis, as well as of evangelization in general, that it is called to bring the power of the Gospel into the very heart of culture and cultures." Again, at the time John Paul established the Pontifical Council for Culture he wrote in a letter to Cardinal Casaroli: "Since the beginning of my pontificate, I have considered the church's dialogue with the cultures of our time to be a vital area, one in which the destiny of the world at the end of the twentieth century is at stake."[9]

Many of Pope John Paul's most eloquent statements on the symbiosis of religion and culture were made on his travels to Third World countries, but he also addressed the issue during his 1987 visit to North America in talks and homilies before black Catholics, Native Americans, and the Hispanic communities.[10]

Inculturation is not simply a utilitarian appropriation of "certain cultural elements, religious or otherwise, that form part of the cultural heritage of a human group and use them to help its members to understand better the whole of the Christian mystery" (*Catechesi Tradendae*, no. 53). The pope sees an "organic and constructive link" between Christianity and culture: "The synthesis between culture and faith is not just a demand of culture, but also of faith. A faith which does not become culture is a faith which has not been fully received, not thoroughly thought through, not fully lived out."[11]

John Paul recognizes that catechesis in a multicultural church raises doctrinal and practical issues. The eucharistic liturgy illustrates the basic problem. Almost from the beginning Christians have celebrated the Lord's Supper in different languages and rites. Language is chiefly a matter of translation, but rites taken as a whole embody cultural phenomena that extend beyond language and rubrics. Differences in linguistic and cultural expression, and even schism between East and West, have not denigrated the significance of the Eucharist as the sacrament of unity. In the more narrow context of the Roman rite, however, there seems less latitude for cultural adaptation. The use of the vernacular notwithstanding, customs, dress, music, dance, and other forms of cultural expression are not allowed to obscure the substantial unity of the rite. What are the parameters of inculturation that permit the assimilation of one expression and not another? Publishers of catechetical materials and catechists in the field need answers to questions of this kind.

There is the delicate problem of retaining positive elements in local cultures while simultaneously safeguarding the integrity of the Christian message. As a form of ministry of the word, catechesis plays a prophetic role. It critiques false values, judges truth in light of the gospel and church teaching, and challenges elitism, racism, ethnocentricity, tribalism, and all forms of individualism and divisiveness. The *Catechism for the Universal Church* cannot be expected to address specifics, but it could draw on the addresses and writings of Pope John Paul to provide pastoral principles and guidance in the most problematic area that catechists face.

Twenty years ago the consultation process played an important role in shaping the *General Catechetical Directory*. The provisional text sent to the episcopal conferences for their critique was a pedestrian document that did not seem to address issues of the day. As a result of the consultation, however, two changes were made that considerably enhanced the general directory and made it a useful model for national and regional directories. First, the outline of doctrine was thoroughly reworked into the form that was eventually published under the heading "The More Outstanding Elements of the Christian Message." Second, part 1, "The Reality of the Problem," was added. The purpose of part 1 was described as follows:

> Since the essential mission of the church is to proclaim and promote the faith in contemporary human society, a society disturbed by very great sociocultural changes, it is appropriate here, with the declarations of the Second Vatican Council in mind, to sketch some features and characteristics of the present situation by pointing out the spiritual repercussions they have and the new obligations the church has as a result.

Despite the negative tone of the above introduction, the paragraphs describing the world and the church presented a fair statement of the opportunities and obstacles faced by ministers of the word.

A similar introduction to the *Catechism for the Universal Church* would go a long way in forestalling the charge that it offers an abstract presentation of Catholic doctrine far removed from today's world and the daily life of Christians. Truth may be timeless, but as Pope John Paul II insists, it is always incarnate in a particular culture.

It is no small order to expect a work of modest size to offer a "compendium of the whole of catholic doctrine, both of faith and of morals." Nor is the task made easier by saying, "it is intended to serve as a 'point of reference for the Catechisms or compendia that are drawn up in different regions'" (0016). Frequent references to Vatican II and even lengthy quotations do not insure that the *Catechism for the Universal Church* is faithful to teachings of the council or has captured its spirit of *aggiornamento*. The criteria for deciding the structure and contents of a new catechism cannot be divorced from the people, beginning with the bishops, for whom it is intended and the times in which they live. The provisional text marks a good beginning, but much more work remains to be done.

The Structure
of the Catechism

Lawrence S. Cunningham
The University of Notre Dame

There is, alas, far too much of this "shoehorning" of extraneous matter in the text.

This draft, in short, suffers from what computer people would call "information overload."

Because the First Vatican Council is so closely identified with the definition of papal infallibility, it is easy to forget that the fathers of the council debated at length the utility of a universal catechism. They intended to adapt the catechism of Cardinal Robert Bellarmine (which was written based on classes the great theologian conducted for laybrothers and children in Rome in the 1590s) to the needs of the day and impose it by precept on the church. The pressure to move to the infallibility question effectively sidetracked action on the universal catechism, and despite the debate and the expressed mind of the council, the catechism issue became a dead letter for the time.

The conciliar discussion on the catechism in Giovanni Mansi's *Amplissima Collectio* makes interesting reading. There was a genuine debate on: (a) whether a universal catechism was needed; (b) if it was needed, whether it would be mandated for the whole church; and (c) what shape the catechism should be.

The bishops were not of one mind. Some of the Germans were quite happy with the catechism of Peter Canisius. Others (notably Augustine Verot of St. Augustine, Florida) wanted no mandated catechism until the fathers of the council could see a finished project. Still others wanted a single catechism to supplant the plethora of catechisms that were then in use in their territories and not totally free from eccentric opinions or odd formulations. What all the bishops seemed to agree on, however, was that a catechism would provide an instrument of unity in the presentation of the faith.

Nearly a century later the preparatory commission for the Second Vatican Council toyed with the idea of a universal catechism but decided not to press the issue. The question of a catechism remained in the air, but it was not until the extraordinary synod of 1985 that the Vatican, at the special urging of Cardinal Bernard Law of Boston, decided to provide such a book. Pope John Paul II decided that the catechism should not be for the faithful but for the bishops, who would use it as the working model for catechisms suitable for their locality. Furthermore, the pope wanted a final draft for presentation to the bishops in 1990 (the twentieth-fifth anniversary of the closing of Vatican II) with publication to follow in 1991. What came to the bishops in late 1989 was a draft composed by the seven episcopal writers charged with producing the document. This draft was to be critiqued before it was amended and corrected for presentation to the bishops in late 1990.

In a 1987 report on the status of the catechism, Cardinal Joseph Ratzinger described the intention of the work as providing "an organic and synthetic exposition of the essential and fundamental segments of Catholic doctrine in matters of faith and morals in the light of Vatican Council II and in respect of preceding tradition in the church" in such a fashion as to have the characteristics of "essentiality, of integrity and of comprehensibility" so that it could be a "'reference point' for national and diocesan catechisms, which will be subsequent versions and necessary adaptations to suit local conditions."[1]

My remarks will be directed to the issue of the structure of the catechism. Does this draft of the catechism present itself to its readers (i.e., all the bishops) in an understandable and coherent way, taking into account the culture in which we live while paying due deference to the classic expressions of our faith as they have come down to us in the church's tradition? The glossary of terms, prepared by Archbishop William J. Levada of Portland, Oregon, was added expressly to insure that we possess, in the words of Cardinal Ratzinger, "a common fundamental basic language in the catechetical field." As a result, an ancillary question is, Does the glossary provide us with the fundamental language needed for all catechetical discussion in the church?

Behind these questions is the more basic question concerning the structure of the catechism: Is the catechism so written that these other goals are met? My remarks will examine the consequences of the decision to follow the ancient tradition of presenting the catechetical material as devolving from the classic triad of commentary on the creed, the

Lord's Prayer, and the Decalogue plus the later addition of a section on sacraments.

The Structure of the Catechism

The present catechism takes its basic structure from a framework that has a long history in the church: doctrine developed from the creed; ethics derived from the Decalogue; a section on the sacramental life of the church; and spirituality from a meditation on the Lord's Prayer. Catechesis on the creed, the Decalogue, and the Lord's Prayer dates from the early church. The section on sacraments is a postmedieval addition responding to an enhanced sacramental theology available after the rise of scholasticism and, subsequently, in response to the radical revisions of sacramental theology made by the Reformers. Only the glossary of terms is without a long tradition, but its putative purpose is to construct a common language of catechetical-theological discourse.

Catechism (from the Greek "to instruct") was an essential part of the process for those who desired baptism in the early church. By the fourth century this instruction, given by the bishop in the Lenten season before the Easter baptismal ceremonies, was loosely structured on the articles of the creed.[2] The creed itself developed most likely from the threefold act of faith in the persons of the Trinity embedded in the prebaptismal ceremonies. The creed had its own tortuous development. By at least the end of the third century it was already shaped much like our present Apostles' Creed (at least in the West; the Apostles' Creed is not known in the East). When Bishop Cyril of Jerusalem gave his famous course of instructions to the catechumens in 348, discourses six through eighteen were explanations of the creed as it was known in the city at that time.[3]

Later in the century, again in Jerusalem, we possess an eyewitness account of how this teaching was done. In her *Peregrinatio*, Sister Egeria tells how the bishop taught every day in Lent those who were inscribed for baptism after they had been assembled and exorcised by the presbyters. Her words deserve quoting:

> His whole subject is God's law; during the forty days he goes through the whole bible beginning with Genesis, and first relating the literal meaning of each passage, then interpreting its spiritual meaning. He also teaches them at this time all about the resurrection and the faith. And this is called *catechesis*. After five weeks' teaching they receive the creed, whose content he explains article by article in the same way as he explained the Scriptures, first literally and then spiritually.[4]

Cyril's sermons spawned any number of worthy imitators. We possess, for example, the *Explanatio symboli ad initiandos,* which may be constructed from notes taken at lectures by St. Ambrose in Milan. Four sermons (nos. 212–15) of Augustine were given during the handing over of the creed (*traditio symboli*) to catechumens in Hippo. We also have the influential work of Rufinus of Aquileia *Commentarius in symbolum apostolorum* (ca. A.D. 404) with its precious information about the development of creeds.[5]

By the sixth century the formal liturgically rooted catechumenate was in steady decline in the West. That decline brought with it, naturally enough, a concomitant decline in the formal catechetical lectures that were integral to it.[6] One thing that did survive was the conviction that a handy compendium of belief should possess the three formulas: the creed, the Lord's Prayer, and the Decalogue. All through the Carolingian and Ottonian period, episcopal synods and imperial decrees repeatedly directed parish priests to instruct the faithful at least in these rudiments of the faith. By and large these instructions meant that the three formulas should be memorized. Godparents were admonished to see that their charges learned these rudiments of the faith, and parish priests were encouraged to use them as the basis for instruction.

Other educational strategies were employed by the church, ranging from the art of the churches to the sermons from the Sunday pulpit. But the ancient enshrinement of the creed, the Lord's Prayer, and, to a lesser extent, the Decalogue never lost its central place in the church even after instruction was detached from the liturgical setting where it once was placed. The persistent hold that these formulas had on the church is shown by their use as legitimate topics for extended commentary by theological writers.

For example, in the Lenten season of 1273, Thomas Aquinas gave a series of vernacular sermons in the late afternoon for the benefit of both students and the public. His secretary, Reginald of Piperino, took extensive notes on these conferences held at the church of San Domenico Maggiore in Naples and translated them into Latin after the death of the saint in 1274.[7] We know that St. Thomas spoke on the creed and the Lord's Prayer. There is good evidence that he also lectured on the Decalogue and possibly on the Hail Mary, but these latter conferences may have been given earlier in Rome.

By the end of the Middle Ages innumerable examples of catechisms based on the creed, Lord's Prayer, and Decalogue were available in most Christian countries. For example, this template served for Luther's *Small Catechism* (1529), the instruction appended to the *Book of Common Prayer*

(1549), the *Heidelberg Catechism* (1563), the *Summa doctrinae Christianae* of Peter Canisius (1554), and the *Catechismus Romanus* (1566) mandated by the Council of Trent. The latter work, it should be remembered, was designed not for lay use but for the instruction and education of priests. In 1597 Robert Bellarmine wrote a catechism for children (*Dottrina cristiana breve*) and the following year the *Dichiarazione più copiosa* for catechetical teachers. It was Bellarmine's work for children that the fathers at Vatican I wished to adapt for a universal catechism.

In our own day the German episcopal conference commissioned a catechism that was published in 1985.[8] Structured on the Nicene Creed, this catechism, largely written by Father (now Bishop) Walter Kasper, contains within it an apologia for using this time-honored framework for catechetical writing. Despite the impatience of some with the older formulations found in the creeds, the introduction to the German catechism insists that there is good reason for maintaining the creedal template: "They [the creeds] always contain more than an individual time or an individual Christian can grasp. So they must always be unfolded and interpreted. But they cannot be given up, or we would break off community with those who have believed before us in great unanimity. But the church and the individual Christian would then lose their identity."

The Creed and Catechism: Some Reflections

Based just on the schematic survey given above, clearly a catechism derived from reflections on the creed has a long and hallowed tradition behind it. It is also clear that in its beginnings catechetical instruction took place within the context of the liturgy, and the material of that instruction derived from the symbolic handing over and handing back of the creed (*symbolum fidei*). The persistence of the creedal structure of catechetics paid implicit homage to this old usage, but it also had a useful pedagogical function: one could learn the creed by rote and from that schema a systematic course of instruction could follow. As Marianne Sawicki has noted, the creed and the Lord's Prayer were the "curriculum" upon which the teaching for the catechumenate was based.[9]

At the same time, we need to recognize that the creed historically had deep roots in the worship of the church. Creeds had doxological as well as pedagogical and doctrinal functions. How impoverished does the creed become when it is detached from the context of the praying community? Frans Jozef van Beeck has recently published some cautionary words that are worth noting:

From a theological point of view, therefore, it would appear necessary to state that the renewal of the church demands that the *teaching* of the *Christian faith* retrieve its connection with *Christian worship*. This can be expected to have two beneficial results. It will restore the *baptismal profession of faith*—and hence the faith of *all* members of the church—to the center of the church's teaching. It will also retrieve an organic understanding, rooted in worship, of *salvation history,* and in the context of that narrative, of the *hierarchy of truths*.[10]

We must, therefore, be cautious lest a wedge be driven between worship and doctrine. What the church believes must be seen as part of its total tradition, and that tradition must be seen as a totality that encompasses not only right belief but right worship. After all, this is what orthodoxy most fully means. A simple canon of criticism, then, can be used in judging a catechism: Does it state the faith of the Christian assembly in such a way that it moves beyond mere affirmation of truths (as, for example, propositions) to a full encapsulation of the good news?

The Universal Catechism: A First Reading

The provisional text of the *Catechism for the Universal Church* is a bulky 434-page manuscript broken down into nearly 3,700 separate paragraphs and issued *sub secreto* for comment and/or emendation. After a prologue and introduction, the catechism is structured around an explanation of the Apostles' Creed, the seven sacraments, the Ten Commandments, and the Lord's Prayer. The authors of this catechism say explicitly that their intention is to follow the example of both Reformed and Tridentine catechisms by using the four "pillars" of creed, sacraments, Decalogue, and Lord's Prayer (0011).

It should be noted, however, that the writers do not follow these "pillars" with exactitude. The elements of the Apostles' Creed, for instance, are often amplified by reference to the Nicene Creed, since, as they say, it is "often more explicit and more detailed" (1014). Furthermore, the headings sometimes paraphrase the creedal statements by the addition of words (1294) or, for reasons that are not clear, by restating a phrase in Latin (1320). Generally, the translation of the Apostles' Creed employed is that of the International Commission on English in the Liturgy, which is identical with that of the International Commission on English Texts.

It is not my task to assess the theology of this catechism. My concern is a simple one: Is the traditional structure employed by this catechism useful pedagogically to provide that "organic and synthetic exposition of the essential and fundamental topics of catholic doctrine concerning faith and morals" (0017) which Cardinal Ratzinger sees as the aim of this comprehensive work? In short, as a structure does this catechism work toward its intended end?

Before answering this question we should make a few very preliminary but necessary observations to do justice to both the question and the answer.

First, this book is a catechesis and not a work of critical theology. Furthermore, it is catechesis that explicitly sees itself in historic continuity with ancient catechesis. For this reason it makes no reference to nor does it critically engage historical-critical biblical exegesis, just to cite a conspicuous example. Indeed, even before the catechism discusses Scripture in general, it already assumes a christological reading of the Psalms (see 0114 for an example) and understands Scripture as fully interpreted only "in the heart of the church" (0280) with the church being the final arbiter of the meaning of Scripture (0283).

We note this understanding of Scripture here not as a criticism but to locate the general tone of the catechism, which uses Scripture more like the liturgy and less like critical exegesis or current systematic theology. Fragments of Scripture or citations are cited frequently either as useful loci or proof texts of certain doctrinal formulations or as spiritual garnishes to the argument at hand.

Second, we should note that while the catechism is meant to be universal, and despite many allusions to the Greek patristic tradition and the Eastern liturgical sources, this is a catechism that is fundamentally Western both in its shape and in the way it develops theological themes and issues. The Western European provenance, culturally speaking, of this work must be recognized. Structurally this catechism is universal only in the more restricted sense of adopting the widespread assumptions of Western theological development. This is true both of the text of the draft and the glossary, if one can fairly judge from the glossary sample provided. The glossary seems almost lexical in nature and requires no further comment since it is a timid species of a theological dictionary.

The decision to organize the work around the Apostles' Creed is a Western framework because the creed is not common in the East. Also, the divisions of doctrine, sacraments, morals, and spirituality reflect a kind of theology that developed in the West and gave shape to both "sacred doctrine" and catechesis. This shape is a late medieval development in the church triggered by both an evolution in liturgical practices and the general illiteracy of the times.

This Western tone is evident if one compares the universal catechism with a contemporary one written from the context of Eastern theological developments.[11] Written by a team of French Orthodox pastors and now widely used in English-speaking Orthodox circles, this highly successful catechism is directed to those who instruct as opposed to the students themselves. What is most apparent about this work is its basic structure. The catechism develops an organic telling of the story of salvation from the Old Adam to the New Adam. It traces out the entire scope of the biblical vision from Eden to the New Jerusalem. Its only appendix is a compilation of prayers, some reflections on prayer, and a brief meditation on the Lord's Prayer. Most significantly, this catechism is meant to be studied from within the context of the liturgy and according to the unfolding of the life of Christ as it is proclaimed by the church in its corporate witness as an assembly of believers who hear and respond to Word and sacrament. Its framing device is biblical, beginning with Genesis and ending with John's Revelation.

Theologies differ not only in content, emphases, and presuppositions but also in what for a better word I would call "taste" or "style." Orthodox theology tends to be more cosmic, Platonic, and trinitarian. It is more preoccupied with a high Christology and, deriving from that, a more "sacred" sense of church, liturgy, and sacraments. One cannot promiscuously mingle styles, but awareness of the tensive differences between them serves as a useful corrective to the imbalances of each. There is, then, no invidious purpose in my comparison of the framework of the two catechisms. However, reading both of them in tandem does help to see the structural shortcomings of the draft of the universal catechism from a pedagogical and kerygmatic perspective.

As I reread the universal catechism draft I kept before my eyes this question: Were I to rewrite this draft, what organizational changes would I make to insure a better and less diffuse text?

Some Concrete Suggestions

The catechism's divisions based on creed, sacraments, Decalogue, and Lord's Prayer needlessly complicate and obfuscate the work as a whole. That complication arises from treating doctrine and praxis atomistically and not holistically. In other words, too great a conceptual gulf separates the assent of faith from the response that should spring naturally from that assent. As a result, the text becomes overintellectualized (a persistent temptation in Catholic theology) and spiritually undernourished. Furthermore, treating matters that are so organic in their theological context as separate and atomistic tends to underplay organic connections. It also downplays that "hierarchy of truths" that the Second Vatican Council tells us "vary in their relationship to the foundation of the Christian faith" ("Decree on Ecumenism," no. 11).

Let me cite some conspicuous examples of this lack of organicity.

The catechism takes the basic utterance "I believe in one God" (1019ff.) and develops in a systematic way the unshakable foundation of biblical faith in the unicity and unity of God not only as known but as revealed in being and love (1029). However, one must plow through over two thousand paragraphs before reaching a consideration of the worship of God when it is discussed under the rubric of the first two commandments of the Decalogue (3300ff.). In that latter consideration there is a section on atheism and idolatry both ancient and modern. The text then moves to a consideration of the obligation to worship under the commandments (3320). Prefacing that discussion is a small-print note that clearly indicates the structural weakness of the present organization of the work: "The subject matter which is covered from the point of view of morality in the following sections III to VI, is treated from a liturgical and a spiritual standpoint in Part II and the Epilogue respectively."

Without the constraint of the "four-pillar" structure, the authors could have enunciated in one organic manner the revelation of God as God who is worthy of worship alone and, in that worthiness, stands as an existential "No" to all forms of idolatry while simultaneously acting as polar opposite to those who deny his reality in the name of autonomy or self-sufficiency. This basic affirmation of the reality of God could have been further contextualized as an indispensable aspect of all biblical worship and as the beginning place to understand the links that exist between the three Abrahamitic faiths. Finally, a steady focus on the reality of God would have shown the inappropriateness (purely as a matter of symmetry) of inserting a paragraph on the taking of saints' names in a discussion on the name of God (3376–77) simply because the occasion affords the opportunity of talking about the biblical significance of naming. There is, alas, far too much of this "shoehorning" of extraneous matter in the text.

Examples of this kind could be multiplied, but I will give only one more because of its richness as a theological category: the doctrine of creation. Creation is discussed explicitly in section 1 of the catechism under the rubric of the creedal affirmation of God as "creator of heaven and earth." After a consideration of God as sole creator and the Christian understanding of the trinitarian nature of creation, the catechism quickly moves to God's free act of creation, the notion of "creation out of nothing," God's sustaining power over creation, the end of creation, and

divine providence (1110–34). The section ends with a longish consideration (1135–43) of the problem of evil. The exposition of creation reflects
the somewhat impoverished shape of the manual's old tract *De Deo
Creante*, although the later section "of heaven and earth" does mention in
passing the equality of the sexes in creation and their obligations of
stewardship toward the earth (1195ff.). One does not have to be an
enthusiast for "creation spirituality" to see that this is a very limited consideration of creation.

This arrangement is unsatisfactory because in later discussions
where the doctrine of creation is central one finds either no discussion of
what went before or a passing glance at the doctrine. Thus, in part 2
where the liturgy is discussed, a small-print coda (2122; small print signifies ancillary information) says that the liturgy uses signs and symbols
that refer to "creation" and that these "cosmic elements" which put us "in
mind of God" become the bearers of the saving actions of Christ. If the
creedal section on creation were better integrated into the section on
sacraments, it would have been possible to link creation not only to the
liturgy but to the whole notion of sacramentality that is at the core of the
Catholic Christian understanding of the economy of revelation.

Likewise, one finds at most parenthetical references to the doctrine of
creation in part 3 (ethics). Had the doctrine been more centrally highlighted, the section would look less like a grab bag of natural law theory,
casuistry, moral theology, and homiletics and more like a theologically
grounded catechesis. Thus, the section on natural law assumes the doctrine of creation (see 3094 and 3096) but does not root its discussion in it.
The introduction to its discussion on sexuality when considering the
sixth and ninth commandments cites the doctrine of creation but satisfies
itself with a generous slice of Pope John Paul II's *Familiaris Consortio* as the
basis for doing so.

Finally, creation stands as a fountainhead for any systematic theology
of prayer since both creation and the New Creation are pure and
unmerited gifts. The natural human response to that gift is a gratitude
that is not really distinguishable from adoration. While the issue of
prayer and worship repeatedly get addressed in the catechism, it is not
done in any integrated way. It is a minor issue in the section on the creed
(thus underscoring the Western penchant for detaching theology from
spirituality); central to the discussion of the liturgy in part 2 of the catechism; treated prescriptively in part 3; and then receives a direct but very
brief consideration (4001–4126) in the commentary on the Lord's Prayer
in the epilogue.

The scattered character of this catechism results from the decision to divide the work according to the old formula of the four pillars of creed, sacraments, Decalogue, and Lord's Prayer along with the inherited scholastic tendency to divide and classify theological materials. The net result of this decision is to treat heterogeneous materials under rubrics that are not organically related. The use of the "pillars" has the further unhappy consequence of artificially dividing doctrine, praxis, and spirituality when it is possible and desirable to treat them more organically and holistically.

This nonorganic character of the catechism reflects the use of the pillars in late medieval times as a pedagogical tool for teaching the faith outside the context of worship to mostly illiterate people. There was a two-step process in mind: memorization of the formulas of the creed and other pillars and then a very simple explanation of what each phrase meant. This was the bare minimum that was expected for fundamental Christian literacy. A reading of the introduction to Luther's *Small Catechism* makes this strategy clear. The *Large Catechism* was seen to be an amplification of the small one for people of greater literacy or intellectual capacity.

The use of this traditional structure, detached from its ancient roots in the liturgy, can provide comprehensive coverage of the faith (as this draft demonstrates), but the price paid is a lack of organic unity and a certain imbalance in favor of facticity. This draft, in short, suffers from what computer people would call "information overload." One could not imagine using it as a text for teaching. Happily, the authors themselves see it as a kind of template cum reference book. It serves the latter function better than the former.

This flaw, while grievous, is not fatal since, as the authors of the catechism say, the work is meant to be the resource for those "whose responsibility it is to compose and/or to approve national and/or diocesan catechisms" (0018). It is not a substitute for such catechisms nor is its aim to propose "catechetical methods" (0020). Furthermore, this catechism admits to a certain lack of thematic unity in exposition by urging that it be read as a "unity" and by encouraging the reader to follow the cross-references to allow the reader an "overall view of a theme and its interconnections" (0021). In short, the catechism is a "compendium" and a "point of reference for the Catechisms and compendia that are drawn up in different regions" (0016).

There is a lesson to be drawn from these statements. If this general framework remains in the final version of the catechism, those producing particular catechisms will have to think long and hard about ways of shaping their works so that the fundamental mysteries of the faith are highlighted not only as creedal statements but as affirmations with a doxological and kerygmatic character. The thicket of loosely related facts must be pruned in such a fashion that there shines forth the One in whom "the fullness of God was pleased to dwell" (Col 1:19). What we have before us now is a compendium; what we need are people who can turn it into a coherent proclamation of the Catholic faith. To do that, based on this document, will require rare skills and a willingness to question the very framework within which this work was written.

Scripture
in the Catechism

Mary C. Boys, S.N.J.M.
Boston College

The catechism tends to assemble Scripture texts without regard for the theological perspective of the source. Snippets substitute for sustained explication.

As a commentary on the Scripture, the catechism is an unreliable guide.

Whenever the church has given voice to its faith, it has drawn from Scripture, as the writer of Hebrews says, "in many and various ways." During its history the church has found the Scriptures a source for responding to numerous needs: apologetics, devotion (e.g., *lectio divina*), liturgy, aesthetics, and theology. The texts have been appropriated according to need. Seldom have they been expounded with careful attention to methodology.

Church documents typically cite Scripture without due regard for historical context. Even the bishops at Vatican II, who restored the centrality of the Scriptures, employed considerable latitude in their use of the Bible. Most of them had little in-depth involvement with the biblical movement that had helped to inspire the council. As Enzo Bianchi points out, "Their interventions were by no means inspired by the Bible even when they incorporated a formal recourse to it."[1]

That Scripture tended to be used in ecclesial documents of an earlier age as "prop and proof" is not surprising.[2] Today, however, the church must be faithful to its continuing tradition of interpreting the Scriptures when it writes a document like the *Catechism for the Universal Church*. This means taking seriously the inheritance of *Divino Afflante Spiritu*, the 1943 encyclical that set in motion historical-critical studies.

Grappling with the implications of historical and literary criticism in the *Catechism for the Universal Church* implies a transformative process, not merely rearranging or adding a thin veneer of the "latest thinking." A tension is implicit in this transformative process. Long-standing and familiar articulations of belief need to be expressed in a more nuanced fashion in order to reflect the findings of scholarship.

Other strains are evident as well in this catechism. One tension arises from the different genres synthesized in this "compendium of the whole of catholic doctrine" (0016). The propositional language of creeds and councils warily coexists with the narratives of Scripture. The prosaic coherence of this catechism awkwardly meets the poetic and parabolic character of the biblical text.

Other tensions arise from the different goals of exegetes and of the catechism's authors. On the one hand, the authors teach the certainty of faith ("Revelation . . . teaches us with the certainty of faith," 1241). On the other, because scholars often pursue densely complex questions, exegetes tend to avoid claims to certainty. The catechism illustrates this tension particularly in the sections on Jesus (1259–1530). Here categorical assertions abound. In the view of many Scripture scholars, however, the evidence demands more modesty. As Daniel Harrington says, "The more we know, the less we know. . . . A good deal more is known about Palestinian Judaism in Jesus' day than was known forty years ago. But in another sense we know less. Or at least we are less confident about simple and neat pictures."[3] Presumably, lack of confidence about simple and neat pictures makes composition of catechisms a precarious business.

These are not altogether unhealthy tensions. A catechism offers a synthesis; exegesis provides analysis. One should not expect a catechism to employ all the rigorous techniques of exegetes or to draw upon Scripture only according to the canons of the modern scholars. The Bible belongs to the church, not merely to the academy. Nevertheless, readers should find the *Catechism of the Universal Church* to be a reliable commentary on the Scriptures. Given the importance accorded Scripture study since Vatican II, one should expect to find an integration of the salient insights of critical scholarship into the life of the church. This catechism ought not to reverse the course of the church's biblical scholars.

The Principles

Even a cursory reading of the catechism reveals the pervasiveness of Scripture. Direct citations and references swirl through virtually every paragraph. The sheer volume of citations and references—thousands of passages employed to embellish, inspire, and prove—creates such a busy picture that the task of sorting out the patterns becomes imperative.[4] It is by scrutinizing the patterns that one discovers that the catechism has a straightforward, if inadequate, hermeneutical foundation. This is clear both in its explicit principles (0275–99) and in their employment throughout the document.

The authors, following Vatican II's "Dogmatic Constitution on Divine Revelation," establish from the outset that proper interpretation of Scripture requires cognizance of what "the human authors have really intended to mean and what God has indeed intended to make known to us by their words" (0275). The catechism mandates, therefore, that the church must take account of the special conditions of time and culture, such as literary forms, and ways of feeling, speaking, and telling stories (0276). It insists that Scripture is not to be read merely as a historical document but as an inspired work needing the guidance of the Spirit (0277).

Then the catechism lists three criteria for interpreting Scripture in conformity with the Spirit: attentiveness to (1) the content and unity of the whole of Scripture; (2) the context of the living tradition of the whole church; and (3) the analogy of faith, that is, to the coherence of the truths of the faith. These criteria deserve study. They not only offer a clue to the pattern of textual use, but they also signal problems that occur throughout the document. A word, then, on each principle.

The Unity of Scripture

The unity of Scripture, grounded in the unity of God's plan (0279), is crucial to the way the catechism draws upon biblical texts. But the way the catechism explains this principle obscures the distinctive standpoints of the various biblical books. The catechism tends to assemble Scripture texts without regard for the theological perspective of the source. Snippets substitute for sustained explication. For instance, in the paragraph describing Jesus' messianic entry into Jerusalem, John, Luke, Matthew, the Psalms, and Zechariah all are paraded in a sort of dizzying litany (1434). The life of Jesus is presented as a harmony, thereby obscuring, as Elizabeth Johnson points out, the distinctive Christologies of the New Testament writers.

Similarly, the authors have conflated biblical texts with patristic and conciliar teachings. As a result, the catechism offers a superficial congruence of sources. Thus, it exemplifies what the Pontifical Biblical Commission called one of the "hazards" of the classical approach to Christology:

formulating doctrine about Christ in language more dependent on the theologians of the patristic period and the Middle Ages than on the New Testament itself.[5]

The major consequence, however, of the emphasis on the unity of Scripture is the concomitant claim that the Old Testament is related to the New as promise to fulfillment (0287). Though it "still keeps its own value as Revelation," the Old Testament's "inexhaustible content" (0292) is brought forth by typological readings. Typology—using persons, situations, and events from the past to throw new light on present experience—plays a central role in the catechism, even if it is left undefined. Grounded in the assumption of promise and fulfillment, typology permits the authors of the catechism to read the Old Testament as a book about Jesus Christ:

> The coming of the Son of God on earth is so considerable an event that God wished to make ready for it during long centuries before; through rites and sacrifices, figures and symbols, he has made everything converge upon Christ; he foretells him, announces him by the mouths of a succession of prophets; he stirs up in the hearts of the human race a burning expectation of that coming. (1364)

Among the types most frequently discussed is that of the so-called Suffering Servant (1140, 1380, 1444, 1454, 1457, and 1563). Jesus' sacrificial death fulfills "in particular the prophecy of the suffering Servant"; he himself presented the meaning of his life and death in light of this image (1444). Through his obedience even to death, "Jesus accomplished the substitution carried out by the suffering Servant who 'offered his life in atonement' (Is 53.10), 'while he was bearing the faults of many' (Is 53.12) whom he justifies, 'taking their faults on himself' (Is 53.11)" (1457). It is in the songs of the Servant that the "features of the Messiah are above all revealed" (1563).

Such assertions stand in tension with recent biblical scholarship. Most exegetes would take issue with the claim that Jesus understood himself to be the Suffering Servant. They also would debate whether the writers of the New Testament so understood him. Around many points there is little debate, as exegetes (1) reject the sort of predictive prophecy and messianic proof-texting evident in the catechism; (2) situate the texts of the so-called Suffering Servant songs (Is 42:1–4; 49:1–6; 50:4c–11; and 52:13–53:12) in the context of Second Isaiah's consolation to the exiles; and (3) emphasize the complexity of the texts, particularly with regard to the identity of the Servant. The Servant may be the personification of the people of Israel, a righteous remnant of that nation, a corporate personality, the prophet himself, the Davidic dynasty, Zion/Jerusalem—all have been argued. The catechism prescinds from the exegetical problems by its simplistic identification of Jesus as Servant.

That Christians should identify Jesus with the Suffering Servant is understandable, since classic texts allow for, in Paul Ricoeur's phrase, a "surplus of meaning."[6] The songs of the Servant now form part of the constellation of images crucial to Christian identity, but they are robbed of their depth when read prosaically as predictive prophecy.

It is curious that typology should figure so prominently in the catechism when earlier ecclesial documents point to its problematic character. As early as *Divino Afflante Spiritu* we find the exhortation to exegetes to "scrupulously refrain from proposing as the genuine meaning of Sacred Scripture other figurative senses."[7]

The 1985 *Notes on the Correct Way to Present the Jews and Judaism in Preaching and Catechesis in the Roman Catholic Church* acknowledges that typology, though constant in tradition, makes many uneasy and indicates "the sign of a problem unresolved" (no. 3). It proposes that those who use typology "should be careful to avoid any transition from the Old to the New Testament which might seem merely a rupture" (no. 4). Further, it recognizes that although the church and Christians "read the Old Testament in the light of the event of the dead and risen Christ," this is a "Christian reading of the Old Testament which does not necessarily coincide with the Jewish reading" (no. 6).[8]

Not only does the catechism ignore the acknowledged problem with typology, it does not teach how the early church made use of the Scriptures. By reducing prophecy to prediction, the authors have done injustice both to the Prophets and to the dynamic by which the early church saw a new dimension in the texts they had inherited as Jews. The New Testament writers followed exegetical practices common in first-century Jewish life, but their "christological eyes" glimpsed new layers of meaning in their texts. The catechism, preoccupied with typology, overlooks this process. Despite the claim that the Hebrew Bible still has its own value (0292), the dominant impression is that its worth is primarily as preparation.

Typology need not rest on such a basis. Freed from its apologetic moorage in promise-fulfillment categories, typology becomes an essential tool for interpreting the present in light of the past. Typology, used within the Hebrew Bible itself (e.g., Is 43:16–18), exemplifies one of the oldest principles of biblical interpretation among Jews and Christians. It shows how "later verbal symbols throw light on earlier ones in a cascade of imagery that convey [sic] some sense of the divine."[9] The catechism, however, provides little guidance for how the church might more adequately use typology. Since typology is so important in liturgy, this is an unfortunate omission.

The authors do make note of one tradition of interpretation, that of the four senses of Scripture: literal, allegorical, moral, and anagogical (0282). They include the Latin quatrain variously attributed to John Cassian (d. ca. 435) and to Augustine of Dacia (d. 1284). The section is a strange insertion, with no explanation of its development or reference to its limitations. The catechism itself does not make use of the four senses, except in the epilogue on the Our Father (4015). Stylistically it seems odd. The section reflects the proclivity of the authors to offer formulas without context. Christians (and Jews) have been struggling for a long time to articulate how texts have multiple meanings. The four senses were one solution proposed by medievals—and not the only medieval solution. Their formulation is not adequate today, but their quest to transcend the literal sense bears immense relevance. This section, therefore, deserves expansion.

Surely one of the missed opportunities of the catechism is the failure to acquaint readers with the distinctive contours of the Catholic use of Scripture. The story of the varied uses of Scripture in the life of the church is a dramatic one. But in a document so lacking in historical consciousness, readers gain no sense of the many twists and turns of a story that could be so instructive for moderns.

The Living Tradition as Context

One contribution of the catechism is that it draws from the breadth of the Christian tradition. The images of Scripture are supplemented by conciliar formulations and by the sayings of early Christian writers and saints. The catechism bears witness to the nearly two thousand years of interpretation that provide a context for the church's reading of Scriptures. Yet inattention to the development of tradition weakens this witness.

Another glaring omission is the catechism's disregard for the implications of an emerging tradition, the ecclesial teachings expanding *Nostra Aetate*, no. 4, on the relation of the church to Judaism. These teachings eclipse supersessionism, the notion that the Christ-event so overshadows the revelation to Israel that the prior revelation has been rendered obsolete. The catechism, however, is a supersessionist document. Its understanding of "Old" Covenant, messianism, Pharisees, the Law, and the death of Jesus lacks the conceptual shifts evident in official promulgations from Vatican commissions and in papal addresses and, most recently, in two documents from the bishops of the United States.

Despite one use of the term "First Covenant" (0111), the catechism typically speaks of the "Old Covenant" (0316, 1321, 2708, 2712). It includes Pope John Paul II's remark to the Jewish community at Mainz, West Germany, that "the Old Covenant has never been revoked" (0285, but on November 17, 1980, not 1950), yet gives no indication of how that covenant continues to be lived in Judaism. Little in the catechism indicates that the Jewish people continue to exist (1522 includes the only reference to the 1985 *Notes on the Correct Way to Present the Jews*). Jews seemingly exist only to prefigure Christians. Though God formed a people Israel through the covenant, "all this came about to prepare and foreshadow the making of the new and perfect covenant in Christ" (1667).

The catechism is ambivalent toward the Pharisees (1385, 1415, 1417, 1420, 1423, 1430). It points out that Jesus' relations with the Pharisees were "not entirely or always polemic" (1415). This seems to echo the 1985 *Notes*, no. 16 ("His relations with the Pharisees were not always or wholly polemical"). The catechism, however, does not follow the more nuanced presentation of the Pharisees that continues in the *Notes*. It asserts that the principle of integrality of the Law was "dear" to the Pharisees in both letter and spirit (1420):

> Their special emphasis on it [the Law] led the Jews at the time of Christ to a level of extreme religious zeal (cf. Rom 10.2). In such a situation, the only alternative to hypocritical casuistry, rejected by Jesus (cf. Mt 15.3–7) was an opening to an unheard-of intervention from God (cf. Is 53.1): the perfect carrying-out of the Law in the place of all sinners by the only Just One (cf. Is 53.11).

It is unfortunate that the catechism retains the accusation of "hypocritical casuistry." It is deplorable that it includes this citation from Maximus the Confessor (ca. 580–662):

> "Being unable by his promises to persuade the Lord to transgress the commandment of the love of God, the devil tries by his machinations to make him break the commandment of love for one's neighbour. . . . But the Lord . . . did not hate the Pharisees that the devil had stirred up against him. . . . O war of contradictions! Instead of hatred, he shows love, by goodness he drives out the father of evil." (1385; ellipses in catechism)

Here the catechism reflects its lack of integration of the implications of biblical studies. Rather than admitting that recent scholarship challenges the church to rethink its presentation of Jesus in light of new perspectives on the debate between Jesus and the Pharisees, the authors juxtapose certain modern conclusions—that Jesus' relationship with them was more complicated than a simple polemic—with obsolete assertions in direct contradiction of other ecclesial documents.

A far superior summary appears in a recent publication from the Committee on the Liturgy of the National Conference of Catholic Bishops:

> Jesus was perhaps closer to the Pharisees in his religious vision than to any other group in his time. The 1985 *Notes* suggest that this affinity with Pharisaism may be a reason for many of his apparent controversies with them. . . . Many scholars are of the view that Jesus was not so much arguing against the Pharisees as a group, as he was condemning excesses of some Pharisees, excesses of a sort that can be found among some Christians as well. . . . After the Church had distanced itself from Judaism . . . it tended to telescope the long historical process whereby the gospels were set down generations after Jesus' death. Thus, certain controversies that may actually have taken place between church leaders and rabbis toward the end of the first century were "read back" into the life of Jesus.[10]

Similarly careless in its biblical scholarship is the catechism's presentation of the Messiah (1259–69; 1434, 1441, 1545, 1560–66). Two problems appear. The authors caricature Jewish understandings of messianism: Jews "put their hope in a glorious Messiah" (1441). Second, the authors place so much stress on Jesus as the fulfillment of messianic prophecies that they devote little attention to the eschatological dimension, to that time when God will be all in all (but see 4073–78, on the petition "Thy kingdom come").

Would that the catechism had found room for this paragraph from the 1985 *Notes* (no. 10):

> Attentive to the same God who has spoken, hanging on the same word, we have to witness to one same memory and one common hope in him who is the master of history. We must also accept our responsibility to prepare the world for the coming of the Messiah by working together for social justice, respect for the rights of persons and nations and for social and international reconciliation. To this we are driven, Jews and Christians, by the command to love our neighbor, by a common hope for the kingdom of God and by the great heritage of the prophets. Transmitted soon enough by catechesis, such a conception would teach young Christians in a practical way to cooperate with Jews, going beyond simple dialogue (cf. *Guidelines*, IV).

Other supersessionist strains are apparent in the discussion of priesthood and the Law. Though there was a rite consecrating one to the priesthood of the Old Covenant (2708), "this priesthood remains however powerless to effect salvation, needing endlessly renewed repetition, without resulting in a definitive sanctification (cf. Heb 5.3; 7.27; 10.1–4)" (2709). Similarly, the new law of Christ "surpasses the old and accomplishes its promise." Not a written code but a reality inscribed in our hearts, the new law alters both the content and spirit of the old (3122–23).

Regrettably, the catechism, which leaves untranslated most Latin formulations, always renders the Hebrew Torah as "law." Such a translation does injustice to the complexity of Torah. Is it a polemical translation? Though the catechism points to the connection between law and liberation (3110–15), it asserts the superiority of Christian fidelity to the will of God. It also does injustice to the Israelites' "root experience," the Exodus, by speaking of it only as a deliverance from the slavery of sin rather than as a deliverance from slavery in Egypt (3110). As David Hollenbach, S.J., points out later in this book, the catechism tends to separate major religious ideas such as liberation and covenant from ethical ideals such as human dignity and solidarity.

Finally, in her article in this collection, Elizabeth Johnson, C.S.J., correctly points to the catechism's affirmation of Vatican II's teaching that the Jewish people as a whole are not responsible for the death of Jesus. But it seems a curious omission in a catechism structured around the creed to ignore the role of Pontius Pilate (1448–52). Pilate, after all, has explicit mention in the creed. How instructive it might be for the church to understand that Pilate was not merely a weak person ruled by mobs of angry Jews, as the evangelists portray him. In general, this section on the trial of Jesus is presented in a simplistic fashion.

The Analogy of Faith

The third criterion for the interpretation of Scripture is that one be attentive to the coherence of the truths of the faith. Presumably, this means that one takes care to fit one's rendering of biblical texts into a larger tapestry. But does the catechism itself cohere?

It reads more like a collection than a synthesis. The authors provide insufficient guidance for distinguishing the more central confessions of faith from more derivative teachings. In terms of Scripture this stems in part from the failure of the catechism to honor its own dictum about literary forms and cultural context (0276).

For instance, the infancy narratives (1364–78) are accorded the same historical status as the passion narratives (1441–52). Even more problematic is the literalistic treatment of angels (1154–64; 1215–18; 2025, 2124), of the devil/Satan (1219–20, 1229), and of Christ's descent into hell (1471–81). The reader finds an explanation neither of apocalyptic language nor of the historical conditions that gave rise to this type of discourse. Believers need to be given more assistance in decoding mythological language. Otherwise they will either reject it as an artifact of an outdated worldview or embrace it with the naïveté of the fundamentalist.

The emphasis on coherence correlates with another difficulty: inadequate or anachronistic use of terms. For instance, the catechism reflects a narrow notion of apostle. The authors call upon St. Ambrose's (ca. 339–397) reasoning that the creed has twelve articles because there are twelve apostles (1009) and note that "among the twelve apostles chosen by the Lord, Simon Peter holds the first place" (1397). Yet nowhere is there the fuller New Testament understanding that "apostle"—one who is sent—may include more than the "Twelve." Or that women, such as Mary of Magdala, might be apostles.

This equation of apostle with the Twelve continues in the section on the sacrament of order. To say that "the Lord Jesus chose men to make up the college of the twelve apostles (cf. Lk 6.12–16), and the apostles did the same when they chose their successors" (2747) is, at best, anachronistic. Also anachronistic is the claim based on Matt 16:19 that the "power to bind and loose signifies authority to pronounce doctrinal judgements and disciplinary decisions in the Church" (1398).

Moreover, the authors make the apodictic assertion that "the Church, listening to her Master, recognises that she is *bound for ever* by this choice [the selection of men alone] made by the Lord himself" (2747, emphasis added). One would never know that the Pontifical Biblical Commission has unanimously concluded that the New Testament does not settle the question of the ordination of women in a clear fashion.[11]

Since content and form are inseparably related, the genre and style of the catechism reveal its content. By its relentlessly didactic style, the catechism belies its intent of an *organic* exposition (0021, emphasis added). By its compilation of scriptural citations to explicate doctrines, it gives the impression, albeit unintentionally, that the Bible exists primarily to verify doctrinal formulations.

Insofar as this document has educational implications, its form suggests explanation may overwhelm experience. Those who take seriously the educational process will be dismayed by this document. Its tone is one of transmission, not of dialogue. It is alien to the more dialogical tone of recent episcopal pastorals in the United States. One senses that the authors of the *Catechism of the Universal Church* would be ill at ease with this statement of the U.S. Bishops: "those who teach in the name of the Church do not simply instruct adults, but also learn from them; they will only be heard by adults if they listen to them."[12]

Final Questions

Perhaps because the catechism aims to expound everything, it loses coherence. That, too, is a temptation for this author. Because Scripture is so prevalent in the catechism, one is tempted to take on a host of other instances. In the interests of brevity, it seems more judicious simply to list some final questions pertinent to the use of Scripture:

Is the discussion of Mary excessive (0220, 0303, 0310–11, 0335, 1091, 1245, 1259, 1264–66, 1276, 1320, 1356, 1459, 1567, 1571–77, 1756–66, 1767–69)? Does it depend too much on typology (e.g., as the "burning Bush of the definitive Theophany" [1575]), and does it represent an example of dogma overwhelming Scripture? Moreover, as Elizabeth Johnson asks, does the catechism present an adequate Mariology?

Can any ecclesial document prescind from cultural conditioning? The prologue states of the catechism: "It is not its function to supply the adaptations demanded by the 'enculturation' of the christian faith" (0020). Does not this qualification assume that inculturation is merely a matter of translation or adaptation?

Can a document intended for the universal church expound so much with so little reference to women? Aside from the many references to Mary, few others are included, and then only with brevity: Sarah (0304, 0306, 1321); Teresa of Avila (0124), Thérèse of Lisieux (0290, 1027), Joan of Arc (1023, 1264), Catherine of Siena (1041, 1185); the "holy women" (1497, 1499); Eve, Anne (why not the Hebrew form, Hannah?), Deborah, Ruth, Judith, and Esther all compressed into one paragraph (1321; see Elizabeth Johnson on their "weakness"). In the section on the creation, man and woman are regarded as partners incomplete without the other. But, as Lisa Cahill notes later in this book, the assertion that they are "complementary as masculine and feminine" (1197 and 2804) rests on problematic grounds. And will not readers sensitive to the importance of inclusive language be needlessly offended?

The English version of the catechism quotes Scripture according to the Jerusalem Bible. Given the criticisms of this translation, should not the catechism use a more reliable English translation?[13]

Finally, I realize my remarks have been largely negative. The catechism abounds with valuable material. It is an instructive work from which all can learn. Ultimately, however, it disappoints. The *Catechism for the Universal Church,* unable to integrate the salient insights of historical-critical scholarship, will only confuse and mislead the very people for whom it is intended as a point of reference. As a commentary on the Scripture, the catechism is an unreliable guide.

PART 2

THE CREED IN
THE CATECHISM

God in
the Catechism

John H. Wright, S.J.
Jesuit School of Theology, Berkeley

No doubt faith is a kind of obedience, . . . but its fundamental nature is much more openness, trust, acceptance, and commitment.

The paragraphs that are given on the relation between faith and science are not adequate.

If an opening paragraph of the prologue of the *Catechism for the Universal Church* (0003) had served as introduction and guide for the teaching on God, we would have a considerably different and much improved document:

> Those who have received the grace of giving a welcome to the call of Christ and of answering it freely, have felt themselves urged on by the love of Christ (cf. 2 Co 5.14) to proclaim everywhere in the world the Good News of the merciful Father, of his Son who has given himself up for us (cf. Gal 2.20), of their Spirit of Love poured into our hearts (cf. Rom 5.5): "We cannot promise to stop proclaiming what we have seen and heard" (Ac 4.20).

This paragraph points out how much our knowledge of God is a matter of personal experience, how the revelation of the Holy Trinity is the disclosure of God acting in history to save us, and how the reception of this revelation through faith is a free and joyful act that leads to grateful proclamation. Unfortunately, the tone set here does not pervade the exposition of our belief in God, though it is not entirely absent. Often there is an endeavor to treat the doctrine of God religiously, within a context of divine love and human faith and service. Thus the catechism makes abundant use of Scripture and Vatican II documents.

However, this religious context is sometimes overshadowed by juridical and philosophical considerations, and the citations from Scripture and Vatican II are often used for proof texts rather than for conveying the sense and intent of the original documents.

My comments will deal chiefly with the first and eighth articles of the Apostles' Creed: "I believe in God the Father almighty, creator of heaven and earth. . . . I believe in the Holy Spirit." I will treat the first article on God, the Father and creator, under eight headings: our knowledge of God (0102–0233), our language about God (0140–44), the biblical teaching on God, the attributes of God (1016–48), Father and the Holy Trinity (1049–96), creation of heaven and earth (1097–1182), creation of human beings (1183–1213), and the fall (1214–53).

"I Believe in God"

Our Knowledge of God

The catechism at the beginning makes some helpful allusions to human nature as religious and points to the different world religions as the source of reflection on God (0102–19). In the next section, on "Man's 'Capacity' for God" (0120–49), after noting the questions posed by the human spirit, it moves immediately to a discussion of "the ways of approach to the knowledge of God" (0125–39). These "ways" turn out to be not the roots or ground of religious questioning and worship but "proofs" for the existence of God.

While indicating some of the limitations and difficulties of these proofs, the catechism gives the impression that people ordinarily come to God first by way of natural reason. This may not be the intent of the catechism, but by not putting the activity of natural reason as a component within the total sphere of graced human activity, the catechism leads one to suppose that this kind of purely natural theology is a normal process, whereas it is doubtful that it ever actually takes place.

Vatican I, the authoritative teacher on this matter, was concerned to show what human nature is radically capable of in opposition to fideists; it did not intend to declare what in fact takes place. The main point is that without a natural human capacity to know God, human nature would be closed to God and thus not truly open to the possibility of God's revealing self-communication. Revelation would not come to it as gift and fulfillment.

In discussing divine revelation and faith (0201–64), the catechism says almost nothing about ongoing or continuous divine revelation. Scripture speaks of this as the divine light that always shines in the darkness without being overcome by it (cf. Jn 1:4–5), or as the anointing by the Holy One that gives all believers the truth (1 Jn 2:20–21), or as "a spirit of wisdom and of revelation in the knowledge of him" (Eph 1:17). The catechism itself later says, "If . . . we ask the Holy Spirit to 'come', he will reveal to us many other places where 'his prayer' (Rm 8.27) and the compassion of the Savior take him" (1602). With no attention being given earlier to ongoing revelation, it is much more difficult to understand special historical revelations and their transmission.

The catechism beautifully states that God "gives himself" to us by revealing his "loving plan" (0202). But instead of developing the meaning of "self-giving" and its relation to the revelation of the loving plan, the catechism at once begins a discussion of the revelation of the plan. It gives "stages of revelation" that reflect a fundamentalist reading of Scripture: to our first parents, after the fall, to Noah, and then to Abraham and Israel (0209–20). The use of biblical stories is surely not out of place, but if they are used from the beginning, part of catechesis from the beginning should be some indication of how they are to be understood so as to grasp the meaning intended by the sacred author. It is most important that what is learned in catechism not have to be unlearned later, to the confusion and dismay of the faithful.

The catechism rightly speaks of faith as the human response to God's revelation (0301–58). But the primary description it gives of faith is "obedience," even after speaking of it initially as abandonment and self-gift to God. No doubt faith is a kind of obedience, and this aspect needs to be taught, but its fundamental nature is much more openness, trust, acceptance, and commitment. To speak of it primarily and at length in terms of obedience (0303–10) gives faith a tone of law and constraint that ill accords with the joyful freedom of faith and with the abandonment and self-gift with which the section begins.

It is understandable in context why the catechism says that God alone is the object of faith (0312–21) since faith is being considered as a response to God's self-revelation. But to understand what faith in God means it is helpful to see faith more generally as a universal and even natural human activity, which is then transformed and specified in a particular way when human beings respond to God. St. Thomas's treatment of faith is illuminating in this connection (cf. *Summa Theologiae* 2-2, q. 1, a. 4).

Our Language about God

In the section on natural knowledge of God there are a few paragraphs on language about God (0140–44). This needs to be expanded to clarify that while concepts of God (like Being and Creator) may be analogous, all our images of God (like King, Father, and Husband) are metaphorical, including those in Scripture. This means that even our most sacred images are time conditioned and reflect the cultures in which they arise. Thus, though it is correct to speak of the religious novelty and even revolution introduced by Jesus in addressing God as "Father" (1049) and in teaching his followers to do the same, still "Father" is a metaphor. The same truth of intimate love and protection may be conveyed by other metaphors. John Paul I, in keeping with many mystics, spoke of God as "Mother."[1] The catechism should make this possibility clear, lest male imagery so dominate our language about God that the divine mystery and transcendence is compromised. I do not, in fact, recall any female imagery of God in the catechism.

Biblical Teaching on God

The catechism gives no indication of the growth in the Bible's teaching on God. This failure obscures the gradual way in which God's self-revelation came to us and therefore the way in which God normally deals with us. From a tribal deity immanent in the history of his people, one God among others, God comes to be understood as the One God, transcendent creator of heaven and earth. Finally, he is manifested as the "Father" of Jesus Christ and our "Father."

The Attributes of God

In dealing with the attributes of God the catechism deals primarily with uniqueness or oneness, Being, love, and (in the context of "Father") almighty power. It treats these largely in connection with the revelation of the divine name.

It asserts that God's oneness is the first revelation God has made to us and the basis of all our faith in God (1019). It is hard to know what this means. Strict monotheism among the Hebrews was certainly preceded by a kind of practical monotheism, which denied not the existence of other gods, only their significance for them. Revelation and faith were certainly present in this early period.

The implications of faith in the one God (given in 1023–28), while important aspects of the Christian life, seem for the most part only very remotely implied. The basic implication of faith in one God is that he alone is to be worshiped as God. It is not clear, for example, how it implies "the proper use of created things" (1026).

Much is made of the revelation of the divine name in Ex 3:13–15. However, the episode may reasonably be interpreted as God's refusal to reveal his name ("I am who I am"). The meaning attached to the name came from actual use among the Hebrews rather than from this revelation. One cannot attribute to the biblical story the later teaching of the medieval theologians that God alone IS, is *ens a se, ipsum esse subsistens* (1038–41). This may well be an excellent way of understanding God, but is it revealed? Is it a matter of faith or of philosophy?

I think the catechism is correct in seeing that the revelation of God as love is "the keystone of all truth about God" (1042). But to say that this means the revelation of the Blessed Trinity at the passover of Christ seems to go beyond the evidence (1043).

Father and the Holy Trinity

The section on the Father and the Holy Trinity gives the impression that the teaching on the Trinity was clear and acknowledged in the time of the New Testament. The expression *Trinity* was not used, as far as we know, before Theophilus of Antioch (*Ad Autolycum* 2.15) around A.D. 181. This makes the heading highly problematic that reads: "The revelation of the name of God as Trinity" before a series of biblical texts (1050–53).

One can in general say that the treatment of the Trinity in the catechism is more an exercise in dialectics than an articulation of Christians' experience of God active in the work of salvation, as had been suggested by the paragraph in the prologue cited above (0003). The effort to show that belief in one God and three divine persons is not contradictory has been allowed to dominate the study of this mystery. For this reason it largely lacks relevance and seems more a challenge to intelligence than an invitation to enter into the mystery of God's self-communicating love. Any study of the Trinity today should begin with the "Economic" Trinity (how it relates to the world), and then proceed to the "Immanent" Trinity (what it is in itself). This first makes it clear how important it is for us that God is Father, Son, and Holy Spirit and then shows that this is not an absurd belief.

"Almighty" is rightly picked out for special emphasis, since it occurs in the creed. It corresponds to a biblical emphasis on God as active and creating: the living and true God. But it is important to recall what was said earlier about the revelation of God as love and contextualize the discussion of God's power by a reaffirmation of his love. Otherwise one easily allows a theology of divine omnipotence to become a theology of predetermination and predestination. The catechism says:

> Nothing is therefore impossible for him (cf. Jr 32.17) and he disposes of his work as he wishes (Jr 27.5); he is the Lord of the universe, in which he has established the order that remains entirely obedient and available to him; he is the Master of history: he governs hearts and events as he wishes (cf. Est 4.17b; Pro 21.1; Tb 13.2); "Everything that he wishes, he does" (Ps 113.11). (1085)

Alongside texts like these we should place: "What more was there to do for my vineyard, that I have not done in it? When I looked for it to yield grapes, why did it yield wild grapes?" (Is 5:4).

In this connection, the catechism gives some helpful cautions and directions (1088–89). It should add that in acknowledging that God is almighty and thus can do whatever is intrinsically possible, we do not thereby clarify what God's omnipotence actually embraces, since it is not easy for us to determine what truly is intrinsically possible. Because we can conceive or imagine something does not mean that it is truly possible. We can conceive a totally different kind of universe; but that does not mean the universe we conceive is objectively possible and therefore that God could make it. We can conceive another way for the human race to come to be besides evolution, but that does not mean God might have been able to do it that way.

Creation of Heaven and Earth

To say that the world was created for the glory of God (1124) calls for some explanation, lest it seem that God seeks to acquire something for himself by creation. Glorifying God is itself our way of participating in the divine life and goodness which is the end God ultimately intends in creating (cf. *Summa Theologiae* 1, q. 44, a. 4). God intends his glory not for his benefit but for ours.

To describe God's providence as "authority" (1130) is, of course, legitimate, but it can be misleading. The word itself fails to convey wise, loving, powerful concern for creation, even when this is said to characterize it. Furthermore, while the "plan of God" reaches the least details (1131), it is not a predetermined scenario of all that happens but the arrangement by which God, who makes all things possible that are possible, draws good from everything that happens, even from what he does not want to happen (like sin).

The treatment of the "problem of evil" (1135–41) is in general quite good. It avoids the Augustinian notion that all suffering is punishment for sin, at least for original sin. But it would be helpful to make explicit the importance and reason for created freedom, which makes sin possible.

The catechism takes up the angels under the creation of heaven (1154–64). Personally I favor the existence of angels. But it seems to me that it is too much to say just now that their existence is a matter of faith (1154) and therefore to imply that everyone who questions their existence is a heretic. Biblical scholars are trying to discover to what extent speaking of these created spirits is a culturally conditioned way of describing both God's activity and evil forces outside individual persons, rather than divinely inspired affirmations of their existence.

The Fourth Lateran Council, to which the catechism refers (1153), was concerned to condemn all forms of dualism that would admit an evil principle independent of God. In this context it said that God created the angelic and worldly creatures and that he made the devil good, but that the devil made himself evil by his free will. The council was not intending to teach the existence of angels and devils, since at that time no one questioned their existence. The only question was whether evil spirits were creatures of God or independent beings. Since the question of the existence of angels concerns many people, it would be well for the teaching authority of the church to invite serious and religiously inspired discussion of this matter.

Under the creation of the earth the catechism has a long discussion on the work of six days (1167–82). This pattern of six days was used by the Priestly writer of Genesis 1 to inculcate the need of Sabbath observance. The order given in Scripture (1167) does not intend to teach the succession in which things were made. The catechism gives the impression it does when it says "[God created] . . . all in an order that Scripture marks out in a series of six 'days' (Gn 1.3–31)." To speak this way is an effort at "harmony" that does not recommend itself either to scientists or to exegetes, as the catechism itself recognizes (1168). Finally, it is hard to see what is gained by continuing to use this framework of six days in modern catechesis; it would be enough to refer to it in the explanation of Genesis 1.

The paragraphs that are given on the relation between faith and science are not adequate (1171–73). Contemporary culture is so dominated by scientific ways of thought that contemporary catechesis must treat this matter more fully and in a way that will not have to be unlearned at some later time.

Creation of Human Beings

God is said to create the human soul "immediately" (1191) and that it is therefore not "produced" by the parents. This terminology is taken from earlier councils and from Pope Pius XII. But in the context of evolution, "immediately" need not be understood as a creation "outside" the body followed by "infusion" into the body, as was often said in the past. The divine power at work within matter in the process of evolution and in the procreative activity of the parents and the development of the embryo may cause a "within" or spiritual principle to exist that is required by the organization of matter that has been brought about by both created and divine activity. As Karl Rahner has observed:

> We must assume here the concept of an essential self-transcendence on the part of an existing creature sustained by God as its ultimate cause, and on the basis of this assumption we can freely assert that the development of biologically organized materiality is orientated in terms of an ever-increasing complexity and interiority towards spirit, until finally, under the dynamic impulse of God's creative power, and through a process of self-transcendence of this kind, it becomes spirit.[2]

The catechism presents the creation of the human race without any reference to the process of evolution and with the presupposition of monogenism. To present this as matter of faith in contemporary catechesis seems unwarranted. It is clear today that this was not the intent of the inspired writers, whether of the P and J traditions in the Pentateuch or of Paul in the New Testament. The truth of faith is that the human race has come to be, not by accident, but by the loving intention of God. Everything else is a matter for scientific investigation and theological speculation.

The Fall

The narrative of the fall in Genesis 2 and 3 was the endeavor of the sacred writer to provide an answer to the ever-present vexing problem of sin and suffering as he and the community of Israel experienced it: How can things be so awry if God is a good creator?

To answer this question he told a story, a symbolic narrative, which taught that the responsibility for this condition lies with the human beings, not with God. What God intended was symbolized by the tree of life in a garden of paradise. Human resistance early in the history of the race blocked this divine intention and brought upon the race the disorders we see around us and experience within us. To what degree and in what ways the original divine intention actually was realized among human beings was not the point of the story. When the literary genus of the story was not understood, it was easy to give detailed descriptions of a state of original justice (1202–7). But this description is not a matter of Catholic faith.

Just as I personally favor the existence of angels, I favor the notion of a sin of the angels. But I do not favor saying, "The *faith* of the Church teaches us about the fall of the bad angels (I), the fall of our first parents because of original sin (II), and the promise of Redemption after their fall (III)" (1214, emphasis added). The evidence of Scripture and tradition adduced in support of these positions is given without attention to context or original intent. And it is hard to know what it means to say, "the fall of our first parents *because of* original sin" (emphasis added).

The quotation from John Paul II (1220) about the power of Satan is enlightening, but it does not deal with a fundamental problem: Why is Satan's action "permitted by divine providence"?

The doctrine on original sin (1221–38) needs to be reworked very thoroughly and carefully. First, it should be recognized that it is not a central truth of biblical teaching, though it is found there in some way. There is no allusion to it in most books of Scripture, in either the Old Testament or the New Testament. It was St. Augustine who made it the linchpin of his theological system. The reference to its analogical nature as sin (1236) also needs to be clearly explained. Likewise we should be careful not to attribute all the evils we experience to a solitary first act of disobedience (1230–33). In many ways the story of the fall of Adam and Eve is the story of every man and woman. St. Paul points to this when he writes "inasmuch as all have sinned" (Rom 5:12).

"I Believe in the Holy Spirit"

My comments on the eighth article of the creed will fall under six heads: introductory remarks (1531–34), knowledge of the Spirit (1535–37), mission of the Spirit (1538–40), symbols of the Spirit (1541–50), the Holy Spirit in Scripture (1551–82), and the Spirit, the church, and the Trinity (1583–1609).

Introductory Remarks

The introduction (1531–34) to the matter on the Holy Spirit begins very well by citing the two passages in Paul where the presence of the Spirit is manifested in the cries of believers: "Jesus is Lord!" and "Abba, Father!"

(1531). It seems, however, an understatement to refer to these as express-ing "knowledge of faith." Both are exclamations of praise and thanksgiv-ing, not just expressions of knowledge.

It does not seem correct to say that the Father is the "origin of the Deity" (1533), for then he would be his own origin, since deity belongs to him. Strictly speaking, deity or the divine nature has no origin; the Son and the Spirit, divine persons, have origin. The Father is the origin within the deity of the Son and the Holy Spirit.

The association of the final divine works in the creed with the Holy Spirit is very much to be commended. It makes clear the mission of the Spirit within the church (1534).

Knowledge of the Spirit

The introduction to the eighth article of the creed (1535–37) gives the sources of our knowledge of the Spirit within the church but fails to note the "anointing of the Holy One" (1 Jn 2:20) or the inner witness of the Spirit, a theme prominent in Johannine writings. Scripture, liturgy, tradi-tion, and the witness of the saints, especially in martyrdom, are very important (1536). But we should not neglect the inspiration that is given to all believers: "If you love me, you will keep my commandments. And I will pray the Father, and he will give you another Counselor, to be with you forever, even the Spirit of truth, whom the world cannot receive, because it neither sees him nor knows him; *you know him, for he dwells with you, and will be in you*" (Jn 14:15–17, emphasis added).

Mission of the Spirit

I find the language about "the *joint* mission of the Son and the Spirit" (1539 and 1604, emphasis added) novel and confusing. As far as I can dis-cover, it is not the language of Scripture, of Vatican II, of John Paul II in *Dominum et Vivificantem*, or of any other church document. John Paul dis-tinguishes and interrelates the two missions in this way: "How intimately this mission [of the Spirit of truth] is linked with the mission of Christ, how fully it draws from this mission of Christ, consolidating and developing in history its salvific results, is expressed by the verb take."[3]

No doubt where the Son is sent there the Spirit is sent also, by reason of divine concomitance. But the mission of the Son in the incarnation for the salvation of the world does not yet mean the mission of the Spirit for the salvation of the world but a mission to Jesus for the unfolding of his messianic mission. The mission of the Spirit to the world of believers comes after the glorification of Jesus (Jn 7:39). Thus, although there is a mission of the Holy Spirit to Jesus who is sent in the incarnation, to call this a joint mission is not at all clarifying. The mission of the Holy Spirit after Jesus' resurrection also involves *per concomitantiam* an invisible mission of the Son, who also dwells in us (cf. Rom 8:9–10). But to refer to a "joint" mission obscures the special, new presence of the Spirit, who is making us a community (*koinonia*, 2 Cor 13:14) and assimilating us to Christ (2 Cor 3:18).

What does it mean to say (in 1540) that "the Breath of the Father [the Holy Spirit] . . . inspires him [the Word] to speak by the prophets"? The Nicene-Constantinopolitan Creed acknowledges that the Holy Spirit spoke through the prophets, not that the Spirit inspired the Word to speak through the prophets. Even more obscure later in the paragraph is the reference to the "conjoined and mutual" mission. Does this mean that the Son and the Holy Spirit send each other, as "mutual" would lead one to think?

Symbols of the Spirit

The notion of "symbolic names" (1544) is elusive. If the Holy Spirit were actually called all of these things or addressed under these titles, it would be appropriate to refer to them as names. But this is not so with many of them, even in poetry (e.g., "seal" and "hand"). Would it not be more accurate simply to speak of "symbols of the Holy Spirit"?

In discussing water as a symbolic name of the Holy Spirit (1544), the catechism says that the epiclesis consecrating the water makes it an efficacious sacramental sign of new birth. No doubt this blessing is important, but even without it, water when used with the baptismal formula is part of the efficacious sacramental symbol. And the consecrated water, without the baptismal formula, is not an efficacious symbol of rebirth. It is likely, too, that "to drink of one Spirit" in 1 Cor 12:13 does not refer to baptism but to the Holy Eucharist, in view of 1 Cor 10:3–4, 16, 21.

In referring to the anointing of Jesus by the Holy Spirit (1545) no reference is made to Act 10:38, which is a significant passage in this regard.

The Holy Spirit in Scripture

In the section "The Spirit and the Word of God in the Time of the Promises" (1551–66), many references to the Spirit in both the Old Testament and the New are given. This gives the impression that already in the Old

Testament the Spirit was understood in a personal way, as later in the New. However, as John McKenzie observed many years ago: "In summary, the spirit in the OT, originally the wind and the breath, is conceived as a divine dynamic entity by which Yahweh accomplishes His ends: it saves, it is a creative and charismatic power, and as an agent of His anger it is a demonic power. It remains impersonal."[4] Even in the New Testament the meaning of (Holy) Spirit is not the same in all places. It is important to note this development of meaning and not give an erroneous impression. This is especially true of the section "The Expectation of the Messiah and of his Spirit" (1560–66).

For example, Is 11:1–2 is cited as if it were a revelation of the Holy Spirit (1562). If this is not the intention, it should be stated somewhere. John Paul II writes, however, "The Messiah of the lineage of David . . . is precisely that person upon whom the Spirit of the Lord 'shall rest.' It is obvious that in this case one cannot speak of a revelation of the Paraclete."[5]

"The Spirit of Christ in the Fullness of Time" (1567-82) contains much valuable material and is well organized. Once again, to give a correct impression, it would be well to distinguish various ways in which the term "Spirit" is used in the Scriptures and not mingle them together indiscriminately.

The Spirit, the Church, and the Trinity

In "The Spirit and the Church in the Last Times" (1583–98) much is said that is very helpful. However, it seems too much to say, "On that day [of Pentecost] the Blessed Trinity is finally fully revealed" (1584). No doubt all the elements of the doctrine of the Trinity were then available, but they were not yet put together to reveal the Blessed Trinity to us "fully." This language about the Trinity being "fully revealed" occurs in another connection (1043) as noted above, and with the same kind of overstatement.

It is not clear what is being excluded by saying that the mission of the church is not "added on" to that of Christ and of the Holy Spirit (1598). Certainly the mission of the church is continuous with the mission of the Son and the Holy Spirit, but it is distinct from their mission, precisely because the church as a communion of human believers is distinct from the Holy Spirit who makes them a communion. The mission of the church is a created participation in the divine mission of the Son and the Spirit.

Conclusion

While the treatment of the first and eighth articles of the creed, "God the Father almighty, creator of heaven and earth," and "the Holy Spirit," contains many valuable insights, it is so pervasively marked by inaccuracies, questionable interpretations, omissions, lack of proper contextualization, misplaced emphases, and a failure to note developments of theological and biblical scholarship of the last twenty-five years that it is hardly redeemable in its present form.

Jesus Christ in the Catechism

Elizabeth A. Johnson, C.S.J.
The Catholic University of America

The figure of Jesus comes across as a cold fish, knowing everything, in complete control, at the same time totally submissive, moving through his paces, not very inspiring.

The ghost of Apollinaris haunts this catechism.

This Christ is far above our human struggles, and so rather useless for preaching, evangelization, and catechesis.

Overview

The *Catechism for the Universal Church* intends to present a synthetic, organic, complete, and precise picture of what the church believes, and to do so as a point of reference for national catechisms. How does it go about presenting Jesus Christ and the long-promised salvation that he announced and even brought about? And how might this serve the catechesis of the world church?

In keeping with Christian life itself, the placement of Jesus Christ in the catechism is central and pervasive. The opening and closing lines of the whole catechism refer to Christ. Each of its three main divisions of creed, sacraments, and commandments keeps a steady eye on his significance. In the creedal section under "I Believe in God the Son" (part 1, section 2), fully 276 paragraphs (1254–1530) deal with his life and meaning. In addition, christological material appears in connection with creedal confession of the Father, the Spirit, and the church. The section on liturgy and sacraments positions Christ at the center of Christian worship, and the ethics section presents him as the exemplar and inspiration of Christian moral life. The epilogue presents the Lord's Prayer as the prayer that Jesus taught his disciples to say.

In an extended sense, the entire catechism is a presentation of Jesus Christ and the life of the people who believe in him. This pervasiveness has both positive and negative effects. On the one hand, it gives a good Christian tone to the catechism and holds the potential for making the faith intelligible as the following of Christ. On the other hand, it fragments material that should be kept together for clear understanding.

For example, Jesus' role as revealer of God as Father and even as triune is presented cold in the first article of the creed before the outline of his historical life is limned in the second. The crucial role of the Spirit in Jesus' messianic ministry is relegated to the later creedal article on the Holy Spirit. Jesus' identification with the poor in his ministry is miles away from the moral teaching that, following his example, a Christian ought to have a preferential love for the poor. That follows 2,367 paragraphs (from 1390 to 3757) filled with all the sacraments and the first six commandments.

This fragmentation is a prevailing problem of the structure of the catechism itself. It splits faith from life, doctrine about Jesus Christ from the life of discipleship, and both of these from prayer and spirituality. Better integration needs to be achieved in the final draft to make the Christian faith intelligible as a whole.

The long creedal segment "I Believe in God the Son" intends to be a synthesis of the church's christological belief. I will concentrate on this section since it makes explicit the guiding view of Jesus Christ that appears in bits and pieces throughout the rest of the catechism. The chief sources used are the Gospels and the Pauline letters, which are quoted repeatedly and at length. There is also a liberal sprinkling of citations from other New Testament books, teachings of the first seven ecumenical councils, writings of patristic and medieval theologians such as Gregory of Nyssa and Thomas Aquinas, the liturgy of East and West, and papal statements.

The curious judgment seems to have been made that apart from magisterial teaching no other contribution since Council of Trent should be used. Thus, although relatively minor figures are quoted, there are no references to the christological work of major biblical, patristic, or theological scholars of the twentieth century.

The structure of the catechism's Christology as a whole is patterned on the traditional tract "On the Incarnate Word" (*De Verbo Incarnato*) used in manuals for the last several centuries. It is a Christology "from above," a descending Christology. It starts in heaven with the preexisting Son of God, traces his descent into the world of human history to die for our sins, and ends with his universal reign in glory. The center of gravity and interest lies in the dogmatic teaching that in Jesus Christ there are two natures, human and divine, in one divine person, with emphasis on the divine. This becomes the primary filter through which his story is told and his significance perceived.

Accordingly, the narrative line of the creed that the catechism is following is fleshed out by the insertion of doctrinal material. Confessing that we believe in "Jesus Christ, God's only Son, our Lord" becomes the occasion for teaching about Christ's divine sonship with evidence from Scripture, the Nicene debate against Arius, the confession of Ephesus against Nestorius, and the declarations of Chalcedon and Constantinople II. Similarly, the creed's next affirmation about Jesus' conception and birth brings in further explanation of the incarnation complete with technical language about the two natures and their union. Here as in the manuals we also find inserted the teaching about Mary, her immaculate conception, virginity, and motherhood.

Noting that the creed skips over all the years between Jesus' birth and death, the catechism inserts a section on the "mysteries" of the life of Christ. These are to be contemplated with the eyes of faith, which will reveal that in each instance we are dealing with the mystery of recapitulation, of redemption, and of revelation. Thus are presented the mysteries of the childhood and the hidden life of Jesus, followed by the mysteries of his public life from baptism to transfiguration. Throughout these mysteries Jesus is presented as an example for Christians to follow in his submission, abasement, poverty, and prayer.

The creed is picked up again with confession of the passion and resurrection. Jesus' death is treated at length in terms of sacrifice and satisfaction, with the theme of substitution woven in. The articles on his descent into hell, resurrection on the third day, ascension, and future return in glory to judge the living and the dead are unrolled with a view to their significance for the redemption of every individual. This ultimate stage of glory remains closely united with the first, that is, with the descent from heaven realized by the incarnation: "By the right hand of the Father we mean the glory and honor of the divinity, where he who existed as Son of God before all worlds as God, consubstantial with the Father, took his seat bodily after his incarnation and the glorification of his flesh" (1513, quoting John Damascene). Thus the Christology of the catechism comes full circle with Christ the Lord back in glory and reigning now through the church while the salvation that he wrought seeks to be accomplished throughout the world.

Gains

While following a dogmatic Christology from above, several advances of the catechism over the neo-scholastic manuals' presentation of Jesus Christ can be highlighted. A genuinely new and welcome note is sounded here as the catechism strongly endorses Vatican II's teaching that the Jewish people as a whole are not responsible and should not be blamed for the death of Jesus. The historical complexity manifested by the Gospel accounts of the trial of Jesus is acknowledged. And since all of us are sinners, the church makes "Christians responsible for the murder of Jesus with which they have often burdened the Jews" (1452).

From its acknowledgement that Jesus is "a Jew born of a Jewish mother" (1254), to its acknowledgment that many Pharisees were decent characters, to its condemnation of blaming all Jews for the death of Jesus, this is not a Christology that could be used to promote anti-Semitism in the traditional way. However, its explanation of Jesus' relation to the Jewish tradition and its Law, fulfilling it by setting it aside, is ecumenically highly problematic.

There is also some attempt to make the Gospels' view of Jesus' ministry (called in the catechism his public life) count for christological understanding. Brief generic mention is made of his proclamation of the Kingdom of God, his parables, "miracles," invitation to sinners, and the way in which his ministry could have occasioned historical antagonisms that led to his death. This is not a Christology that totally ignores the adult life of the Messiah. In accord with Vatican II, the catechism is also highly inclusive in the scope and depth it allows for the reach of Christian redemption. Given its powerful insistence on Jesus Christ's relation through human nature to every person, this Christology would not support a pessimistic or narrow ecclesiocentric universe. These are all gains.

Critical Problems

While the catechism presents major truths of the faith, its view of Jesus Christ is marked to an unfortunate degree by partiality, incompleteness, and imprecision. The difficulties arise in at least three areas: reading the biblical sources, interpreting tradition, and connecting with twentieth-century experience.

Using Scripture as Proof Texts

The catechism quotes the Scriptures constantly in presenting Jesus Christ. But it does so in a fundamentalist way, with little regard for the insights about the New Testament forged in the last half-century of Catholic biblical renewal. It says the right thing: we must acknowledge literary forms, pay attention to the authors' intent, their way of telling stories in their cultural context, and so on (0275–76). But it usually does not do the right thing when it comes to actually using biblical texts about Jesus Christ. Instead, it uses biblical texts literally to prove preconceived dogmatic understandings.

Through blood, sweat, and tears biblical scholars in the church have forged a remarkable path of reading biblical authors with respect for the authors' intent. The harvest has been rich for Christology. We now realize that the New Testament presents us with not just one view of Jesus but a diversity of views within the one faith, views, moreover, that cannot be harmonized. Mark's Christology of the misunderstood, suffering Messiah is different from John's Christology of the Word made flesh who calls his disciples friends. Each reflects a different experience of the church community that generated it. One cannot be collapsed into the other, but each contributes a witness and insight that nourishes the faith of later believers.

Biblical scholarship has also traced a genuine development in the way Jesus' disciples and later believers came to understand and confess him, from before the resurrection to after it, from a Jewish context to a Hellenistic one, from an implicit to an explicit Christology, from a functional understanding of his messiahship (what he does for us, how he relates to us) to an ontological one (who he is in his being that enables him to do this). Apostolic preachers explicated what Jesus said and did in the light of that "clearer understanding" that they enjoyed after the resurrection. There is continuity but also difference between Jesus' historical life, the church's early preaching, and the text of the written Gospels. This three-stage schema was given official recognition by the Pontifical Biblical Commission in 1964 and reprised in Vatican II's "Dogmatic Constitution on Divine Revelation."[1]

Unfortunately, the draft of this official catechism ignores the official church position on biblical interpretation. In the interest of its own agenda it does violence to the Gospels' christological variety and presents a false uniformity as historical fact. Failing to distinguish between levels of Gospel tradition, it constructs doctrinal propositions upon biblical texts that cannot support them. Approaching the Scripture with a predetermined format, it overlooks much that is at the living heart of the Gospel witness.

For example, despite what Paul or Mark might have actually thought about Jesus, they are quoted as if they had a full-blown Nicene Christology. Despite the late and highly developed character of John's Christology, the "I am" statements in this Gospel are taken as the verbatim words of Jesus and used to prove his divinity. Scripture texts are strung together in an indiscriminate manner with little regard for their integrity. Thus, Jesus as the Son of God in a divine transcendent sense is demonstrated by a literal reading of Peter's confession in Mt 16:17, Paul's conversion experience in Gal 1:15–16, Luke's rendition of Paul's preaching in Acts 9:20, as well as Jn 20:31 and 1 Thes 1:10 (1271). On balance, what is going on here is a sophisticated form of proof-texting, familiar from the manual style of theology. Scripture is pressed onto a procrustean bed. It is as though the biblical renewal had never happened.

In 1984 the Pontifical Biblical Commission issued a document called "Scripture and Christology" in which it analyzed eleven ways Scripture was being used to present Jesus Christ. The catechism belongs to the first way, called the "classical or traditional theological approach," which presents a dogmatic system enriched by biblical texts. The biblical commission's cautions about this way are applicable to the catechism at every point. Not being open to critical questions in the exegetical area, it takes certain details to be historical when they are actually the result of literary convention for a theological purpose. It too easily accepts the word-for-word authenticity of certain sayings attributed to Jesus in the Gospels, even though they are recounted differently in different books. This leads it to construct doctrinal propositions upon conservative conclusions in biblical interpretation that are controversial, thus setting out on a deceptive route.[2]

The way this draft of the catechism uses and misuses the Scripture has a negative impact in at least three directions. First, it does harm to the way the contemporary church has learned to read the Scriptures, in the process veiling the distinct and irreplaceable witness of the Word of God itself. Second, it makes christological doctrine unbelievable by constructing its supports on historically shaky ground. Not that the doctrine is not true. The old apologetics does not work with the new exegesis. Anyone who learned this catechism would be set up for a crisis of faith as soon as he or she encountered modern biblical interpretation.

Perhaps most serious of all, it takes the life out of the church's living memory of Jesus, so recently revitalized by new reading of the Gospels. With telling insight John Paul II wrote of Jesus Christ, "It is his life that speaks, his humanity, his fidelity to the truth, his all-embracing love. Furthermore his death on the cross speaks—that is to say the inscrutable depth of his suffering and abandonment."[3] These are precisely the things that have power to awaken faith and discipleship. Thanks to the biblical renewal, the word of Jesus Christ's life is being heard more clearly. The synoptic Gospels have been rediscovered in their own integrity. Space has been made for Jesus' historical existence in all its authenticity. The witness of his fidelity stands out starkly against the background of historical conflict and contingent events. The power of the resurrection shines dramatically, and the hope it generates moves to the heart of faith. The living memory of Jesus watered by the Scriptures is renewing the church.

The imposition of a preformed system onto the Gospel texts robs the story of Jesus of its vitality and hinders the word of his life from being heard. It is instructive to note some of what it omits in telling the story of Jesus. The prophetic nature of Jesus' ministry and his role as the eschatological prophet are overlooked. Nor are we told about his table fellowship with all manner of people, the concrete stories of his parables, his inclusion of women in the circle of disciples, the Johannine story of Jesus' washing the feet of his friends at the Last Supper, or the final anguished cry from the cross. The agony in the garden is given only fleeting mention in another connection.

As a result of a dogmatic manner of reading the Scriptures, the figure of Jesus comes across as a cold fish, knowing everything, in complete control, at the same time totally submissive, moving through his paces, not very inspiring. Half a century ago Karl Rahner labeled this picture of Jesus Christ "mythological" in a pejorative sense and laid at its doorstep a great deal of the responsibility for this generation's difficulty with the faith.[4]

The catechism states explicitly that it will interpret the whole of Scripture as a unity (0279). But what it has done is use Scripture to support one particular dogmatic view of Jesus Christ, filtering out whatever in Scripture does not support this view and pressing biblical insight into a neo-scholastic mold. Instead of giving a total and integral biblical picture of Jesus, it delivers only a partial and distorted one. Like a Shakespearean character doomed to tragedy by a fatal flaw, what follows from this biblical option leads to a debilitated end: unsubstantiated claims about Jesus Christ made in pseudorealistic historical terms that do not hold up under scrutiny. And this is presented as the belief of the church.

A One-Sided Emphasis on Divinity

The christological tradition went forward through the centuries in a variety of ways: in the actual discipleship of believers, including even martyrdom; in deep streams of spirituality focused on different aspects of the humanity of Jesus Christ; in liturgy, theology, and in precise doctrinal formulations. In keeping with its neo-scholastic paradigm, the catechism focuses only on the latter, missing the opportunity to teach about the richness of the church's heritage. Even in presenting dogma about Christ, an inability to conceive how humanity can flourish in all freedom in close union with God leads to a one-sided emphasis.

Through controversies galore during the first seven centuries, the church crafted the doctrine that in Jesus Christ two *physis* concur in one *hypostasis*, or as we say in English, two natures unite in one "person." The twentieth-century renaissance in Catholic patristic scholarship has shown that the point of this doctrine is salvific. Its fundamental interest is to protect the faith of the church that in Jesus Christ God has truly entered human history and thereby saved us. Every element here is vital. Only God can save. Just as importantly, what is not assumed is not redeemed. The genuine humanity of Jesus Christ is as crucial theologically as his divinity.

The catechism affirms this theoretically, but it does not carry through on its implications. Part of the difficulty is with vocabulary. There has been a semantic drift of the word *person*, so that its meaning today usually connotes a psychological reality in a sense different from its original ontological meaning. Thus, to say that Jesus is a divine person who has assumed a human nature is inevitably to lead people today to think that in Jesus there is a divine psychology operating out of a human body.

This is not the intent of the dogma. Rather, in rejecting monophysitism, it affirms that the human nature of Jesus Christ possesses a genuine, spontaneous, free, spiritual, active center, a human rational soul which as creature faces God in a genuinely human attitude of adoration, obedience, and a most radical sense of creaturehood. The catechism, however, uses the word *divine person* in an ontological/psychological sense, and so gives an interpretation of the dogma that does not do justice to his genuine humanity.

More profoundly the disinclination to affirm the full-blooded humanity of Jesus Christ is rooted in a fundamental dualism that pervades the catechism. This dualistic view separates matter and spirit, body and soul, humanity and God into opposite camps. There is competition between them, so that there has to be less of one to make room for more of the other. To attribute all the messiness of humanity to Jesus would be to compromise his being genuinely the Word of God.

Knowing how to embrace unity in difference, however, makes clear that this is a false dichotomy. Given the nature of God as love, genuine human autonomy grows in direct and not in inverse proportion to union with holy mystery. Nowhere is this more true than in Jesus Christ, whose unique union with God renders him the most truly free and personal of us all. But this antidote to the poison of ancient dualism has not been swallowed by the catechism. Instead, it affirms one-sidedly that the Son of God who possesses in identity the absolute divine being assumes a human nature as his own and thus becomes a human being while remaining himself. It gives no substantive play to the equally important truth that this human being can pray, adore, weep, be surprised, receive the gift of being heard, experience the claims of God's will upon him as something authoritative and alien, and even feel in a creaturely way to the point of abandonment by God.

These problems revolve around the disputed theological question of Jesus' psychology. Biblical scholars caution against presuming that we can grasp with certainty what Jesus did or did not know in any detail, including his own self-identity in an explicit way. Nor has this ever been definitively defined by the church. But the catechism presents as certain doctrine the disputed theological opinion that Jesus knew everything clearly and knew it from the first moment of his existence. According to the catechism, when Jesus says he does not know something about the future as in Mark 13:32, he really means that it is not his mission to reveal it (1280, 1311). When he uses the title Son of God for himself, he is affirming his eternal preexistence (1273). Modern biblical exegesis does not support these positions. Neither does a theology that takes seriously in a contemporary context that Jesus Christ is genuinely human.

In its review of the early christological heresies and the councils that dealt with them, the catechism, while repetitive about Arius, who denied Christ's divinity, is strangely silent about Apollinaris's views, something that the manuals included. This bishop taught that to preserve the sinlessness of Christ and the unity of his person he could not be said to have a human soul. Rather, in a kind of divine transplant the Word of God substituted for his human mind and will, making him human flesh on the outside but inwardly divine. This view was condemned by various synods and the second ecumenical council at Constantinople (A.D. 381). The truth that Jesus Christ had "a rational soul," which insured a genuine human psychology, was incorporated into the confession of Chalcedon.

Although this early chapter in the development of doctrine is omitted, the ghost of Apollinaris haunts this catechism. It cannot admit any recognizable form of human knowledge or human freedom into Jesus' experience. It quotes Cyril of Alexandria frequently, for example, to defend Mary as the Mother of God but never notes that this same Cyril also wrote, "We have admired his goodness in that for love of us he has not refused to descend to such a low position as to bear all that belongs to our nature, included in which is ignorance."[5] Such selective reading of the tradition delivers a truncated view of the humanity of Jesus Christ. He walks around like God dressed up in human clothes; he is an actor who has his lines memorized in advance; his humanity is a puppet whose strings are pulled by the divine. This Christ from above never really gets his feet on the ground.

"He worked with human hands, he thought with a human mind, acted by human choice, and loved with a human heart. Born of the Virgin Mary he has truly been made one of us, like us in all things but sin."[6] This lovely and often repeated phrase of Vatican II tellingly does not appear in the catechism. Instead, Jesus Christ's humanity is presented in scholastic fashion as merely the perfect "instrument" of the divine purpose to save us (1455). This is a brittle and inadequate analogy, far removed from contemporary valuation of the human in both secular and religious discourse. Theologically this presentation of Jesus Christ is one-sided, and so the radical depths of the incarnation are covered over. Existentially and religiously this Christ is far above our human struggles, and so rather useless for preaching, evangelization, and catechesis.

An Inadequate Theology of Redemption

If anything good can be said to characterize this century of mega-death it is the growing sense that we are all one world. This is coupled with a breakthrough of the desire for freedom and human rights. In keeping with the catechism's scriptural proof-texting and doctrinal dualism, its view of redemption does not deliver a good news in keeping with this consciousness.

Jesus' crucifixion under Pontius Pilate is analyzed at length using the major metaphors of sacrifice and substitution, while redemption is presented as a work of satisfaction thanks to Christ's love for sinners. There is so much more that should be said. Scripture uses multiple ways of speaking of what God has done for us in Jesus' death and resurrection: reconciliation, victory, liberation, and justification, to name a few. In addition, tradition carries alternative theologies of redemption. Not only does the catechism present only one such theology, it does not try to connect its theology with the horizon of contemporary people who have no experience of temple sacrifice or of feudal satisfaction practices. Nor does it deal with the critical pastoral problem that at face value such a theology casts God the Father in the vengeful role of the executioner, desiring the death of his son.

Regarding the fruits of Christ's sacrifice, the emphasis is on the individual person's being saved from sin: the cross won grace now being mediated to the individual through the sacraments. What is overlooked is the crucial reality that the individual is always constituted by a network of relationships. The insight that salvation includes human community, social structures, ecological connectedness, and right order is not integrated. Correspondingly, the personal response of faith is highly privatized. The catechism's vision does not encompass a faith that does justice, except remotely.

There is also a peculiar, relentless emphasis on submissiveness, both for Jesus and for those who believe in him. A relatively long treatment is given to the hidden life of Jesus at Nazareth, about which we know nothing certain. The hidden life is presented with emphasis on his "long years of voluntary submission" "every day" to Mary, to Joseph, to his Father in heaven (four times in 1376). The Jesus of the public life is held up as an example of abasement, while his death on the cross is the supreme instance of his submission to the will of his Father. This is what won salvation, and believers are pointed to these examples as the model for their behavior, generically.

Such a picture is simply not true to the Jesus of the Gospels, who is depicted as courageous, groundbreaking, and even opposed to authority when his sense of mission for the good of people required it. He is sent not to teach submission but "to proclaim release to the captives, recovering of sight to the blind, to set at liberty those who are oppressed" (Lk 4:18, not quoted in the catechism). Nowhere do the Gospels depict him as commanding obedience, nor extolling it as a virtue. The salvation that Jesus brings occasions liberation, not a new submission.

I would think that anyone who has watched the people of Eastern Europe mass together with their candles and flags to insist on freedom; who knows the grinding poverty of the poor of the Third World and their rightful desire for a life more in keeping with human dignity; who knows the debilitating effect of systems of domination, be it of men over women, whites over blacks, armed military groups over unarmed civilians; anyone with a pastoral sense who is aware of the deep movement in our world toward freedom would know how dangerous and repugnant it is to propose submission/obedience as the message of the gospel.

Borrowing a page from the Frankfort school, we may ask *cui bono*? To whose good is this telling of the story of Jesus with the central metaphor being submission? It would seem to be at the service of an ideology that supports vested interests, interests that would prefer to have present power structures remain unquestioned. The good news of salvation on its way from God in Jesus Christ gets lost in this telling.

Exclusive language and sexist presuppositions also weaken the good news that this catechism presents. The language is a major drawback, given that English is one of the three official languages of this draft of the catechism (the other two being Spanish and French). Thus the maneuver of going to the original Latin and retranslating cannot be performed.

"Man" constitutes a special problem. It is used generically to mean all human beings ("The single end of the practice of the moral life is to lead each man to become what he is" [3803]). And it is used specifically to mean adult males ("Only baptized men can validly receive this sacrament" [2747] of ordination, although it would be interesting to take this in a generic sense). There is also an abundance of son, brother, and fraternal language in describing the new life in Christ: "Thanks to the Spirit who transforms us to the image of God, we become 'adopted sons' of the Father united to Christ" (3169). Is it truly expected that through such catechesis girls will be thrilled to find that Christ has made them into sons? Hardly. In truth girls and women were not much in mind when the catechism was written, except marginally.

Besides the exclusive language, an androcentric perspective pervades the catechism. Speaking of women who prefigured Mary's role in salvation history, for example, it states: "Against all human expectation, God chooses what is weak and feeble (cf. 1 Cor 1.27) to demonstrate the faithfulness of his promise: Anne, the mother of Samuel, Deborah, Ruth, Judith, and Esther, and many other women" (1321). Now, to outfox a ruthless leader, charming one's way unarmed into his tent and then cutting off his head as Judith did, may be called many things. But unless one has gone down the rabbit hole, "weak and feeble" is not one of them.

In truth all these women are presented as weak because of their gender. But at least they are mentioned. There is a deafening silence about women's participation during the ministry of Jesus and about their keeping faithful vigil at the cross—both attested to in Scripture. The androcentric perspective compromises the catechism's value, casting it primarily in the service not of the universal church but of its dominant half.

Mary

As with Jesus Christ, material on Mary is scattered throughout the catechism. Three Marian dogmas—the immaculate conception, divine maternity, and virginity—are found under the third article of the creed, and her assumption into heaven is found under the ninth. As with Christology, a critical reading of Scripture is ignored in favor of assimilating certain biblical texts to a dogmatic perspective. The immaculate conception, for example, is said to be supported by the angel Gabriel's salutation to Mary as "full of grace" (1322), whereas the original text reads "highly favored one" and Luke did not have the remotest idea of this doctrine. Predictably, the Markan Gospel's negative view of Mary which places her outside the circle of disciples in 3:31–35 is omitted, and differences between the Gospels' portraits of Mary are harmonized.

The traditional manualist perspective is considerably enriched in the catechism by Vatican II's teaching about Mary in relation to Christ and the church, and this is a gain. However, its interpretation of the council is not always trustworthy. Example: with an appeal to the "Dogmatic Constitution on the Church" (no. 63), Mary's virginity is presented as a sign of her faith "unadulterated by doubt." Not only does the constitution not connect Mary's virginity with an absence of doubting, but the words in quotation marks do not even appear.

The presentation manages to remain a privilege-centered Mariology, freed from the excesses of earlier times yet not successful in rendering Mary credible as a genuine woman whose life was a "pilgrimage of faith," a felicitous phrase of the council omitted in the catechism. Nor are the council's warnings about excesses in the Marian cult mentioned. Overall, the catechism's view of Mary is analogous to its presentation of Jesus Christ: containing some truths of the faith but flawed by biblical superficiality, dogmatic dualism, and pastoral dubiousness.

Conclusion

While commendably seeking to be synthetic, organic, complete, and precise, and while containing some of the treasures of the faith, the catechism's overall presentation of Jesus Christ is marked to an unfortunate degree by partiality and imprecision. For all of its presumed good intentions and its incorporation of some insights of Vatican II, this is not a catechism representing the spirit and insights of that council. Rather, it presents a neo-scholastic theology of Jesus Christ and redemption liberally salted with scriptural proof texts. We can do better than this. If this draft is not substantially revised, even essentially redrafted and rewritten, it may well function best as a "point of reference" of what not to do in drawing up a catechism for this country.

The Church
in the Catechism

Avery Dulles, S.J.
Fordham University

The catechism overlooks the corporate significance of non–Roman Catholic churches and ecclesial communities in God's saving plan.

One wishes that the questions of papacy, episcopacy, collegiality, and magisterium could have been discussed more thoroughly and less frequently.

The *Catechism for the Universal Church,* in its present draft, suffers from several inner tensions, partly induced by the conflicting desires of those who called for this work at the Extraordinary Synod of 1985. Aspiring to be a pedagogical tool in the style of the sixteenth-century catechisms, it adheres to the four-part structure of Apostles' Creed, sacraments, commandments, and Lord's Prayer (0011). Presenting itself as a "compendium of the whole of catholic doctrine, both of faith and of morals" (0016), it seeks to incorporate in an "organic" way (0021) the authoritative teaching of the magisterium, including that of recent popes and councils. Beyond this, the new catechism attempts to be faithful to the inspiration of Vatican Council II as "the great catechism of modern times" (0010). Finally, it wishes to draw extensively on sacred Scripture, the church fathers, and the liturgies, including those of the ancient East (0017).

The various aspirations impose different and partly incompatible priorities. Can a complete and coherent presentation of Catholic doctrine be achieved in the framework of the traditional four-part catechetical structure? And can an authoritative synthesis of traditional teaching be combined with the generally open and phenomenological approach of Vatican II?

These tensions are evident in the treatment of ecclesiology. Vatican II, named as the principal source (1613), made the church its primary theme, but in the catechism ecclesiology plays a minor role. It is limited to some twenty pages (pp. 153–74) out of more than four hundred. Vatican II intended to bring the church abreast of the present day and to address the experience of contemporary believers. But the present catechism, concerned with fidelity to the past, is unabashedly dogmatic in its approach. It offers a timeless ecclesiology based on authoritative testimonies.

The linkage between the church and faith is repeatedly emphasized. After describing the church as body of Christ and bride, the catechism declares: "It is only with the eye of faith that one can see the Church in the way that she is described in these quotations from the council" (1655). In discussing the four "notes" of the church, which were used apologetically in much Counter-Reformation ecclesiology, this catechism affirms that faith alone can recognize the church as one, holy, catholic, and apostolic (1683). Although we do not believe *in* the church, in the way in which we believe in the three divine persons (0319, 0321, 1612), we believe *with* and *within* the church, which is, so to speak, the first believer (0342). The church "teaches us the faith" (0343). No one can be a believer in solitude, without the support of the believing community (0336–37).

In summary, we have here a "descending" ecclesiology, an "ecclesiology from above." The catechism focuses on the divine origins of the church and contemplates the church with the eyes of faith. Such an approach, though perhaps appropriate for an authoritative catechism of this kind, is not necessarily suitable for actual religious instruction. The catechism is not intended to preempt the good judgment of the teacher or prevent the use of other catechisms that may be better adapted to particular groups or individuals. Some readers may require more explicit treatments of contemporary objections or difficulties. A more experiential or phenomenological approach may be appropriate. The universal catechism, as its prologue makes clear, is intended as an exposition of doctrine and not as enjoining a particular catechetical method. The method of instruction should be varied according to the age and culture of the students (0020).

The four-part structure of the catechism forces some artificial separations. The church, taken up in part 1 (the creed) under the ninth article ("I believe in the holy Catholic church"), is separated from the sacraments (part 2), from the new life of the Christian in the Spirit (part 3), and from the life of prayer (part 4). Within part 1 the church is treated between the Holy Spirit and the communion of saints. The ecclesiology is anticipated in the article on the Holy Spirit, insofar as the Spirit constitutes, sanctifies, and sends the church. The ecclesiology is rounded out by the section on the communion of saints, to which a section on "Mary—Mother of the Church" is appended.

The Church as Sacrament

The section on the church is divided into three articles: the mystery of the church, the church as people of God, and the four traditional "notes." In the first article, on the church as mystery, the catechism chooses its basic model of ecclesiology. Equating mystery with sacrament, it speaks of the church as the sacrament of Christ, that is to say, the manifestation and communication of Christ, who is himself the great sacrament of salvation (1615). The church, as the sacrament of the mystery of salvation (1615, 1700), is the sign and instrument of intimate union of human persons with God and with one another in God (1588, 1614, 1628, 1658). The theme of the church as sacrament prepares in some ways for the treatise on the sacraments that will come in part 2 of the catechism (cf. 2088).

The various images of the church in Scripture and Vatican II are explained as presenting different aspects of the one inexhaustible mystery that is the church. Special attention is given to the images of the church as mystical body and as bride, both of which emphasize intimacy with Christ. The mystical body, according to the catechism, is "more than an image," for the church is a real and visible extension of the living Christ—mystical because it is accessible to faith alone and because it belongs to God's plan of salvation (1642). The image of the bride supplements that of the mystical body by suggesting the otherness between the church and Christ, who does not absorb it into himself (1652). The Holy Spirit is the "soul" of the mystical body (1650). The church is also the temple in which the Holy Spirit is pleased to dwell (1602, 1637, 1664).

The exposition of the church as people of God in article 2 is colored by the sacramental model already adopted. "People of God," according to the catechism, is an image drawn from the Old Testament, which can be applied to the church only when qualified by a new christological and pneumatological (Spirit-centered) focus (1637). Because it has Christ as its head and the kingdom of God as its destiny, the church "has characteristics which distinguish it clearly from all other peoples in history" (1668). One becomes a member by "birth from above," by faith and baptism (1669). The church is a priestly, prophetic, and royal people, hierarchically structured (1673–76; cf. 1672).

The universal catechism does not admit any opposition between the church and the kingdom of God. On the contrary, it identifies them. Church and kingdom "designate the same reality, but from different points of view" (1632). The church here on earth is the kingdom of Christ already present in mystery (1519; cf. *Lumen Gentium*, no. 3), but in the present age the kingdom is still incomplete (1586). "The Church in the glory of heaven will be the Kingdom fully realized" (1633).

This identification of the church and the kingdom runs counter to a great deal of post–Vatican II theology, both Protestant and Catholic, but I do not see how it can be faulted in terms of the council's own teaching, provided that the ecclesial character of all grace and salvation is kept in view. By adverting to the provisionality of both church and kingdom within history—as the catechism does to some extent—one can guard against the danger of triumphalism.

In treating of the origins of the church, the catechism emphasizes that the church is born from the pierced side of Christ (1624) and that it receives its life from the sending of the Holy Spirit on Pentecost (1626). Christ is not only the foundation of the church, he is also its founder (1685). In his earthly ministry he intended to bring about the church, which would exist definitively after the events of Easter and Pentecost. For this last point—which may be polemically directed against theologians such as Hans Küng—the catechism relies on a quotation from a 1985 document of the International Theological Commission (1634), a source that lacks magisterial authority.

Although the catechism several times refers to the present era as "the time of the Church" (1586, 2019), it also teaches that the church is coextensive with all times. The church has its roots in the Old Covenant and has in some sort existed since the time of Adam and Abel (1622); it will reach its consummation in glory at the end of the ages (1621, 1622, 1629). Thus, the church should not be understood simply as the institution existing from Pentecost until the Parousia. It includes the souls suffering in purgatory and the saints gloriously reigning with Christ in heaven (1746).

A distinctive feature of this catechism may be found in its discussion of the "ultimate passover"—a final trial that will shake the faith of the church (1524). This dire prediction is based on several apocalyptic passages in the New Testament, which are understood as denying that the kingdom will be achieved through any historical triumph of the church (1526). Here the universal catechism takes a line that differs from some earlier catechisms, such as the so-called *Dutch Catechism* and the 1985 *German Catechism for Adults*, which interpreted these texts as hortatory and consolatory rather than predictive. In context, the universal catechism is concerned to obviate any claim that the messianic hope of peace and prosperity will ever be accomplished within history (1525). This warning is directed explicitly against fundamentalist millenarism and perhaps implicitly against certain types of Catholic political and liberation theology.

The Notes or Attributes of the Church

Under the four traditional notes that form the theme of article 3, the catechism presents in highly compressed fashion several standard ecclesiological themes. In taking up the unity of the church, the catechism asserts that the church is one both in its causal principles (one Lord, one Spirit) and in its historical realization, which is sealed by the bonds of confession, sacramental communion, fraternal harmony, and pastoral government (1684–90). These paragraphs convey the impression that the church of Christ is simply identical with Roman Catholicism. Whereas the "Dogmatic Constitution on the Church" says that the church of Christ "subsists" (subsistit, Lumen Gentium, no. 8) in the Roman Catholic church – a term chosen by the council to make room for the ecclesial reality of other Christian churches and communities – the present text gives misleading translations, stating that the church of Christ "has its existence" (1687) and "exists" (1736) in the Catholic church (1736).

Continuing its discussion of the oneness of the church, the catechism describes the wounding of unity by heresy and schism (1692–94) and makes a brief allusion to the ecumenical task – that of overcoming the divisions among Christians. The inadequacy of human powers to achieve the goal of Christian unity is emphasized (1698). Much later the catechism states that all baptized believers stand in a certain relationship of communion with the Catholic church (2266) and that the Orthodox churches have true sacraments and apostolic succession in the ministry (2477). In its ecclesiology, however, the catechism overlooks the corporate significance of non–Roman-Catholic churches and ecclesial communities in God's saving plan. In this respect the catechism falls short of Vatican Council II's "Decree on Ecumenism" (no. 3).

The catechism dwells at some length on the second attribute of the church, holiness (1699–1705), a theme resumed in the article on the communion of saints (1737–54). As in the first chapter of Vatican II's "Constitution on the Sacred Liturgy" and the fifth chapter of its "Dogmatic Constitution on the Church," personal sanctity is affirmed as the main purpose of the church (1700). All members of the church are called to seek intimate union with God through charity in their hearts (1702). The variety of vocations and ways to holiness, elaborated in chapter 5 of the Vatican II "Constitution on the Church," is omitted in the catechism.

As in Vatican II, the church is held to be unfailingly holy (1699; cf. Lumen Gentium, no. 39). Although the church includes sinners among its members, not excepting its ministers, sin always separates the sinner to some degree from the church (1703). Later, in the treatment of penance, it will be mentioned that the sacrament reconciles the sinner both to God and to the church (2523, 2526). In view of the distance existing between the church and its sinful members, the catechism is perhaps justified in not speaking of the church itself as sinful, any more than did Vatican II. The catechism acknowledges, though without great emphasis, that the church, "with sinners clasped to her bosom," stands in need of penance and renewal (1703; cf. *Lumen Gentium*, no. 8).

Vatican II's "Constitution on the Church" placed immediately after the chapter on the universal call to holiness a special chapter devoted to the religious life. This theme is unaccountably neglected in the present catechism. The absence of any discussion of monasticism and the contemplative vocation is surprising in a catechism that in most other respects dwells on the riches of the Catholic tradition.

The third attribute, catholicity, provides an occasion for the catechism to explain the various senses in which the church is universal—for example, in embodying Christ, who has the fullness of divinity, in providing the fullness of the means of salvation, and in being sent to all peoples and individuals without exception (1707–8). The catholicity of the church permeates all its parts and congregations, in each of which the universal church is truly present (1709–10). The variety of particular or local churches is mentioned very briefly, almost in passing (1711), but the theme will be developed at greater length in a later chapter dealing with the liturgy (2105–8).

This later text picks up the idea, prominent in Vatican II, that the mystery of Christ is legitimately understood and celebrated in different ways, according to the variety of local cultures, which are gathered into a many-splendored unity thanks to the catholicity of the one church. If this idea of unity in diversity could be brought out more explicitly in the main treatment of catholicity, the catechism would be enriched. Even a cross-reference to the section on the liturgy would help.

Generally speaking, the present catechism, reflecting a strongly universalist ecclesiology, gives very little attention to the local churches. The particular church is identified exclusively with the diocese (1709). Other local manifestations of the church, such as patriarchates, regional conferences, parishes, and basic communities, are overlooked. The family as "domestic church" is later mentioned in a discussion of marriage (2869) but does not appear in the treatment of ecclesiology.

Under the heading of catholicity the catechism treats the necessity of the church (1713) and the question of who belongs to the church (1714). On these points the language of Vatican II is exactly quoted without added explanation. Like the council itself, the catechism fails to show

how people ignorant of the gospel and of the church can receive the grace
of Christ, which is in principle conferred through faith and the sacraments. Earlier the catechism described the church as the "mother of all
believers" and quoted Cyprian as saying: "No one can have God for
Father who does not have the Church for mother" (0353). The ecclesial
nature of grace and salvation suggested in these passages does not seem
to be consistently carried through in the discussion of catholicity. The
same ambiguity recurs in the treatise on the sacraments, where the
necessity of baptism is discussed (2248–55). It might be unrealistic to
expect the catechism to clarify what the council and many recent theologians have left obscure.

The last note, apostolicity, is understood rather restrictively in terms
of continuity with the ministry of the first apostles (1720). Apostolicity, in
this sense, has reference primarily to the pope and the bishops, who
inherit the transmissible functions of the apostles. The apostles are identified as the original Twelve, or at least with the original witnesses of the
resurrection who were sent forth by Christ himself. Like the apostles, the
bishops are held to constitute a college in which the pope, as Peter's suc-
cessor, holds the primacy (1726–28). At this point the catechism takes up
very briefly the papal office, the relationship of the pope to the episcopate, and the infallibility of the supreme magisterium (1725, 1730–31).
The magisterium was also mentioned earlier, under the "Transmission of
Divine Revelation" (0250). Later, under the sacrament of order, the catechism will return to the themes of apostolic succession and the collegiality of the episcopate (2725, 2729–30).

These repetitions are probably inevitable in view of the structure of
the catechism, but one wishes that the questions of papacy, episcopacy,
collegiality, and magisterium could have been discussed more thoroughly and less frequently. No place is allotted for a coherent treatment
of the structures of government in the church. Some other catechisms
avoid this problem by providing a section on ministry under the heading
of ecclesiology. If this were done, it might be possible to say something
about the varying degrees of authority in magisterial statements (which
are very rarely irreformable), about ecumenical councils (a surprising
omission), and even about particular councils and synods. No mention is
made in this catechism (or most other catechisms) of the synod of bishops or episcopal conferences, in spite of their prominence in the contemporary life of the church.

Even within the present order it might be possible to include somewhere a proper treatment of the ministry of the word. This could be
placed in the section on apostolicity or perhaps in the introduction to the

section on sacraments. Since Vatican II there has been a great flowering of nonordained ministries. Because these ministries are so helpful to the church and so meaningful to many lay persons, their omission in this catechism is regrettable.

A broader conception of apostolicity than we find in the present draft of the catechism could also provide a favorable context for the lay apostolate. This theme, though missing in the section on ecclesiology, is not entirely absent from the catechism as a whole. The task of all the members of the church to announce the gospel and bear witness to it is mentioned earlier in the chapter on the Holy Spirit (1598) and again under the rubric of the church as people of God (1675). Most fully, the prophetic function of the church appears in the last part of the catechism, dealing with the moral life (3145–65). There the whole church is shown as having the duty to proclaim the gospel and to teach the principles of the moral law. The laity are exhorted to play an active part in applying Christian principles to the problems of the day (3159). Although the church's function of building a just society is not strongly emphasized, the catechism does assert the responsibility of the faithful to serve "the common good of human society so that it may conform to the rules of justice and actively support the practice of the virtues" (1676).

Conclusion

In terms of the five models of the church presented in my earlier work, *Models of the Church*,[1] I would characterize the present catechism as clearly favoring the sacramental. The idea of communion, although also present, is interpreted in terms of shared faith and sacramental life rather than as an experience of interpersonal relationships or joint discipleship, as in many presentations of the communion model. The other three models of the church—institution, herald, and servant—are definitely subordinated. While the divinely given functions of pope and bishops as successors of the apostles are mentioned on several occasions, relatively little attention is given to the juridical and social structures that have evolved in the history of the church (institutional model). The church is seen as having a mission to evangelize (herald model) and to promote justice in society (servant model), but its reality is not defined in terms of these responsibilities.

As one who has a certain preference for the sacramental model, I am in sympathy with many directions taken by the universal catechism. In spite of the criticisms that can be made, this work could in some ways serve as "a point of reference," though not as a binding norm, for regional catechisms drawn up in countries such as our own (cf. 0016). But I feel obliged to express certain dissatisfactions with the present draft, which is not an attractive or inspiring presentation of the Catholic faith.

Much of the difficulty arises from the four-part schematization. Useful as the sequence of creed, sacraments, commandments, and Lord's Prayer may be as a touchstone for elementary catechesis, these four headings give a poor framework for the kind of dogmatic synthesis attempted here. The fidelity to Vatican II, moreover, is incomplete. Certain teachings of the council are indeed repeated, but many of its concerns, such as *aggiornamento*, the reformability of the church, the importance of the Word of God, the structures of collegiality, the active role of the laity, the value of the religious life, regional diversification, and ecumenism, are skirted or suppressed. A stronger case for evangelization and for the social mission of the church would be desirable.

In the catechism as a whole, and not simply in the ecclesiology, the biblical citations should be carefully reviewed to assure their conformity with contemporary scholarship. The patristic citations and references, as presently given, seem to interrupt the flow of the argument rather than to be truly supportive. They might better be consigned to footnotes or reduced in number, and in any case translated into English rather than left in Latin, as is frequently the case. A way should be found to distinguish between matters of faith, noninfallible doctrines, and merely theological opinions. The theological preferences of the authors, where they are controversial and unofficial, should probably be excluded and certainly not presented as if they were binding doctrine, as is occasionally done. Finally, the translations from Vatican II should be carefully scrutinized. Some of them, as I have mentioned, are misleading. The quotations from the "Dogmatic Constitution on the Church" in paragraphs 1713, 1719, and 1728, as they now stand, are nearly unintelligible.

PART 3

THE LITURGY, SACRAMENTS, AND PRAYER IN THE CATECHISM

The Liturgy
and Eucharist
in the Catechism

Peter E. Fink, S.J.
Weston School of Theology

The catechism is somewhat faithful, somewhat innovative, and somewhat regressive all at the same time.

The catechism presents a collage of theological insights that clash rather than form a unified whole.

Vatican II's "Dogmatic Constitution on the Sacred Liturgy" (*Sacrosanctum Concilium*) greatly enriched and significantly advanced Roman Catholic understanding of the liturgy in general and of the Eucharist in particular. This enrichment continued in the postconciliar reformed rituals with their attending introductions (*praenotanda*). For the Eucharist, the Roman Missal of Paul VI with its *General Instruction* presents in both the form of prayer (*lex orandi*) and the form of teaching (*lex credendi*) the fullness of eucharistic faith as it is celebrated and proclaimed by the contemporary church.

The proposed *Catechism for the Universal Church* aims to offer a "compendium of the whole of catholic doctrine" (0016). It devotes its entire second part to the liturgy in its many forms under the title "On the Celebration of the Christian Mystery." To assess this treatment of the liturgy and eucharistic faith, it is important to examine the catechism in light of both *Sacrosanctum Concilium* and the *General Instruction of the Roman Missal*, for these remain primary and foundational statements of the postconciliar church's magisterium.

Part 2 of the catechism is divided into two sections. Section 1, "The Sacramental Economy" (2009–2163), presents the liturgy as a whole, including a focus on the Eucharist as a liturgical act. Section 2, "The Seven Sacraments of the Church" (2201–2882), includes additional material on the Eucharist under the heading "The Sacraments of Initiation"

(2401–97). This is itself an unfortunate separation. Further materials on the church's sacramental worship of God are scattered throughout the catechism, especially in the sections on the creed (when treating of the Holy Spirit) and on the first commandment. For this assessment, however, my examination will limit itself to the materials in part 2. After an initial overview, some specific issues will be brought into focus.

Initial Overview

Three questions can be addressed to the catechism in its relation to Vatican II and to the postconciliar liturgical reform. Does the catechism faithfully represent the magisterium as it is set forth in *Sacrosanctum Concilium*, the *General Instruction of the Roman Missal*, and the liturgical texts of the Roman Missal? Does the catechism advance what is contained in these documents in any significant way? Does the catechism depart from the conciliar and postconciliar *lex orandi* and *lex credendi* in a way that either distorts, steps back from, or otherwise bypasses what *Sacrosanctum Concilium* and the *General Instruction* set forth? An affirmative answer must be given to all three questions, for three distinct threads are woven through the catechism.

One thread in the catechism is faithful to the primary vision of the church at prayer as it is set forth in *Sacrosanctum Concilium* (no. 7). It speaks of the liturgy as the action of Christ, the high priest, together with the church which is his body. It locates the liturgy of the church within the sacramental economy of salvation: born when the church itself is born through the outpouring of the Spirit of God, the liturgy serves both the ongoing salvation of the world and the church's anticipation of the fullness of that salvation in the final coming of Jesus Christ.

The catechism admirably recalls the relationship between faith and worship explained in *Sacrosanctum Concilium:* liturgy presupposes faith, on the one hand, and expresses, nourishes, and deepens faith, on the other (no. 59). And true to *Sacrosanctum Concilium* (nos. 37–40), the catechism recognizes and supports a plurality of liturgical form within the unity of the one church. It celebrates the diversity of liturgical expression that is found in both Eastern and Western churches that enjoy "communion in the faith and in the sacraments received from the apostles" (2108).

A second thread, most noticeable in the first section on the liturgy, constitutes an advance on *Sacrosanctum Concilium*. The Vatican II constitution was dominantly a voice from and to the church of the West. It acknowledged that certain of its principles were applicable to the Eastern churches, but its primary objective was the reform and restoration of the liturgy of the Latin rite. The catechism, by contrast, makes a deliberate effort to speak both the Eastern and Western voices of the church.

In particular, the catechism gives strong notice to the spirit and the liturgical traditions of the church of Byzantium. The language, at least in section 1 on the liturgy, is highly mystagogical: it is poetic, prayerful, and inspiring. In sharp contrast to the almost exclusively christological focus that has been traditional in the Latin West, the catechism presents Christian worship in a decidedly trinitarian context, with great attention given to the action of the Holy Spirit. In addition, this section presents more fully than would have been possible in 1963, when *Sacrosanctum Concilium* was promulgated, insights derived from both biblical and liturgical studies throughout the twentieth century.

There is, however, a third thread that presents some troublesome departures from the conciliar and postconciliar magisterium. A major gain of Vatican II regarding the liturgy was its recognition of and insistence on the nature of liturgical action as action of the whole church together. This continues to be affirmed in the catechism, but without the same stress or importance. The ecclesial dimension of liturgical action seems consistently to be played down. The laity more frequently are considered "recipients" of rather than "participants" in the sacramental act. Communion, which is explicitly named in all the new eucharistic prayers of the Roman Missal as communion of the church in the body of Christ, is portrayed instead, or at least with a much greater emphasis, as communion with the divine life. And the fourfold presence of Christ in the Eucharist, which *Sacrosanctum Concilium* (no. 7) affirmed with clarity and force, is somewhat retreated from. There is a return to a focus on the consecrated bread and wine that has dominated and in fact restricted the question of Christ's presence in the Eucharist. This focus returns in an unusual and questionable twist and is treated as a subquestion under the focus on sacrifice.

Thus the catechism presents us with three distinct threads that complicate its stated aim to be a "compendium of the whole of catholic doctrine." The catechism is somewhat faithful, somewhat innovative, and somewhat regressive all at the same time.

Specific Issues

The presence and effect of these three distinct threads can be illustrated by calling attention to several specific issues the catechism deals with. We will look at the following: (a) the ecclesial dimension of liturgy; (b) the operational understanding of sacraments; (c) eucharistic faith; (d) priesthood; (e) liturgical calendar; (f) liturgy of the hours; (g) the role of symbols in liturgical celebration; (h) the relation between the heavenly and the earthly liturgy; (i) inconsistency of language; and (j) the catechism's ecumenical appeal.

Ecclesial Dimension of Liturgy

Vatican II gave a central place to the concept of the church as sacrament: "For it was from the side of Christ . . . that there came forth 'the wondrous sacrament of the whole church'" (*Sacrosanctum Concilium,* no. 5; see also *Lumen Gentium*). This more fundamental use of the term *sacrament* is at the root of the sacramentality of those actions of the church that have been traditionally named *sacraments.* The church as sacrament, moreover, allows all sacraments to be called actions of the whole church.

The church as sacrament does appear in the catechism, but almost in passing and without the same centrality. The catechism prefers to use the term in regard to the economy of salvation as it unfolds in the time of the church. Christ is the sole mediator of the new covenant; he still lives and intercedes for us and no one succeeds or replaces him; he alone brings about salvation by the ministry of his church through the sacraments (2021). The sacraments emerge in this treatment without their fundamental rooting in the church as sacrament; they become vehicles of grace available in and through the ministry of the church rather than acts of public worship "performed by the Mystical Body of Jesus Christ, that is, by the Head and his members" (*Sacrosanctum Concilium,* no. 7).

The catechism makes an obvious and disturbing shift away from the inclusive language of Vatican II that spoke of the whole church as the primary agent in sacramental worship and thus called attention to the essential ecclesial dimension of Christian worship. To speak of the laity only as recipients of sacraments seriously limits this ecclesial dimension.

This shift is evident in many places, for example, in how the liturgical action of the church is located in the economy of salvation. *Sacrosanctum Concilium* (nos. 5–8) offered an unfolding of the economy of salvation and located the church's celebration of the liturgy within it. God, who desired salvation for all, spoke in many ways through the Prophets, and in the fullness of time sent his Son, whose humanity united with the Person of the Word was the instrument of our salvation. In Christ came our reconciliation; in Christ the fullness of divine worship was given us. From

Christ came forth "the wondrous sacrament" of the church sent forth to preach salvation in word and to enact salvation in sacrament. Christ continues to be present in the church associating the church with himself in his act of worship of the Father and his act of salvation of humanity. Liturgy (word and sacrament) gives a foretaste of the heavenly liturgy "toward which we journey as pilgrims."

The catechism also offers an unfolding of the economy of salvation, but one that follows the eucharistic anaphora of St. Basil of Caesarea (employed in East and adapted as Eucharistic Prayer IV in postconciliar Latin liturgy). It begins with creation and sin and the constancy of God's faithful covenant. From this comes the time of promise and the time of fullness, where the mystery of salvation is accomplished in Christ, from his incarnation to his ascension (which is the paschal mystery). The Spirit inaugurates the last times. "It is at this time that the economy of salvation, having been accomplished 'once and for all' becomes our present liturgy of the mystery until the Lord's second Coming in glory" (2012). The role of the church is given scant notice in this unfolding of the economy.

A second place where this shift is obvious is in the section that asks, "Who celebrates the church's liturgy?" *Sacrosanctum Concilium* (no. 7) called the liturgy "an action of Christ the Priest and of his Body, which is the Church." The catechism announces that "the liturgy is the 'action' of 'the whole Christ' (*Christus totus*)" (2123), though it does not spell out the meaning of the term as Christ together with his church. Instead, it turns immediately to "those who already celebrate it beyond the signs" (i.e., those beyond death) who even now take part in the "heavenly liturgy." It draws out the relation between sacramental liturgy and the heavenly liturgy ("The sacramental liturgy celebrated here below shares in this heavenly liturgy") and calls on Revelation to give a rich description of this heavenly liturgy.

Stressing again (2125) that the Spirit and the church make us share in this eternal liturgy, the catechism only then speaks of the assembly of the baptized as the assembly that celebrates. Rather than speak of the united assembly with many ministers to serve it, it immediately announces the specific role of the ministerial priesthood (to act in the person of Christ the Head). The catechism does not deny that the whole church celebrates the sacred liturgy. It affirms it clearly in its summary remark (2129). Its major concern, however, is to call attention to the role of the ordained in the action of the church: Christ must be represented in the church by ordained members to ensure that certain liturgical acts are "truly saving acts of Christ himself" (ibid.).

In the end it is a question of nuance and emphasis. Vatican II gave strong emphasis to the ecclesial dimension of Christian worship. As a result, the greatly relativized treatment of the ecclesial dimension in the catechism stands out. Vatican II clearly gave primacy to the liturgical assembly as a whole in its insistence that "the full and active participation by all of the people is the aim to be considered before all else" (*Sacrosanctum Concilium*, no. 14). The concerns in the catechism seem to have shifted: it gives primacy to the heavenly liturgy in which the earthly liturgy shares and to the ordained priesthood that represents Christ as head of the church.

Understanding of Sacraments

Sacraments are named "diverse sacramental expressions of the same paschal mystery" (2083). The language used here is derived more from the East than from the West. "The sacraments are not 'things' as religious rites are, but divine-human 'energies', 'powers' coming from the Body of Christ . . . joint works (synergies) of the Holy Spirit and the Church" (2084).

Four characteristics of sacraments are given. Sacraments are: (a) *of faith*—they presuppose faith and also nourish, strengthen, profess, and proclaim it (2086); (b) *of Christ*—the church is Christ's body present sacramentally; sacraments manifest what the church is (2087); (c) *in the church*—sacraments are "of the church" because she herself is sacramental, that is, the place where the Holy Spirit is at work; and (d) *of salvation*—sacraments confer the grace they signify; they are effective because the power of the Holy Spirit is at work and sanctifying because the Spirit conforms those who receive them to the sacred humanity of the Son of God (2090).

This is a further illustration of the shift away from the ecclesial dimension of the liturgy that was so strong in Vatican II. Again, it is a question of nuance and emphasis. Stress is given to the reception of sacraments rather than to their enactment by the church in assembly. Stress is also given to the church as the place where sacraments are celebrated rather than to the people who celebrate. What seems to dominate is an older image of sacraments as "vehicles of grace" entrusted to the church rather than as actions of people that express and manifest the nature of the true church (*Sacrosanctum Concilium*, no. 2).

Eucharistic Faith

Chapter 3 of section 2 is devoted to eucharistic faith. The language of the chapter is more didactic and doctrinal than that found in the first section.

There is also a noticeable shift in source material that is drawn upon. In the earlier section the new Roman eucharistic prayers, as well as some Eastern prayers, were cited in abundance, with only minimal reference to the Roman Canon (Eucharistic Prayer I). In this section the Roman Canon is the text cited almost exclusively. Likewise, the earlier section cited Vatican II in abundance; in this section the Council of Trent seems the principal guide. This shift in language signals a more radical shift in the way the church's eucharistic faith is presented.

Two major ingredients of eucharistic faith have dominated theological attention in the West: the real presence of Christ and the sacrificial nature of the Eucharist. There is a noticeable difference in the way these two issues are treated in the Council of Trent, Vatican II, and the catechism. Trent treated eucharistic presence and eucharistic sacrifice as two separate but equally important issues. Vatican II brought them together, with the primacy given to Christ's presence. As *Sacrosanctum Concilium* explains, Christ is present in a variety of modes (Word, presiding priest, bread and wine, assembly) in order to accomplish the work of our redemption (*Sacrosanctum Concilium*, no. 7). Sacrifice is a function of Christ's presence; he is present in his sacrifice. The catechism reverses this and gives priority to the dimension of eucharistic sacrifice.

The notion of sacrifice dominates the catechism's presentation of eucharistic faith. The context is set by the particular understanding that is given to the Last Supper "command formulary" ("Do this in memory of me"). While this formula was cited earlier to mean repeating Jesus' words and actions, here it is used to mean "offering Christ," "commemorating Christ," "commemorating his sacrifice." In this context the elements of eucharistic faith are given a preferred order of treatment: (a) memorial (of his death and resurrection), (b) sacrifice, and (c) presence.

Memorial is rightly seen as telling the events of God's wonders so that they may "become in a certain way present here and now" (2439). This is an echo of earlier sections that stressed the realism of liturgical celebration. But in this section the term *sacrifice* is preferred to the *paschal mystery*, which was employed earlier.

Sacrifice itself is given a particular nuance. The "gift of body" contained in the Supper bread and cup sayings is interpreted as *giving for* rather than *giving to*. Drawing on the decrees of Trent, the catechism affirms that the Eucharist is a sacrifice because it represents the sacrifice of the cross, is its memorial, and applies its fruit. While continuing to cite Trent, it neglects a nuance essential to the Tridentine doctrine—that the manner of offering is different. The catechism maintains that "the sacrifice of the cross and the sacrifice of the eucharist are identical" (2445).

Apart from this neglected nuance, the content of faith on eucharistic sacrifice is cleanly presented: the sacrifice is both of Christ and of the church; the Eucharist is the sacrifice of the church because of the intimate union of the church with Christ; it is the whole Christ (head and members) that offers and is offered.

When finally the catechism treats of the presence of Christ in the Eucharist, it does so, as already noted, as a function of sacrifice. Such a presentation of eucharistic faith is questionable. Yet this is not the only departure from Vatican II regarding Christ's presence in the Eucharist. The other, and perhaps even more serious, departure concerns the modes of Christ's presence. *Sacrosanctum Concilium* (no. 7) expanded the notion of Christ's presence to include four modes of presence: Word, priest, food, and assembly. All four modes are the "real presence" of Christ. In the catechism, however, the exclusive focus of real presence is again the eucharistic food: "The eucharistic presence of Christ begins the moment of transubstantiation and remains as long as the eucharistic species exist" (2460).

Another inconsistency appears in the treatment of Eucharist as "the paschal banquet." The earlier language of communion with the Trinity and the more ecclesial sense of communion that is spoken in the so-called "second epiclesis" of the eucharistic prayers ("be brought together in unity") is forgotten. Communion is again identified simply as "the intimate union of the faithful with Christ" (2463).

There is a clear doctrinal priority in operation here. The Mass is (a) the sacrifice that perpetuates the sacrifice of the cross; (b) the memorial of the death and resurrection of the Lord, who commanded, "Do this in memory of me"; and (c) the sacred banquet where, by communion with the Body and Blood of the Lord, the people of God share in the benefits of the paschal sacrifice, reactualize the New Covenant, and prefigure the eschatological banquet (2464).

This doctrinal stress on the sacrificial dimension of the Eucharist is no doubt responsible for what must be the most unfortunate statement in the entire catechism: "Instituted in the context of a meal, the eucharist is not itself a meal" (2413). This is more than a failure of nuance; the statement as it stands is simply false.

True, the Eucharist is not *merely* a meal, and that is surely what the author intended to write. The context makes it clear that the catechism wishes to distinguish the sacramental elements from the community meal or agape from which the eucharistic action was very early separated. The larger context, however, suggests an effort to go further, namely, to focus on the sacrificial element of the Eucharist over against the meal. Eucharistic faith is in serious jeopardy at this point. Vatican II insisted that human sanctification in regard to the Eucharist occurs precisely because it is a meal. According to Vatican II, human sanctification is made manifest in signs perceptible to the senses and accomplished in ways proper to each of the signs (*Sacrosanctum Concilium*, no. 7). The fullness of eucharistic faith is not served by once again separating the meal element from the sacrificial. The two dimensions of eucharistic faith are intimately related: Eucharist is sacrificial meal.

Clearly the catechism is attempting to counter some current losses in eucharistic piety: loss of reverence and awe; loss of the transcendent in concern for the experiential and existential; reduction of the eucharistic banquet to an ordinary human meal. But so blatant a retreat into a mode of discourse so alien, not only to contemporary post–Vatican II consciousness but also to the other sections of the catechism itself, is questionable.

Priesthood

The catechism continues to speak, as did Vatican II (*Sacrosanctum Concilium* and *Lumen Gentium*), of the priesthood of the baptized and the ministerial priesthood of the ordained. It rightly affirms that the latter is in service to the former. A shift in nuance, however, is observed in the manner in which Vatican II on the one hand and the catechism on the other speak of the difference and the relation between them.

The "Dogmatic Constitution on the Church" (*Lumen Gentium*) states: "Though they differ essentially and not only in degree, the common priesthood of the faithful and the ministerial or hierarchical priesthood are nonetheless ordered one to another; each in its own proper way shares in the one priesthood of Christ" (no. 10). The catechism makes the subordinate clause primary: "The priesthood of bishops and of priests differs essentially from that of the faithful, although they are 'ordered to one another; each in its own proper way shares in the one priesthood of Christ'" (2715). *Lumen Gentium* gives priority to the relationship and mutual ordering; the catechism gives priority to the difference.

One suspects that this reverse priority, and a deliberate attempt to affirm it, lies as an undercurrent throughout the document. A clear line is drawn between sacraments and sacramentals, although the texts cited from *Sacrosanctum Concilium* do not support the sharp distinction made by the catechism. Sacraments are instituted by Christ; sacramentals by the church. Sacraments confer grace; sacramentals do not (they prepare people to receive the fruit of the sacraments). Sacraments pertain to the ordained priesthood; sacramentals to the priesthood of the baptized. If there is a deliberate effort in the catechism to stress the ordained priesthood over against the priesthood of the baptized, it would explain the stress given to the eucharistic sacrifice that treats of Christ's presence as a function of sacrifice and evokes the startling statement that "the eucharist is not itself a meal."

This stress on the uniqueness of the ordained priesthood is important. The stress on the relationship between the two modes of Christ's priesthood, however, is equally important. The language of Vatican II was clearly designed to counter centuries of neglect of the priesthood of the baptized and to establish this priesthood in relationship to the ordained priesthood. The truth of the matter is that neither the difference nor the relationship is subordinate to the other. There is a difference in degree and kind between the two, and at the same time a relationship and mutual ordering between them.

Liturgical Calendar

The catechism gives as the primary focus of time "God's today" (2060). This is consistent with its emphasis on realism in the liturgy, Christ present and acting in the here and now. Eucharist is named the "most intense 'moment'" of God's today; it is the center of all sacramental life. Sunday is called the "original feast day"; the Eucharist is its center. Even where culture does not allow for a "work-free" day, Sunday should be kept as a day of rejoicing and gladness. Easter is named the source of the Christian liturgical year that is directed to the time for which we wait in hope.

The date for Easter is given, according to an agreement of all the churches at the Council of Nicaea, as the Sunday following the full moon (14 Nisan) after the spring equinox (2071). Nothing is said either of the continuing discrepancy among the churches regarding the celebration of Easter or of a proposed date upon which all might agree.

The liturgical year is described in terms that were more coherent before the reform of the Roman calendar and that would not apply at all to many Eastern churches whose calendars differ from the West in some important ways (especially in the naming of and celebration of the pre-Christmas season). Advent is named the time both of preparation for the first coming of Christ and of the expectation of the second coming at the end of time. The traditional "third coming," the coming in grace, is not mentioned. The mysteries of the earthly life of Jesus are celebrated between Christmas and Lent. Lent is called preparation for Easter (no mention is made of Christian initiation or reconciliation). The seven weeks leading to Pentecost are said to "follow" Easter (current Roman calendar calls them weeks *of* Easter, not *after* Easter). Easter is envisioned as the "day" of Easter, not the fifty days that culminate at Pentecost. The time after Pentecost (currently named "ordinary time" in the West, still named "after Pentecost" in some Eastern calendars) is called "the time of the Church." This interpretation of the liturgical calendar is at considerable odds with the current Latin Roman Catholic practice and would not make much sense to many Eastern churches either.

Liturgy of the Hours

The liturgy of the hours is given considerable note. Through the "divine office" the paschal mystery celebrated in the Eucharist "enters into and transfigures the time of each day" (2077). It is called "Jesus' own prayer" because its primary content is the psalms; it is the prayer of the priestly people in the one Priest praising the Lord without ceasing and interceding for the whole world.

Nothing is mentioned about the two "hinges" upon which the daily office turns (i.e., morning prayer or Lauds and evening prayer or Vespers [cf. *Sacrosanctum Concilium*, no. 89]) or of distinctions between those bound to choir and those not. The office is spoken of simply as "the praise and intercession that goes up to the Most Holy Trinity from the whole people of God" (2082).

Symbols in Liturgical Celebration

The catechism gives several terms to identify the word *celebration*. It is act (the once-for-all action of Christ) and service (the church serves this action so that salvation "may be accomplished in us") (2111). To this is added community (liturgical actions are actions of "a holy people gathered and ordered under the authority of the bishops" [2112]) and festival (we celebrate Christ our passover [2113]).

In its treatment of signs and symbols, the catechism is content with a somewhat cognitive approach. Citing St. Thomas Aquinas (2121), it names three dimensions of the sacramental sign: calling to mind (*rememorativum*) of Christ's passion; showing forth (*demonstrativum*) of what Christ's passion accomplishes in us; signaling (*prognosticum*) of future glory. *Sacrosanctum Concilium* presented a stronger sense of sacramental signs, naming them both cognitive and performative: "It [the liturgy] involves the presentation of man's sanctification under the guise of signs perceptible by the senses and its accomplishment in ways appropriate to each of these signs" (*Sacrosanctum Concilium*, no. 7).

Earthly and Heavenly Liturgy

Vatican II spoke of the heavenly liturgy as the goal of the church's journey: "In the earthly liturgy, by way of foretaste, we share in that heavenly liturgy which is celebrated in the holy city of Jerusalem towards which we journey as pilgrims" (*Sacrosanctum Concilium*, no. 8). Since the council's primary concern was the reformation and restoration of the liturgy on earth, it did not develop the heavenly liturgy beyond this eschatological note. The catechism, by contrast, not only develops the concept of the heavenly liturgy at length, it seems to give it primacy of place. The earthly liturgy takes on "the appearances of this passing world" (2024). It is celebrated at certain moments, in contrast to the heavenly liturgy which never ceases (2025). The earthly liturgy shares in the heavenly liturgy and makes this heavenly liturgy visible and effective on earth (2028).

The church's tradition of sacramental realism is stressed here: the mystery of salvation is made present within the church's sacraments. Perhaps Vatican II gave such emphasis to the "liturgy from below," to the neglect of the "liturgy from above," that the real presence of the eternal mystery in the earthly celebration was in danger of being weakened. It is not clear, however, that the catechism achieves a balance between the two. If accent on the first can tend to diminish the importance of the eternal mystery that is made present, the reverse accent can return to the preconciliar stress on the eternal that seriously neglected the earthly liturgy that makes it present. The postconciliar liturgical reform would thereby lose much of its urgency.

Language

When the section on the liturgy (section 1) is set side by side with the chapter on the Eucharist in section 2, two radically different modes of discourse can be observed. The first section not only draws heavily on material from the Byzantine East, it employs language (e.g., "divine-human energies," "synergies," liturgy as "epiclesis") that is bound to confuse, if not baffle, most Catholics of the Latin West. It is nonetheless refreshing language from the perspective of contemporary liturgical scholarship.

The chapter on the Eucharist in section 2, by contrast, draws almost exclusively on the Roman Canon and the Council of Trent, losing much of the earlier ecumenical appeal and freshness. Moving back and forth between an Eastern theological framework and the more familiar Western perspective, if held consistently throughout, would have celebrated diversity within the unity of the one church. Instead, the catechism presents a collage of theological insights that clash rather than form a unified whole.

Ecumenical Appeal

The catechism's extensive employment of Byzantine liturgical texts and theological language presents a broader ecumenical appeal than did *Sacrosanctum Concilium,* at least regarding the churches of the East. The first section of chapter 2 particularly gives equal voice to East and West on positions where the two have traditionally differed. An attempt is made to affirm equally both positions on such issues as the *filioque* (the Spirit proceeds from Father *and the Son*) and the agency in eucharistic consecration (i.e., the words of Jesus and Holy Spirit). An attempt is also made to link these Eastern and Western churches to their unity in apostolic origins. But the document will be less appealing to the separated churches of the West.

In the section on eucharistic sacrifice, to give one example, the "fruits of communion" are given as (a) union with Christ, (b) separation from sin, and (c) unity of the church. On this last, reference is made to both the Orthodox churches and the ecclesial communities separated from the Catholic church. Citing Vatican II, the catechism maintains that true priesthood and true Eucharist unite the Orthodox with the Catholic church "'in closest intimacy'" (2477, *Unitatis Redintegratio,* no. 15). But because of the "'absence of the sacrament of Order,'" Protestant communities "'have not preserved the proper substance of the eucharistic mystery in its fullness'" (2477, *Unitatis Redintegratio,* no. 22).

Regarding the second citation, however, the catechism significantly alters the positive tone of the original:

> Although [*Quamvis*] the ecclesial communities separated from us lack the fullness of unity with us which flows from baptism, and although we believe [*quamvis credamus*] they have not preserved the proper reality of the eucharistic mystery in its fullness, especially because of the absence of the sacrament of Orders, nevertheless [*tamen*] when they commemorate the Lord's death and resurrection in the Holy Supper, they profess that it signifies life in communion with Christ and await his coming in glory. (*Unitatis Redintegratio,* no. 22)[1]

What the council puts as subordinate, and in fact softens further by the words *we believe,* the catechism puts as its main affirmation, and without the qualifying "we believe." What follows "nonetheless" in *Unitatis Redintegratio* instead follows "however" in the catechism. ("However, when these communities 'commemorate the Lord's death and resurrection in the Holy Supper, they profess . . . '"). And where the council draws from this the conclusion that "the doctrine about the Lord's Supper . . . should form subjects of dialogue," the catechism concludes from the same that "eucharistic communion with these communities is not possible for the Catholic Church."

Conclusion

The catechism is to be highly commended for the extent to which it continues the vision of the church at prayer that is so richly put forth in *Sacrosanctum Concilium* and in the *General Instruction of the Roman Missal*. It also takes forward strides in giving a strong voice to the Eastern branch of the universal church and not remaining a dominantly Western voice. It is plagued, however, by some underlying agenda that limit if not threaten its effectiveness as a "compendium of the whole of catholic doctrine." Besides praise and commendation, it must be severely critiqued for stepping backward on some very essential matters.

The Sacraments
in the Catechism

David N. Power, O.M.I.
The Catholic University of America

The universal catechism seems to favor a post-Tridentine approach to the sacraments rather than what has developed following the mandates of the Second Vatican Council.

An institutional and instrumental understanding of sacrament still prevails.

The *Catechism for the Universal Church* treats the liturgy and the seven sacraments of the church in part 2, "On the Celebration of the Christian Mystery." Following a short introduction, this part of the catechism is divided into two sections, "The Sacramental Economy" (2009–2163) and "The Seven Sacraments of the Church" (2201–2883). Each section is further divided into chapters and articles.

The two sections have not been well integrated. The first section, treated in the previous essay, is more concerned with the positions of the Second Vatican Council and with the liturgy of Eastern churches, whereas the second section primarily takes up the positions fostered by the Council of Trent and scholastic theology.

The treatment of the Eucharist is discussed in the previous essay by Peter Fink, S.J. Since the material on the other six sacraments is abundant, it is impossible in the confines of this essay to analyze each article in detail. I will therefore address the fundamental plan and approach of this section of the catechism, as reflected in treating of each of the sacraments. First, my essay will describe the approach taken in the catechism. Second, it will suggest that a mystagogical approach would be a better way to meet the intent of the catechism. Third, it will show the problems that arise when the sacraments are presented without an adequate framework to deal with their historical and cultural development and the rich diversity of liturgical traditions. Fourth, it will underline some of the specific issues that arise from the treatment of the sacraments of order and marriage.

The Approach Taken

The section starts off with the statement that sacraments, to the number of seven, were instituted by Christ. As far as the evolution of sacramental number and rite are concerned, the principle adopted by the catechism is that later history clarifies what was there from the beginning. Developments of the canon of Scriptures, of the doctrine of the faith, and of the sacramental treasure are placed on a par with each other: "In [the] Spirit, the Church has gradually clarified the 'dispensation' of this treasure, as she has clarified the canon of scripture and the doctrine of faith (cf. Mt 13.52), as a faithful steward of God's mysteries (1 Cor 4.1)" (2084).

Once the seven sacraments have been listed, the sacramental system is explained through the analogy with the development of human life, especially physical, that is found in the *Summa Theologiae* (3, q. 65, a. 1) of St. Thomas Aquinas. Apparently this is deemed to afford adequate intelligibility and justification for the number seven and a way of explaining the effects of each sacrament in particular.

All of this means that the teaching of the Council of Trent and of the catechism of the Council of Trent is the prototype for the catechesis on the sacraments. This shows up in the catechism's concentration on institution, essential rite, qualities of minister and recipient, and sacramental effects. This emphasis recurs in treating of each sacrament, whatever other material is incorporated from the Second Vatican Council, the revision of liturgical books, Eastern liturgies, or ecclesiastical writers.

Thus particular credit is given in the mode of treatment to a definition of sacrament given in one of the "In Brief" paragraphs of the previous section:

> The sacraments are symbolic actions instituted by Christ and entrusted to the Church, through which the divine life is bestowed upon us. The visible rites by which the sacraments are celebrated signify and confer the graces appropriate to each sacrament. The sacraments are efficacious signs of grace. They bear fruit in those who receive them with the right attitude and in the right spirit. (2093)

The curlicues do not very effectively camouflage the definition: sacred signs instituted by Christ to give grace.

It is disconcerting to find this approach taken in a document that is intended to serve as resource and guideline for local catechisms. This is especially so considering the more serious efforts of section 1 to take into account the developments of the Second Vatican Council and the revision of liturgical books and rites. Although the section on the seven sacraments does relate each sacrament to the church and writes of its celebration in the church assembly, the paradigm is the life of grace in the life of the individual and the efficacious bestowal of grace on the individual.

One odd result of this approach is the division of the sacraments into sacraments of initiation, sacraments of healing, and sacraments that serve communion. Another is the placement of the full treatment of the Eucharist among the sacraments of initiation, as primarily the sacrament of the nourishment of the life of grace.

The teaching of the Second Vatican Council suggests a more organic approach to the sacraments as ecclesial sacraments, celebrations of the body of Christ. This would present the sanctification of the person as a participation in the organic life of the body, which is a communion in Christ's Spirit. Thus the "Dogmatic Constitution on the Church" (*Lumen Gentium*, no. 11) introduces the sacraments with this statement: "The sacred nature and organic structure of the priestly community is brought into operation through the sacraments and the exercise of virtue." This is rooted in the vision of the church itself as sacrament, sign, and instrument of communion with God and of unity among all people.

In such an organic and corporate approach, the Eucharist would receive first treatment in dealing with the sacramental economy. As stated in a 1967 instruction of the Sacred Congregation of Rites on the eucharistic mystery (quoting from the conciliar "Decree on the Ministry and Life of Priests"), the Eucharist is the true center of the whole Christian life, for both the universal and the local church, and all other sacraments are linked with it and directed to it.[1] This offers a different way of organizing the catechetical material on sacraments than that adopted by the universal catechism.

Though admittedly there is often a tension in the revision of the liturgical books and in the theology presented in their introductions (*praenotanda*), by and large they place sacrament within the larger context of divine economy and church. In the introduction to the revision of the books for the sacraments of initiation, for both adults and infants, the first article has to do with the economy of salvation.[2] Through these sacraments people pass from an economy in which they are subject to the power of darkness to life in Christ, as God's children in the Spirit. This is what is celebrated in the sacraments. In these sacraments, as the second article says, they are incorporated into Christ, formed as God's people, made a new creation through water and the Spirit. Curiously, the catechism refers to these articles by a "cf." but then privileges the analogy with the birth and growth of physical life in its own explanation (2207).

The same reference to economy and to the church as body and community is found as prelude to the revision of the *Order of Penance*. The sacrament is placed within the economy of humankind's reconciliation with God through Christ (art. 1). There follows the recognition that this reconciliation is given and celebrated first in the sacraments of baptism and Eucharist. The sacrament of penance is for sinners in the church who need reconciliation with God, in and through the church (art. 2). Whether reconciliation is with God, through the instrumentality of the church, and hence with the church community, or whether it is with God through reconciliation with the church, is never clearly resolved in the revised order. Consequently, one would not expect to see the matter settled in the catechism.

However, one could expect to see the relation to economy and church given as the foundation to the catechesis of the sacrament and to see other questions related to this. Instead, the sacrament of penance comes across as a practice of individual confession that fosters a sense of sin and inner penance in the life of each person. Lost is a varied celebration of reconciliation, through which sinners are reconciled to God in the church and the whole body is empowered to face and overcome the sin that haunts both church and society.

These references to the revision of the liturgy of initiation and of penance are sufficient to make the point that the universal catechism seems to favor a post-Tridentine approach to the sacraments rather than what has developed following the mandates of the Second Vatican Council.

An organic approach centered on the Eucharist would allow a better integration throughout part 2 of the catechism, of much of the material found in section 1, article 7, "The Paschal Mystery Unfolding in the Church's Life" (2083–92). This article presents the sacraments of the church as sacraments of faith, sacraments of Christ in which he is himself present and pours out the energies of the Spirit, sacraments celebrated in the church that build it up as sacrament of universal salvation, and sacraments of salvation. In the presentation of sacrament under these rubrics, there is frequent mention of the gift and action of the Holy Spirit, which is important to an understanding of the sacraments as acts of the body of Christ.

All these factors in the understanding of sacrament have been given importance in the teaching of the Second Vatican Council and in the revision of liturgical books and rites. Even in article 7, however, where they are listed and explained, one cannot escape the impression that an institutional and instrumental understanding of sacrament still prevails.

This appears particularly in the inclusion of the Holy Spirit in the sacramental economy. The adoption of categories from the Orthodox church is apparent in the use of the phrase "energies" to describe both the sacrament itself (2084) and the gift of Christ given in the sacraments (2087), as in the description of sacraments as "the joint works (synergies) of the Holy Spirit and the Church" (2084). Elsewhere it is said that the energies of the Spirit are at work in the church through the sacraments (2088), and that "the Father grants the appeal of the Epiclesis of every sacrament when the Church expresses her faith in the coming of the Spirit of the Promise" (2090).

The important insight in all this is that pneumatology can underpin a catechesis of sacrament in a way that has never hitherto been done in the Western church. An understanding of the church as the body of Christ united in the Spirit would foster an organic approach to all the sacraments as expressions and celebrations of the church. Unfortunately, the basic ecclesiology of the article is weak and fails to integrate pneumatology with Christology. One gets the impression that the church is thought of primarily as Christ's institution, sacrament, and instrument. Thus it is the place in which he is at work through the Spirit or in which the Spirit is itself at work in conjunction with this instrument. "Joint work" is, as noted, the particular interpretation given to the image of "synergy." Hence it is not surprising that this very article, which attempts to integrate the ecclesiology of the Vatican Council, should conclude "In Brief" with the above-quoted definition of sacrament.

Doctrine or Mystagogy?

The catechism frequently refers to the liturgies of the sacraments, both past and present, of both the East and the West. This enriches the presentation and can lead to a better understanding of sacramental rites. However, the celebration is not taken as the starting point of catechesis as happened in the mystagogical catechesis of the early church, where instruction on the meaning of the sacraments was associated with their liturgies. Rather, the starting point of the catechism is the doctrinal teaching of the church, and principally the teaching of the Council of Trent or the theology of the scholastics of the High Middle Ages.

Early ecclesiastical writers, of both East and West, are often quoted. But the general assumption seems to be that nothing either before or after the Council of Trent merits attention on its own. Nothing can complement rather than corroborate the post-Tridentine approach or indeed offer an alternative approach. The general format for the treatment of each sacrament is to locate its institution in the Scriptures, determine its essential rite, define its effects, and explain the requirements for minister and recipient. Contemporary issues, such as the need for individual confession or the difficulties confronted by the married in the contemporary world, are addressed, but within the classical scholastic framework.

This may well be a lost opportunity to develop a truly contemporary mystagogy with the revision of liturgical rites. The catechesis intended by this document is for persons familiar with the life of the church and with its sacramental celebrations. Even children who are being prepared for first communion, for the sacrament of penance, or for confirmation are not unfamiliar with these rites. They belong to a church in which these sacraments are constantly celebrated.

Hence there is room for a retrieval of an early church practice that based the instruction on the sacraments on their celebration, for persons familiar with it.[3] This could be done in the spirit of what is described in the *Order of the Christian Initiation of Adults* as the period of postbaptismal catechesis or *mystagogia*. This is a truly integrating approach, for it associates instruction on the meaning of the sacraments with their liturgies, with the hearing of God's Word within these liturgies, with the experience of Christian community, and with the apostolic thrust of the Christian life (*OCIA*, nos. 37–40).

It needs, of course, to be a truly contemporary mystagogy, not simply an attempt to copy the mystagogy of early Christian centuries.[4] That practice gives us the model of a catechesis on sacrament and Christian life for those who have already experienced the rites. The model also provides room for the inclusion of the Scripture in which the mystery of God's economy is meditated.

Oddly enough, the catechism includes a less fortunate aspect of this mystagogy in its doctrinal exposition when it explains the effects of baptism through a reading of the text of the blessing of the water. The use of Scripture in that blessing, as in early mystagogy, proceeds from a typological reading of Old and New Testaments, whereby the types of the Old Testament are fulfilled in Christ and the church, and the mysteries of Christ's flesh prefigure the life of grace.

The advantage of this typology is that it presents a unified reading of the economy of grace, with Jesus Christ as central point. The problem is that it allows no inner consistency to the Hebrew Scriptures or to the story of the people of Israel, and hence in times past it was often accompanied by a virulent anti-Semitism. Use of the Scriptures proclaimed in the liturgical rites of our day would have to be based on a more critical reading of the text of both Old and New Testaments (for more on typology see earlier article by Mary C. Boys, S.N.J.M.).

The model of mystagogy still can be adapted to contemporary church life. Guidance along these lines is often found in the introductions to the new liturgical books. Thus the *Rite for the Pastoral Care of the Sick* addresses the dilemma of human illness and suffering, for humanity as such and for Christian people in particular.[5] The sacrament is related to the Christian economy, in which Christ is healer and savior and in which the church carries on a ministry to the sick that is inherent to the church as sacrament of Christ. The rite presents a wide variety of scriptural readings that are proclaimed and heard in the celebration of this sacrament. It joins the blessing and anointing with oil with prayers that evoke the mystery of Christ and the Spirit and that place the hope for healing within the horizon of eschatological hope. Specific doctrinal questions do have to be clarified, such as those regarding the minister, the subject, and the effects. But the ritual shows how these can be addressed within the context of celebration and within that of the church's experience of human frailty and of its ministry of healing.

Staying with this example of the sacrament of anointing, the catechism's own intentions would be better served by a more mystagogical approach. It opens the article on this sacrament (2601ff.) with a citation from the "Dogmatic Constitution on the Church" (*Lumen Gentium*, no. 11), which explicitly locates the sacrament as a sacrament of the whole church, and not therefore simply as something intended for its sick members. It then describes the reality of illness in human life, relates it to the paschal mystery of Christ, and evokes the church's mission to the sick and suffering. Sample scriptural references are scattered through these paragraphs of the catechism (2602–9) to make certain points, but no Scripture text gets attention as such. It would be more efficacious, and more directly related to the nourishment of the life of faith, to provide a reading from and reflection upon some of the texts included in the lectionary of the order of celebration. This would locate the catechesis within the community experience, within the hearing of God's Word, and within the recourse in faith to Jesus Christ.

After this introductory paragraph the catechism cites the Council of Trent to explain the sacrament of the sick and completes it with a citation from Paul VI's "Apostolic Constitution on the Sacrament."[6] Paul VI makes the point that the liturgical tradition was obscured when the sacrament became viewed as extreme unction. Next the catechism treats the subject, the celebration, and the effects of the sacrament, with a variety of references to Trent, Florence, Vatican II, John Paul II, and the Scriptures.

This is all rather higgledy-piggledy, and there is clarity only when the reader gets to the "In Brief" section. There the straightforward doctrinal approach prevails, without reserve. The relation of these final summaries to the rest of the text may illustrate a basic problem with the catechism, which is probably counter to the very intention of its authors. Because the rest of the matter is somewhat disorganized and tries to account for a variety of matters, while at the same time adopting an essentially doctrinal approach, those using the catechism may rely too much on these summaries in developing their books and curricula. This would belie the intent of the catechism to relate sacraments to celebration, to scriptural and liturgical traditions, to the life of the church as a living body in the Spirit, and to the paschal mystery of Jesus Christ.

A more successful catechesis would take the celebration, its rites and texts, as starting point and context. The doctrinal issues would be settled within such context. Within the context of celebration the child or adult believer can better appreciate the mystery of Christ, the life of the Spirit, the nurturing and apostolic life of the church, and the transformation of human realities through God's love and grace. Within that context one also can see the reasons why certain doctrinal or disciplinary decisions are made about the sacraments. I have illustrated this point with reference to the sacrament of anointing, but the same procedure could be adopted for all the sacraments.

Historical Awareness

The catechism adopts a doctrinal and institutional approach that favors a development that looks like an unfolding of a treasure. The supposition appears to be that both the sacraments themselves and the teaching on them existed from the first days of the church and simply needed to be explicated in the course of time. Having opened this section on the seven sacraments with the blanket assertion that they were instituted by Christ, the document follows the scholastic and Tridentine example of locating the moment and manner of the institution of each in particular. By and large, it repeats what was said in the Tridentine decrees. Occasionally the authors show themselves aware of the problems inherent in historical reconstruction, but this does not dissuade them from attributing the essentials of each sacrament to Christic institution. Consequently it is impossible for the document to account adequately for the history of the sacraments themselves or for sacramental doctrine.

We are told, for example, that explicit testimony to infant baptism is found in the second century, but that it is "very probable" that infants where baptized even in early days, when whole households were baptized (2240). We are then told that this is "immemorial practice" (2241) and that this practice corresponds to the responsibility of parents to nourish the life that God has given to their charge (2242). A previous number (2239) has already mentioned that adult baptism was originally the most common situation and still is today in missionary territory. Further on, in referring to the necessity of baptism, the catechism allows that an implicit desire for baptism suffices for salvation for adults who have not heard the gospel (2250a). It then attempts to maintain both the imperative that children must be baptized and the hope that even without it they may be saved (2253–55).

I have brought these different points together to show how failure to see things in their historical and cultural context both misrepresents history and makes it difficult to address current issues. At any given time or in any given culture, the reality of church life and of its interpretation of the gospel makes these diverse practices comprehensible. The location of adult baptism today "in mission territory" avoids any explanation of why it was customary at one time in Christian families. It also ignores the increasing practice of adult catechumenate and initiation in countries where Christianity has been long established. Likewise, the tendency to present infant baptism as both necessary and preceptive sets aside the real problems connected with the baptism of infants in families of marginal relationship to the church.

Similar and even more serious problems are found in the treatment of the sacrament of penance. Despite the genuine attempt to place the sacrament in the broader context of the whole of the church's penitential practice and exercise of mercy (2508–23), the catechism finds it possible to state: "Through all the changes which this sacrament has known over the centuries, a *fundamental structure* can be discerned: it comprises two equally essential elements; on the one hand *acts of the person* who is converted through the action of the Holy Spirit: namely contrition, confession and satisfaction; on the other hand, the action of God through *intervention of the Church*" (2532, emphasis in text).

The clear intention is to uphold the practice of individual confession as the generally normative practice for today's Catholics (cf. 2565). As a result, history is distorted through a biased reading, and it becomes impossible to allow for a context within which current practices may continue to develop, with attention to all the factors at work in developing a sound practice of sacramental reconciliation.

Again, the institutional and doctrinal approach thwarts the cate-

118   LITURGY, SACRAMENTS, AND PRAYER

chism's best intentions. If the church were consistently presented as the body of Christ taking shape in history and culture, if sacramental celebration were consistently taken to be the expression of this self-realization in the power of the Spirit, and if sacramental catechesis were mystagogical in form, the document's inner inconsistencies could be avoided.

This provided an excellent starting point in treating the plurality of liturgical traditions (2105–8) in the previous section on the sacramental economy. There we read that "the unfathomable richness of Christ's mystery is such that no liturgical tradition can exhaust its expression" (2106) and that "the existence of different liturgical traditions is in fact linked to the Church's Mission itself" (2107), and that furthermore "the mystery of Christ is celebrated according to the culture of each local church" (2108).

Acknowledgment of this rich liturgical and cultural diversity occasionally recurs in treating individual sacraments (e.g., in differentiating between the Western approach to confirmation and the Eastern chrismation, or in reference to marriage rites in East and West). But the principles quoted are not taken as foundational for a sacramental catechesis that takes history and culture seriously.

In the approach suggested by a sacramental mystagogy, this reference to historical development and to the variety of liturgical traditions could put sacrament and its celebration in the context of contemporary church life, with its growing diversity of cultural traditions and with its need to face contemporary situations. It also would have allowed for a vital and appreciative ecumenicity. For Roman Catholics in particular, a sense of living communion with Eastern churches can be enhanced through an appreciation of their liturgical traditions. Liturgy and sacraments can also be an avenue to fuller mutual accord with the churches that have sprung from the Reformation. Division on the number of the sacraments is overcome to a great extent through a more fundamental sacramental principle that takes the church itself as sacrament and looks upon sacramental celebrations as expression of this fundamental being.

Based on such a comprehension, Catholics can appreciate not only the celebration of baptism and of the Lord's Supper in other churches but also the rituals of marriage, ordination, anointing, penance, and confirmation that these churches retain in a variety of ways. Doctrinal and liturgical differences do not evaporate in this approach, but a greater mutual appreciation of ecclesial reality is fostered.

As it is, the churches of the Reformation get short shrift in this catechism, with only the acknowledgment of baptism as bond of unity between all Christians and of the elements of eucharistic celebration that they are deemed to retain. Because there are doctrinal similarities between the Eastern churches and Rome on apostolic succession, episcopacy, and priesthood, these churches are taken as partners in dialogue in dealing with sacraments. This ignores the greater cultural affinity, even in liturgy and more actual contact, between members of the Roman rite and the churches of the Reformation. To explore and explain this affinity at a catechetical level, in a spirit of mutual appreciation, would be an important step toward ecclesial reconciliation.

Sacraments Which Serve Communion

Under the heading of "Sacraments Which Serve Communion," the catechism treats of the sacraments of order and marriage as it continues to pursue the distinction of sacraments given by St. Thomas Aquinas. According to this distinction, all the other sacraments serve the life of grace of the individual, whereas these two are meant to prepare people for the service of others.

It is a peculiar heading to use, since the Eucharist, which is not treated here, is par excellence the sacrament of ecclesial communion in Christ and the Spirit. The distinction is peculiar to uphold in the wake of the ecclesiology of the Second Vatican Council that emphasized the active participation of all the baptized in the prophetic, kingly, and priestly offices of Christ, for the building up of the body and the exercise of its apostolic mission.

The distinction is also in part contradicted by the catechism itself. From the outset of chapter 3 (2701ff.) the catechism uses the image of consecration to show that the consecrations peculiar to order and marriage are founded upon the consecration received by all in baptism (2703). The catechism also says that in the sacraments of initiation Christians are already called to the mission to evangelize the world (2701).

The heading is a somewhat inauspicious prelude to the treatment of the two sacraments. Their treatment in the catechism is given special attention in this essay because it seems to embody problems that are fundamental to the entire treatment of sacraments.

Order

The treatment of the sacrament of order mentions that candidates are ordained to the threefold ministry of sacrament, word, and pastoral care, as was explained in the documents of the Second Vatican Council (e.g.,

Lumen Gentium, chap. 3). However, this section on sacraments stresses the sacramental aspect of order (2704). For other aspects of the apostolic ministry, one is referred to elsewhere in the catechism (0236–42, 1396–98, 1720–26). Apparently the sacramental aspect means the power and ministry of bishop and priest to celebrate the sacraments, in virtue of the reception of the sacramental character. Something of the isolation of the sacramental ministry from the ministry to word and community that the council tried to avoid is thus restored to catechetical teaching.

In any case, the catechetical teaching on order centers on a description and discussion of priesthood (2707–23). Natural priesthood and the priesthood of the Old Covenant are said to be fulfilled in the unique priesthood of Jesus Christ, perfected in his sacrifice, and "rendered present by the Christian priesthood without the oneness of the priesthood of Christ being diminished" (2713b). By this the ordained priesthood is obviously meant, since, referring to Trent, the text speaks of the "joint institution by the Lord of the eucharistic sacrifice and the christian priesthood" (2713). The following paragraphs, however, go on to speak of the double participation in the unique priesthood of Christ through baptism and through order, with accent on the essential difference between the two (2714–15). While it is said that the ministerial priesthood is "wholly at the service of the common priesthood" (2715), it is defined as "a means by which Christ continues to build up and guide his Church."

Using the terms "in the person of Christ the Head" (*in persona Christi capitis*), or simply "in the person of Christ" (*in persona Christi*), and "in the name of the whole church" (*nomine totius ecclesiae*), the catechism (2716–22) explains the action of the ordained minister in sacrament and liturgy. This terminology was used in *Lumen Gentium* and other Vatican II documents.[7] The intention is to show that, on the one hand, Christ is present and active in the church by sanctifying power through priestly ministry. On the other hand, priests also represent all the people in making prayer to God, including the offering of the eucharistic sacrifice. The relation to Christ remains primary even in this second case, since "it is because he represents Christ that [the priest] can represent the Church" (2721).

The use of this terminology harks back to a sharp distinction between the acts performed by the priest in the person of Christ and those performed by him in the person or name of the church, as it was espoused by Thomas Aquinas (*Summa Theologiae* 3, q. 82, a. 7, ad 3). For Thomas the priest consecrated the body and blood of Christ or conferred the sacraments in the person of Christ, but he professed the faith of the church and offered the sacrifice, prayers, and devotions of the people in the person of the church. Thomas made the distinction to highlight the instrumental role of the priest in the administration of the sacraments and in the eucharistic consecration. This seems to be virtually the position adopted by the catechism. It fits very well with its preference for understanding the sacraments as effective signs of grace over understanding them as celebrations of the paschal mystery in the community of the church, Christ's body.

Despite the reference to *Lumen Gentium*, the authors of the catechism appear not to have noticed its effort to bypass this separation of two sets of acts. *Lumen Gentium* in fact reads: "The ministerial priest, by the sacred power that he has, forms and rules the priestly people; in the person of Christ he effects the eucharistic sacrifice and offers it to God in the name of all the people" (no. 10). The expression is awkward because the relation between Christ's offering and the people's offering has not been clearly resolved, but the desire to present their close relation is apparent. The same thing can be seen in the "Decree on the Ministry and Life of Priests" (*Presbyterorum Ordinis*, no. 5), which treats of the sacramental ministry of priests.

Liturgical reforms have stressed the communal nature of eucharistic and sacramental celebration without ever derogating from their hierarchical nature. The tension between these two aspects of sacrament has not yet been clearly resolved in magisterial teaching, and so one would not expect to see it resolved in a catechetical document. However, it is another thing for the universal catechism to choose an approach that accentuates the difference between the acts of the priest as instrument of Christ and those that he performs in the name of the people. This privileges the hierarchical understanding of sacrament against its ecclesial understanding. It privileges the role of the sacraments in giving grace to individuals over against their nature as corporate and symbolic expressions of the body of Christ, sacrament of salvation and human reconciliation.

Another difficulty with the treatment of priesthood that operates against a good understanding of church and sacrament is that it is cut off from any fuller treatment of ministry in the church. One gets little sense in reading this document of the slow and varied development of ministerial structures in the early days of the church or of the variety of charisms and ministries that always have served, and still do serve, the building up of the church and its mission. Early developments are quickly passed over when the Pastoral Epistles are cited as evidence of the apostolic origins of the threefold ministry (2765) or when it is said that the three degrees existed "from the beginning" (2770). While it cannot be rightly expected that the issue of women's ordination be opened up in this kind of document, it is disillusioning to read a justification of the ordination of males alone through an appeal to an action of Jesus himself and later of the twelve apostles (2747). This kind of ahistorical and acritical reading of the New Testament could readily lead to the incredulity rather than to the conviction of the well disposed.

The division of order into the three degrees of episcopacy, presbyterate, and diaconate is not well served by the appeal to the category of priesthood or by the ahistorical reading of church development. Though the document has distinguished order from baptism in terms of the different participations in the priesthood of Christ, it finds ministerial priesthood verified only in the episcopacy and the presbyterate, not the diaconate (2724, 2738). The deacon is said to receive a distinct sacramental character that configures him to Christ the servant of all (2739). Logically this would make the diaconate either a distinct sacrament or not a sacrament at all if the only distinction is between types of priesthood. What the document ends up with are: the baptismal priesthood, the ministerial priesthood, and the diaconate, which has a unique (sacramental) character of service. This logically means an economy of eight, not seven, sacraments.

This section on the sacrament of order cries out for a mystagogical approach, where the point of departure would be the celebration of ordination. The sacrament thus would be clearly located in the life of the church as a community of faith and the body of Christ. The relation of order to the church community would stand out simultaneously as one of presidency and service. Its various ministries of word, sacrament, deaconal service, and pastoral leadership would find their place in the life and apostolate of the whole community. The relation to Christ as both servant and priest would come into focus in the evocation of his memory. The role of the Spirit in appointing leaders and in giving the charism of ministry would be found expressed in the laying on of hands and in the prayer for the gift of the Spirit. The participation of other communities or of their ministries (bishops or priests as the case may be) would also be taken as a fitting testimonial to the place that the episcopal college has in the universal church or that the presbyterate and the diaconate have in the local church.

Marriage

Given the complications of the history of the marriage rite and of its inclusion among the seven sacraments, it is virtually impossible for the catechism to deal with it as it deals with the other sacraments. In fact, this section is as much concerned with the marriage union and with family life as with the sacramental celebration. What is attempted creates a number of basic problems.

First, the treatment given to the sacrament of marriage illustrates a problem that arises from the basic plan of the catechism. It separates the treatment of the sacrament from the treatment of human sexuality and family that occurs in the section on the fourth, sixth, and ninth commandments. Only a simple cross-reference is given where this article treats of marriage in the created order (2850). It also separates the brief section on the family as domestic church (2868–71) from ecclesiology, so that one may be left wondering where the two connect.

A second problem has to do with trying to address new issues in an old framework, pouring new wine into old wineskins. Every recent marital and domestic issue is taken up somewhere in the article, be it divorce, the traditional domination of woman by man, planned parenthood, the openness of marriage to procreation, mixed marriages, or the dissolution of the marriage bond by ecclesiastical tribunals on account of deficient consent (2832). Even virginity gets included, possibly to answer the charge that its age-old presentation as a vocation depreciates marriage (2820–24).

Yet because of a surprising lack of cultural and social consciousness, these problems are not considered in their human context but appear as abstract issues, solved on the basis of doctrinal principles, as though the reality and resolution of each issue were the same in every culture and in every social context. It may be pleaded that local catechisms have to fill out this context, but the universal catechism gives neither implicit or explicit invitation to do so. The very manner of its treatment suggests that this would be accessory rather than essential to the comprehension of the issues mentioned.

A third problem has to do with the use of discriminatory language. This is a question that runs through the entire text of the catechism, but here it is all too evident how outrageous it is. The text bears a demonstrable concern to uphold equality between man and woman and very often mentions the couple "man and woman" or "men and women." Yet in this very context where man's domination over woman is a specific concern, the text does not avoid the generic use of "he" and "man" to describe God and the entire human race, as in this citation: "God who created man through love also called him to love, because man is created in the image and likeness of God (Gn 1.27) who is *himself* love (1 Jn 4.8, 16). Since God has created man and woman in his image, their mutual love is part of this likeness. This love is an image of the absolute and unfailing love with which God loves man" (2803, emphasis added).

A fourth problem is specifically liturgical. The very real difference between the Eastern emphasis on the blessing of the priest and the crowning of the couple, as against a Western accent on the exchange of marital consent, is mentioned several times (2827, 2836). The lack of an ecclesiological and sacramental basis discussed earlier in this essay, however, makes it difficult to draw any rich insight from this divergence. There is a possible openness to this in two statements in the chapter. The first says that marriage is in itself a liturgical act and is therefore appropriately celebrated in the church's public liturgy (2837a). The second says that "marriage brings the couple into an ecclesial *ordo*" (2838b).

These two remarks suggest that marriage finds its Christian meaning within the communion of the church, as a charismatic reality within it, as a service to it, and as a sign of the communion of human creatures in Christ. Its celebration in a sacramental act expresses this reality.

The divergent approaches of East and West to the essential sacramental act can best be seen through a full appreciation of sacrament as an ecclesial act, perfected by a variety of ministries and actions. Couple, priest, and the community that witnesses this marriage together constitute the sacramental action as an ecclesial act. In this one tradition the Western church, despite its very hierarchical approach to sacrament, has constantly attributed active sacramental roles to lay persons. When this is placed in the context of the full sacramental action of Christ's body, it can give fresh insight into all the sacraments, illustrating how the different parts come together, each with its own specific activity, to create sacramental fullness. Against the background of its own tradition and in appreciation of the role of the married in the life of the church community, the celebration of marriage can help to overcome the Western dichotomy between priest and people in the celebration of sacrament and liturgy.

Conclusion

If it were merely a matter of suggesting modifications to the text, one could list a profusion of details that deserve change or correction. There is, for example, the way in which the catechism deals with the necessity for infant baptism (2241, 2249ff.), its treatment of the Eucharist as remedy for sin (2472, 2473, 2518), the definition of sin (2523), or the questionable way in which it relates suffering to original sin (2620) and thus obscures a position taken in the *Order for the Pastoral Care of the Sick*.[8] The questions about the suitability of the text on sacraments are, however, more basic than that.

Much that is rich is presented on the sacraments, drawn from the teachings of the Second Vatican Council, from the revised liturgy, and from other more ancient liturgies. In the end, however, the best intents of the text seem to be defeated by the adoption of the fundamental pattern of the catechism of Trent and scholastic theology. It is hard to see how it can be bettered by simply introducting amendments (*modi*). The introduction of new material only clutters the text, so that finally the only lucid parts of the work are the summaries marked "In Brief." While these enjoy the advantage of clarity, they are all too obviously of a post-Tridentine pattern. A rethinking of the whole approach seems necessary for a current catechesis. The challenge of a contemporary mystagogy on sacrament remains to be taken up.

Prayer in
the Catechism

Monika K. Hellwig
Georgetown University

It seems important that this fourth section be developed further and given the full status that is denied it by its designation as an epilogue to the main body of the text.

The epilogue vacillates between being a line-by-line commentary on the Lord's Prayer and a treatise on prayer in general.

As might be expected, the topic of Christian prayer occurs frequently in the draft of the *Catechism for the Universal Church*. Prayer is dealt with in each of the four parts. Part 1 on the Apostles' Creed ("the faith professed") describes the search for God, the quest to know God. The treatment is sketchy and is perhaps done better in the Dutch bishops' *A New Catechism* for adults which has been in use in a variety of languages, including English, since 1967.[1] This description of the search for God might well be expanded and tested in RCIA programs, because for an increasingly large number of people in industrialized and industrializing countries it may be the most significant question dealt with in the catechism.

Part 2 on the sacraments ("the faith celebrated") deals with liturgical prayer and is analyzed in two essays earlier in this collection. Part 3 on the Ten Commandments ("the faith lived") treats prayer when discussing the first three commandments. Here the catechism deals with the importance of worship, the use of images in worship, the habit of prayer, the meaning and efficacy of prayer of petition, what is meant by the exhortation to pray always, the role and significance of liturgical prayer, and the meaning of Sabbath/Sunday observance.

Thus, many important questions on prayer are discussed throughout the catechism, and most of these topics are not covered in the last part of the draft, the epilogue that is devoted to prayer. Consequently there is a discontinuity in the catechism's treatment of prayer, due in part to composition of the document by different authors for the different sections. But the discontinuity is largely unavoidable given the structuring of the draft around the classic sources: creed, commandments, sacraments, and Lord's Prayer. Because the unfolding of these classic sources is the main purpose of the universal catechism—a purpose that seems urgent in our times if we are not to lose the living tradition of the treasures of our heritage—it seems that the discontinuities in the systematic treatment of particular themes are a price that must be paid. However, for the sake of fully coherent development of themes, it might be good either to introduce some repetition in the epilogue or to insert cross-references. What is suggested in the remainder of this essay is envisaged in the context of that proposal.

The main discussion of prayer in the draft is presented in the fourth part, entitled "Epilogue." The title is unfortunate for several reasons. First, this section, unlike the other three major parts of the catechism, is based on words that the New Testament attributes directly to Jesus. This alone should entitle the section to recognition as a principal part of the exposition of the faith. Second, the Lord's Prayer offers the more biblical perspective of eschatology when it introduces the expectation of the coming reign of God. This biblical perspective of eschatology, so important for our times, is not immediately evident from the classic creeds. Third, this last section of the draft offers the most extensive treatment of prayer in general and personal prayer in particular that is to be found in the draft. An initiation into Christian prayer traditions is more basic in the experience of the individual than an explanation of creedal formulations. Finally, the Catholic church has a particularly rich heritage of prayer traditions, and these are a major component of the treasury of resources that we hold in trust for those who come after us. For these reasons it seems important that this fourth section be developed further and given the full status that is denied it by its designation as an epilogue to the main body of the text.

Strengths and Weaknesses

The epilogue on prayer is largely a commentary, phrase by phrase, on the Lord's Prayer, and as such it stands in a great tradition. It is both instructive and inspirational and has great strengths. Perhaps its most significant strength is its heavy dependence on the New Testament and the wonderful array of patristic excerpts. Moreover, the whole commentary is a serious and nonmoralizing attempt to introduce the reader to the

meaning that the prayer might have had for Jesus and his immediate followers. The prayer is properly situated in its Hebrew context, though this
is sketchy if it is to serve as a resource from which teaching and catechetical aids are to be drawn. A considerable virtue of the commentary is that
nothing in it is inappropriate to the contemporary catechetical context,
nothing is inaccurate or liable to misunderstanding, and nothing is ill
informed in the contemporary explanations that are offered.

There are also weaknesses in the epilogue as it now stands. First,
although there is a splendid array of excerpts from primary sources of the
tradition, these are from the patristic age only, and they are not well
integrated into the contemporary commentary. On the topic of prayer in
general, and in commentary of the Lord's Prayer in particular, a great
wealth of postpatristic primary sources exists in our tradition. It is surprising, for instance, that such figures as Anselm, Bernard, Aquinas,
Bonaventure, Ignatius of Loyola, and Francis de Sales are not included in
the collection. Even more surprising, in this field where women have
made such a great contribution, no women authors are cited. One might
suggest Perpetua, Egeria, Dhuoda, Hildegard of Bingen, Mechthild of
Magdeburg, Gertrude the Great, Catherine of Genoa, Catherine of
Siena, Teresa of Avila, Thérèse of Lisieux, Elizabeth of the Trinity, Edith
Stein, Dorothy Day, to mention just a few.

Second, the commentary is not systematic but gently meditative.
This instructive and inspirational approach is suitable if this is really only
intended as an epilogue to the universal catechism. Yet many extremely
important issues are touched upon that either ought to be dealt with systematically here or should bear references here to other sections where
they are dealt with systematically. Some issues are given short shrift in all
sections and could well be developed in some depth in this last part on
prayer. These include eschatology, the meaning of history, the relationship between Christian commitment and civic responsibility, and the
relationship between prayer and action.

In short, the epilogue vacillates between being a line-by-line commentary on the Lord's Prayer and a treatise on prayer in general. The
weaknesses listed above may be due to this vacillation over form that is
not resolved in the draft.

Detailed Observations

Before giving any suggestions for expanding the treatment of prayer in
the next draft, I will make some detailed observations on the draft's treat-

ment of the Lord's Prayer. The text of the Lord's Prayer (4008) includes the doxology, and textual-historical reasons are given for the inclusion (4009). This is an excellent plan for ecumenical, historical, and liturgical reasons. Given this ecumenical concern, the catechism should use the common English translation of the Lord's Prayer by the International Commission on English Texts.

Using the New Testament, patristic literature, and liturgical text and practice to explain the role of the Lord's Prayer in liturgy and in individual piety is also very helpful (4010–17). This passage in the catechism will certainly enrich catechists and those with whom they share these treasures of tradition.

"Our Father"

The segment immediately following (4018–35) is not so satisfactory. While giving an excellent explanation of the biblical foundations for calling God "Father," it misses the gender question, passing it by without the slightest acknowledgment. This omission will cause more and more negative reactions as feminist theologies reach more and more of the people to whom this manual is to be offered. My suggestion here is not to drop the Father analogy. Its extensive use in Scripture makes that not only undesirable but practically impossible. But acknowledgment can be made that gender is not appropriate to God and is used by analogy with human society and according to the then-existing patterns of authority in human society. It is also possible and desirable to gather scriptural quotations and references demonstrating feminine, particularly maternal, imagery used for divine presence and action in history.

A distinct but related issue arises in the treatment of the plural possessive (the "Our") in the "Our Father" (4036–44). The commentary discusses in a general way the community dimension of creaturehood and salvation yet does not explicitly develop the implications for practical social justice and peace. These issues are clearly contained there and are urgently at the forefront of pastoral concerns in the contemporary church. Some development of those implications is needed, the more so as there seems to be considerable confusion in the Spanish- and English-speaking Catholic church about the attitude of Rome concerning liberation theology and the issues it raises. Efforts of the U.S. episcopate to draw social justice and peace issues to the attention of the faithful have also aroused considerable resentment. The critics argue that such issues are not closely related to the Christian faith but are entirely a matter for political and economic assessment by technical experts. Social justice issues are not clearly expounded in the section on the commandments, as pointed out by David Hollenbach later in this collection. In the epilogue another opportunity is missed, especially as the catechism makes such a serious effort to place the Lord's Prayer in its Hebrew context of expectation of the coming reign of God.

Related to this is the discussion of the Father's being "in heaven" (4045–53). I find the section unsatisfactory in two ways. First, the catechism correctly states that heaven is not a place but a word referring to the transcendence of God. But the text continues to string together quotations using concrete imagery in a way that would lead one to think not only in spatial terms but in a way that suggests discontinuity between what happens "on earth" and what happens "in heaven." It is unsatisfactory to leave matters there. This is an area of much popular confusion, leading to a pervasive devaluing of worldly and historical events and responsibilities in favor of an etherealized and privatized sense of the spiritual life of Christians. Second, this treatment does not seem to bring out sufficiently the eschatological character of the Lord's Prayer.

The next section (4054–57) is very profound, linking the Lord's Prayer to the eucharistic action, although it may be too brief and subtle for some of the people for whom the manual is intended. The same might be said of the following section (4058–70) discussing the "hallowing of the name." This section invokes and extensively quotes biblical and early Christian mysticism in an inspirational but elusive fashion. Because of its power to inspire and illuminate contemporary Christian life, this section might profitably be developed at some length.

Petitions

The later section on the petition "thy will be done" (4079–88) offers some good biblical theology about Jesus as the one who comes to do the will of the Father and who thereby makes the critical difference in the history of the world. Yet, regrettably, the exposition associates believers with the obedience of Jesus (4082) in an entirely passive way, as though the recitation of the petition did not involve an energetic commitment to transforming life, action, relationships, and expectations in the world.

This becomes more specific in the section on the petition of daily bread (4089–4102). This petition is explained as acknowledgment of indebtedness and dependence upon God, and the question whether *epiousios* is correctly translated as "daily" is raised along with some other questions usual in Gospel commentaries. A fleeting reference to the parable of Dives and Lazarus indicates that the petition is for *"our* bread" and therefore implies some concern for others. This is good, and the link with the parable is helpful because it might not spontaneously occur to most Christians praying the petition. But it would be theologically and pastorally important to introduce some reflection on the intrinsic connection between what we ask God to do in our prayer and what God intends to do by the empowerment of our own freedom to act in the world and in the shaping of society and its patterns of relationship.

In the same vein the commentary on the petition for forgiveness makes multiple biblical connections that are most insightful and places heavy and appropriate emphasis on the interconnections between forgiving and being forgiven (4103–9). Yet it misses the important opportunity to speak about the broader issues of reconciliation and peace in society with the concomitant issues of social justice as the true basis of peace. Such elaboration is particularly important because Christian counsels of meekness and forgiveness lend themselves too easily to distortions that counsel fatalism and impassivity in the face of massive suffering of whole victim populations. It would be helpful in this context of the petition for forgiveness to have the catechism's insightful comments on relationships between individuals extended to those larger patterns of relationships for which we are also, though not so obviously, responsible.

Something strange happens in the commentary on the petition not to be led into temptation (4110–16). It seems the commentator had difficulty thinking of any explanation that might be needed at this point. The opportunity is missed for making the connection between this petition and the distortions of "original sin," which calls for complex and subtle discernment in a world where so many accepted values are subtly destructive. Instead of that very practical and very pertinent discussion in which so much might be opened up for fuller understanding, we have here attempts to explain how a good God could let people be tempted to sin. What is really needed is a coherent explanation of the implication in the words of Jesus and the explicit later teaching of the church that conversion to redemptive living is an unceasing lifelong endeavor. Christian living requires a lifelong effort not because the first conversion is insincere but because a world distorted by the consequences of past bad choices and evil deeds is a very complicated and bewildering context in which to live a Christian life.

The final petition, to be delivered from evil (4117–22), is interpreted eschatologically as the biblical context would demand but again avoids references to the meaning and tasks of history that might be helpful and most pertinent at this point. Likewise, the concluding comments on the added doxology (4123–26) miss the opportunity to reflect on what the rule of God might mean for us here and now, in public as well as in private life. The danger is that the familiar words might either lose their meaning for those praying them so frequently or come to substitute for the reality. The naming of God as king in power and glory forever might become thought of as sufficient response to the claims of God's rule.

General Questions

The above comments still leave some general questions to be discussed. One of these is the issue of inclusive language and other gender questions. There is no evidence in the epilogue of any awareness of the issue. As far as the language is concerned, it seems both urgent and, in most cases, very easy to address: for instance, "man is by nature" can be replaced by "people are by nature," "a man knows" by "a person knows."

A further general question concerns the primary sources quoted so abundantly. As mentioned earlier, it is important to continue the chronological sequence beyond the church fathers. In addition, the link between the contemporary commentary or catechetical explanation offered and the primary sources cited might be made much closer by assimilating the former more closely to an extended series of the latter. This would enrich the presentation and more fully realize the purpose of the whole document.

The most important question concerning this fourth part of the draft catechism has to do with the relation between the purpose and the content of the whole document and of this fourth part of the document. If the purpose of the whole document is, as claimed in the prologue, to provide a resource, a treasury, from which to draw for contemporary catechesis, then what is written about prayer might be expanded to offer the riches of tradition. Some additions are suggested below. One reason the style and content of the epilogue are not consistent with the rest of the document may be that the author(s) was unsure about the purpose of this fourth part in relation to the other parts. It needs to be clarified whether what is now the epilogue should simply offer the Lord's Prayer as a classic text accompanied by explanatory commentary or whether it should offer a comprehensive resource on Christian prayer traditions.

Furthermore, it needs to be clarified whether the explanation of the Lord's Prayer is expected to deal theologically with issues such as eschatology and sin or whether it is expected only to give spiritual guidance and inspiration on the assumption that theological exposition of such issues has been fully covered elsewhere. If the assumption of adequate prior coverage is being made, there should at least be cross-references so that a fuller resource is offered for the teaching of the Lord's Prayer.

The fuller treatment of prayer would be particularly helpful in our times. Besides commentary and exposition of the Lord's Prayer, the treatment of prayer might include at least one form of trinitarian doxology, the Psalms as a form of Christian prayer, and the canticles and beatitudes of the New Testament. Biblical texts for prayer play a pervasive role in the liturgy, which is discussed in part 2 on the sacraments, but this does not exhaust what might helpfully be offered to foster and sustain private prayer.

If the final part of the universal catechism is to be thought of as a systematic exposition of prayer, it certainly needs to deal at some length with the traditional categories of adoration, thanksgiving, petition, and contrition, although these are touched upon in the part of the document dealing with the first three commandments. Given the many questions and difficulties that people have with prayer in our times, a discussion of these postures of prayer is needed. Particular attention might be devoted to an explanation of prayer of petition—what Jesus said about it, how we expect prayer of petition to affect outcomes, why we should pray prayers of petition, and so forth.

Finally, it is important to show that prayer is not only the recitation of set formulas. Besides the Jesus prayer of the East, which is mentioned in the text, there are several well-developed prayer traditions in the Western church. For instance, the *lectio divina* as foundation for the "ladder of monks" moves spontaneously from reading of sacred text to reflection on the mysteries and from there to explicit prayer and finally to contemplation or simple presence. Although traditionally connected with the practices of monasticism, this tradition of prayer is most apt and applicable to lay life in our times. A universal resource catechism ought surely to propose this as a way of prayer to be taught to all the faithful. Similarly, affective styles of prayer generally associated with the Franciscan movement seem to respond to the needs being expressed so vehemently in the charismatic movement today. Because this need is being expressed, the time seems favorable to offer the cumulative wisdom of the tradition of affective ways of prayer. Nor would it be amiss to discuss here the role of images, blessed objects, holy water, devotional customs, shrines, and pilgrimages.

Particularly valuable among the Western traditions of prayer are the approaches to prayer described and proposed in the Ignatian *Spiritual Exercises*. These were designed for individuals who needed to be very deeply rooted because in Ignatius's time, as in ours, there was very little cultural congruence or support for the individual Christian living in a world full of contradictions and confusion of values and expectations. A modern offspring of Ignatian prayer traditions also might be mentioned, namely the Jociste tradition of communal reflection on Gospel texts and social situations taken alternately and brought into the focus of the three functions: see, judge, act. This in turn has led to the communal Gospel meditations of the basic Christian communities of our times. Clearly, in each of these three phases, the Ignatian, the Jociste, and that of the basic Christian communities, prayer has been taught very effectively for modern Christians. These traditions, therefore, might well be included in the central resource manual for contemporary catechesis.

Summing Up

It is excellent that this fourth part exists; it ought to be given equal standing with the other three parts rather than being designated an epilogue; its scope might well be extended far beyond that of commentary on the Lord's Prayer to include other biblical texts and a more systematic treatment of prayer; such a treatment might cover theological issues concerned with prayer and should at least bear cross-references to theological discussion of other topics such as eschatology and sin; the broader treatment of prayer should include traditional categories of adoration, thanksgiving, petition, and contrition, but also should include the major prayer traditions of the Western church; the splendid collection of patristic texts should be carried further by the inclusion of excerpts from great Christian texts of women and men of subsequent centuries down to the present; and the commentary would be enriched by being assimilated more closely to the excerpts from the primary sources of the tradition. None of this should be taken as lessening the gratitude we owe to the author(s) of the epilogue in the first draft—gratitude particularly for the profound spirituality of the text and for the solid grounding in Bible and patristics of the commentary on the Lord's Prayer.

PART 4

THE TEN
COMMANDMENTS
IN THE CATECHISM

The Moral Vision
of the Catechism

William C. Spohn, S.J.
Jesuit School of Theology, Berkeley

The language of law dominates the fundamental moral vision of the catechism, just as it did moral theology following the Council of Trent.

A more adult ethics sees the moral life as taking responsibility for discovering humane solutions to the problems of personal and social life.

Did some Roman Rip Van Winkle write the moral section of the proposed *Catechism for the Universal Church*? At first glance it appears that its author has slept through the last thirty years of development in the field of Christian ethics. Since this has been one of the most fruitful eras in the entire history of moral theology, our author has missed a great deal.

Perhaps the experts consulted by the Pontifical Commission for the Catechism lacked exposure to moral theology beyond the average seminary studies of the 1940s and 1950s. What was taught to them became canonized as *the* Catholic tradition. The outline of the catechism's "Part Three: Life in Christ" follows the patterns of preconciliar textbooks: conscience, natural law, sin, virtues, the Ten Commandments. Some biblical material has been interjected, but it only buttresses the legalistic approach that characterized most pre–Vatican II moral theology.

Or perhaps this antiquated presentation comes from a more disturbing strategy. Perhaps it is a deliberate exercise of omission: if moral theology since the council has betrayed its proper role in the church, we should pass over its changes in silence. The document makes no reference to the developments that have reshaped Catholic moral thinking. The openness to human experience and the "signs of the times," the admission that the magisterium is not omnicompetent in complex moral questions, the crisis among theologians and laity following Pope Paul VI's *Humanae Vitae*, the worldwide collapse in the practice of frequent confession, fundamental rethinking on the possibility of mortal sin, the increasing independence of the laity from hierarchical direction in sexual ethics and married life, the retreat from exceptionless, concrete moral norms, the awareness that all magisterial certitudes are historically conditioned, the admission of error in church teaching on slavery, religious freedom, women, and so on, and the shift from avoiding sin to taking responsible action to combat oppression and injustice—all these may be just nightmares for our theological Rip Van Winkle. Like another Washington Irving character, Ichabod Crane, he shakes them off as so many headless horsemen or graveyard fantasies. The problems of 1990 can be met by asserting the confident absolutes of the church of Pius XII. Catechetics should produce docile, loyal Catholics who live by the law and believe that their relationship with God is the same as their relationship with the institutional church.

The text shows some effort to respond to Vatican II's directive that moral theology should be reconnected with the Christian vocation, Scripture, and the life of Christ. Sections are dutifully included to meet this request, and scriptural citations are abundant. However, the additions are only parentheses inserted in an old-fashioned system. The new material does not alter the basic vision: Christian moral life is primarily obedience to laws fixed by God and proclaimed by the hierarchy, with the consolation of sacramental absolution for inevitable human failure. The gospel reveals the "law of Christ" and "to those who love, obedience brings peace" (3223).

There have been three major developments in moral theology since Pius XII that no honest assessment of today's church can ignore. They represent basic changes in Catholic consciousness, not simply flights of theological speculators who "confuse the faithful." They are the shift from law to responsibility, from the particular moral act to the agent, and from the pursuit of an individualistic "perfection" to loving service of the neighbor.

From Obedience to Responsibility

In contemporary moral theology the basic model of Christian moral life has shifted from obedience to divine law to responsible initiative for human and gospel values. But the language of law dominates the fundamental moral vision of the catechism, just as it did moral theology following the Council of Trent. Selecting the Ten Commandments as the structure of Christian obligations reinforces the primacy of law. Law is the "root metaphor" for the moral life since every aspect of Christian morality is seen from this perspective: the moral agent, God, Christ, the role of the church.[1]

For example, "in obeying the natural law man obeys 'the divine law itself—eternal, objective and universal' . . . of which it is the expression" (3095). Moral obligation rests on objective universal norms, the "divine law" in the catechism's terminology. "Human acts are never morally neutral. Conformity with the 'objective norms of morality' places them in the category of good; non-conformity in the category of evil" (3050, see also 3039). Acts are not right because they promote human goodness; they are good only because they are right, that is, in compliance with objective standards. When conscience has to discern what to do in difficult cases, the first point of reference must be the law. "First, that which is unlawful cannot be morally justified; secondly, moral choice should always have as its motive love for the other" (3043).

In this section the fundamental image of God is the sovereign divine lawgiver who manifests his love by helping us obey these dictates through the Holy Spirit, the sacraments, and the magisterium. The catechism regularly locates law above love in the divine action. Accordingly, "To recognize the sovereignty of God, freely accepting his authority and the demands of his love, is the foundation of moral life. God reveals himself as law-giver; his laws constitute the framework within which the universe can develop. He also reveals himself as love, in which man shares and so fulfills his destiny" (3310).

Part 1 of the catechism frames a Christology to support the legal model of part 3. Jesus accomplished redemption by "the perfect carrying-out of the Law in the place of all sinners" (1420). It absolutizes Matthew's account that Jesus did not come to abolish the Law and the Prophets but to complete them (Mt 5:17–19), while ignoring the famous antitheses of the following verses where Jesus reinterprets the Law on some points and alters it on others. Since the document omits the New Testament passages where Jesus challenges the Law, one suspects that it reasons backward from its preferred portrait of the Christian as obedient to moral laws to Jesus as obedient to Law.[2] As we shall see, "obedience" in the New Testament is a much richer symbol than that.

Neither Scripture nor St. Thomas Aquinas requires such a concentration on law. Certainly rules and principles play a role in biblical ethics, but one must do violence to the text to make Christianity primarily a life of duty. The catechism frequently states that the gospel reveals the "law of Christ" for the Christian to obey. The phrase is taken from Gal 6:2 where it actually refers to bearing one another's burdens in fraternal correction, not to obeying a full set of Christian duties.

The term *divine law* covers an impossible range of biblical material in this catechism. It refers variously to the Ten Commandments, the whole way of life of Israel that the Hebrew Scriptures call Torah, "the order of the world which God set in creation and recorded in the divine law" (3021), "universal objective norms" that are not spelled out, "the 'new law' that Christ has revealed in the new commandment of love" (3027), the final dictate of conscience, "the expression . . . of the divine law, defining what is good and what is evil" (3034), and the assistance provided by the Holy Spirit (3123). "Law" is used in a wide range of analogous meanings, but the document treats them all as if they were precise behavioral rules directly mandated by God. The Hebrew notion of Torah means "wisdom" and "instruction" that guide a way of life; it cannot be reduced to the term *law*.

A more accurate reading of Paul would conclude that in Christ "Law" has been replaced by Spirit. The liberating "law of the Spirit of life in Christ Jesus" (Rom 8:2) has supplanted the directive force of Torah that gave Israel spiritual identity and moral guidance. The Spirit, operating through the gifts of the entire body of Christ, guides Christians in the path of personal and communal life. Paul is never reluctant to point out specific attitudes and actions that are incompatible with life in Christ, but obedience to such rules does not constitute the heart of Christian moral life.

In the New Testament the Spirit is not given primarily to conform believers to the law. It leads them to fulfill the requirements of morality but, more importantly, conforms them to the pattern of Jesus' cross and resurrection in the faith community. It enables both individual and community to respond with the values of Christ to the challenges of life. Christian moral life as a whole is a response in trusting gratitude to the gracious overtures of God in Christ. The "obedience of faith" (Rom 1:5) is the personal commitment of one's whole self to God made possible in Christ, a loving response that expresses itself in good deeds.[3] Hence, "responsibility" is a root metaphor for Christian morality that is more theologically based than "law." In Christian ethics it primarily means personal responsiveness to God and neighbor rather than moral accountability, which is the only meaning the catechism acknowledges.

The metaphor of law reinforces an early stage of moral development where clear norms prevail. It also fits an ecclesiology where the faithful are cast as children under the benevolent paternalism of the clergy. A more adult ethics sees the moral life as taking responsibility for discovering humane solutions to the problems of personal and social life. No objective moral norms can provide a blueprint for addressing economic injustice or oppression.

Thomas Aquinas does not dictate an ethics concentrated in laws and principles any more than Scripture does. Traditional moral theology often ignored the analogical status of "law" in Aquinas and applied it literally, missing Aquinas's careful distinctions between eternal, divine, natural, and human positive law. "Law" in Aquinas is a flexible analogy for moral directives that can refer either to the lawmaker's normative design or to its embodiment in the practice of the citizen. Natural law is not the divine plan for creation. Aquinas refers to this as "eternal law," which human reason cannot know directly. Natural law is the embodiment of God's intentions in certain fundamental human inclinations and intelligence, not an objective, universal code of rules. "Divine law" refers to biblical articulations of the natural law (see *Summa Theologiae* 1-2, q. 2, a. 4 and 5), which Aquinas sees of great benefit for recognizing the claims of natural law.

Humans use reason and experience to implement these basic human values in a variety of cultural arrangements and positive laws. Biblical "divine law" assists humans in discovering God's intentions, but it remains subordinate to natural law. In other words, biblical or positive law are expressions of objective human values, not their foundation. Aquinas based his ethics on virtues that habitually implement basic human values through the intelligent exercise of prudence. This was turned into an ethics of divine rules by moral theology manualists who seemed unable to imagine any ethics that was not based on law, command, and obedience.

The catechism insists that there are objective, eternal norms that absolutely command and forbid specific actions. It mentions no difference between enduring, cross-cultural values and the culturally bound norms that express them. More technically put, this confidence in objective norms rests on a questionable theory of knowledge that holds that language can exhaustively grasp the "essence" of experience. Once the right term is found, no further development or change is necessary.

At other points the catechism admits the tentative character of all human efforts to speak about God. Theologians who forget the symbolic, analogical character of religious language run the risk of reducing the mystery of God to formulas. Moral theologians have often made the same error in canonizing moral norms as objective and universal in their attempts to resolve the complexities of human experience. Human values are objective and universal, but they will always be expressed in norms and institutions subject to change, bias, and cultural limitation. It is doubtful that the assistance of the Holy Spirit can exempt any theology from human finitude.

The attempt to restore objective, unexceptional moral rules to the center of Catholic morality provokes skepticism for those aware of history. If the magisterium has the power to discover eternal norms, why has it erred on a number of issues and changed on others? One suspects a basic stratagem here: because the author does not want certain teachings to change, he claims that they are beyond history and experience. Since these laws are transcripts of eternal divine decrees, they are immune to development or criticism.

A glance at history proves embarrassing for this objectivist account. How would it explain papal decrees approving the burning of witches, tolerating slavery, and condemning religious freedom? If the magisterium can deduce God's will from universal principles, why does it allow different applications of general social principles while insisting that sexual norms be applied exactly the same way in every case?

The Moral Act and the Moral Agent

Contemporary moral theology teaches that the moral quality of an act cannot be determined apart from the moral agent, whose basic commitments, dispositions, and social relations help define the morality of any act. The catechism presupposes that the proper focus of morality is the individual act measured against objective divine law. Attendant circumstances and the agent's intentions may diminish the agent's culpability but do not affect the act's moral goodness or evil (3050–52). Because individual actions are instances of universal, objective patterns, they are not unique. Woe to morality if circumstances and intentions become the measure of morality: "The consequence of such thinking which breaks all connection with the natural and objective order of things divinely established is to make man himself both the source and centre of moral life" (3054).

The unnamed targets of such condemnation seem to be the large numbers of moral theologians who are often called "proportionalists." They do not believe that acts can be morally defined apart from the particular circumstances and intentions of the agent. They hold that most moral decisions involve a trade-off of specific values and disvalues that can be justified only if the human goods fostered are reasonably proportionate to the disvalues tolerated in the particular action. When moral norms are considered apart from specific facts and intentions, they illumine specific situations of choice but do not automatically prescribe what to do or not to do.

Proportionalists point out that traditional moral theology always considered act, intention, and circumstances together in judging moral good and evil (as Lisa Sowle Cahill and David Hollenbach, S.J., explain in the following essays). For example, we cannot make a moral evaluation of an act of giving money to the poor until we know whether the agent is motivated by philanthropy or a yen for publicity. Exceptionless moral norms ("Commit no murder") usually include a term that refers to intention and circumstance. Unlike the morally neutral "homicide," "murder" includes a judgment on act, intention, and circumstances; it means "unjustified homicide."

The proportionalists doubt that God inscribes objective divine laws ("instructions for use") in the human person. They hold with Aquinas that natural law is not a cosmic moral code but a process of using virtue and intelligence to work out the human response to life's varying challenges. The catechism agrees with Cardinal Joseph Ratzinger that moral norms are objective products of God's will and "can only be witnessed to, but not produced or annulled by some calculated analysis."[4] In this view a morality founded on human values rather than on these divinely established norms was denounced by Vatican II as "man's desire for autonomy which refuses all dependence on God" (*Gaudium et Spes*, no. 20). The leading proportionalists, such as Josef Fuchs, Richard A. McCormick, and Bruno Schuller, make no such claims for independence from God.

Mortal Sin

Finally, the catechism ignores the postconciliar rethinking on mortal sin. A preconciliar objectivist account gave the impression that individual infractions of certain serious norms constituted mortal sin. In a more personalist account, the fundamental turning away from God through decisions that violate others is what is "mortal." Individual acts must be placed in the context of the agent's fundamental stance toward God. Specific acts are symptoms and occasions of a more pervasive self-disposition or fundamental option that affirms or denies God through those particular acts. This redefinition of the self, a negative conversion, could not occur with the frequency feared by Catholics in the recent past. The widespread disaffection from frequent confession indicates that fewer Catholics live in fear of slipping into genuine mortal sin. If the catechism addressed this historic collapse in sacramental practice, the authors might have to admit that the average Catholic no longer finds the older teaching on mortal sin to be credible.

This debate over moral acts is not merely an academic squabble. At stake is the proper pastoral care the church should offer. Do moral rules adequately cover all the relevant cases? If so, the church should proclaim the norms, note the rare exceptions, and offer the faithful the consolation of pastoral plea bargaining and forgiveness when they fail to follow the rules.

Moral Discernment

A different pastoral approach is called for if moral choices are not so uniform. Since moral principles cannot foresee every specific configuration of persons, values, and concrete possibilities, pastoral care must be more flexible. Specific moral norms illumine the situation of choice but do not automatically dictate what to do. In that case the church should proclaim the relevant values and principles while training the faithful to discover where they are being called. This practice is called moral discernment. This course of pastoral education was recommended by Karl Rahner almost twenty years ago:

> Consciences must be formed, not primarily by way of a casuistic instruction, going into more and more concrete details, but by being roused and trained for autonomous and responsible decisions in the concrete, complex situations of human life which are no longer completely soluble down to the last detail, in fields never considered by the older morality, precisely because they were then unknown and even now cannot be adequately mastered by a rational casuistry.[5]

Christian moral discernment means the art of sorting out one's options by drawing on fundamental commitments and religious aspirations, memory, the experience of the community, and the life of Christ. It recognizes that basic moral principles set the outer limits of moral action but turns to the Gospels and community experience for the values that shape this way of life. Reason is informed by faith, as Richard A. McCormick writes: "It is reason shaped by faith and . . . this shaping takes the form of perspectives, themes, insights associated with the Christian story, that aid us to construe the world theologically."[6]

These resources equip the Christian to interpret experience in the light of the gospel but do not assure a predictable outcome in every case. Catechesis and moral education should give the highest priority to developing a moral perspective shaped by the Christian story to serve as the basis of moral discernment. The moral prohibitions of the Ten Commandments serve as the outer limits of Christian action, just as civilized societies recognize fundamental human rights that the state cannot transgress. However, we need other forms of moral guidance for living humanely in the vast space within the boundaries set by general principles.

Mainstream Catholic moral theology, which is not represented in the catechism, realizes that the fundamental stance taken toward God and neighbor must be the central concern in a church community where many are baptized but unconverted. The catechism remains in a legal, act-centered framework in its description of mortal sin—"conscious and deliberate breaking of a law of God in a grave matter" (3077). Aquinas's formulation comes closer to a relational view of sin: "God is not offended by us except in so far as we act against our own good."[7] This means that moral education should explain how certain actions destroy ourselves and others and, consequently, are destructive of our relationship with the loving God.

Moral theology in the past generation has decisively "turned to the subject." Not a mass-produced human nature but the whole person becomes the measure of moral good. This turn was encouraged by the council. The official commentary on Vatican II's "Pastoral Constitution on the Church in the Modern World" (*Gaudium et Spes*) states that "human activity must be judged insofar as it refers to the human person integrally and adequately considered."[8] Moral theology today considers the person as an emerging self whose perception of value has been shaped by experience, history, culture, and community. Acts take on meaning as parts of a whole life, not in isolation. Since we become what we do, our character is the result of our actions and the interpretation we give them. Some communities provide us with more adequate interpretations than others, but none, not even the community of faith, exhausts the mysteries of human love, suffering, commitment, and compromise. The council understood that we remain "a pilgrim people" in our moral journey. That modesty seems to have been forgotten by the catechism in its attempt to "restore" certitude to every detail of moral teaching.

Vatican II learned from the "signs of the times" and the testimony of human culture that comes primarily through the laity in the church. The catechism seems to take just the opposite tack: "In the evolution of modern society there emerge new sensitivities (concerning, for example, solidarity, social justice, the absolute rejection of war), new demands and hopes (for example, equality of rights, liberation movements, feminism, mastery over life), which sometimes make the perception of values and moral obligations less easy to arrive at" (3041).

Certainly the appreciation of human freedom and the authority of conscience are signs of the times that Vatican II could endorse in contemporary culture. The catechism offers several paragraphs on the value of conscience but approves it only insofar as it agrees with the teaching of the church (3033–44). The cautious paragraphs on freedom are an afterthought inserted into the text at paragraph 3048. Here "freedom is the source of the moral quality of acts, establishing them as properly human, voluntary and moral" (3048b). How this is reconciled with the statement two paragraphs later that conformity to "objective norms of morality" makes acts morally good is not explained.

Moral objectivity does not exist in a timeless, transcendent dimension above the vicissitudes of human experience. The objective points of reference for Christian discernment are always incarnated in specific histories and communities. Tradition, Scripture, human wisdom, and scientific data are "objective" but they do not exist in isolation from particular subjects in specific contexts. As such, they are conditioned by the limitations common to humanity. When all the gifts of the Holy Spirit operate (that is, when consultation in formulating the magisterium's teaching extends beyond court theologians), the church becomes a community of moral discourse that charts the way in face of new moral problems. As John Mahoney, S.J., writes:

> It may appear, then, that the various current attempts to incorporate particulars into the science of moral theology . . . is a move to throw a bridge across the gap between "objective" and "subjective" morality and to judge that, far more frequently than has been suspected, what diverse individuals consider God requires of them is in actual fact what God does "objectively" require of them, as legitimate personal diversities.[9]

Once it recognizes the linkage between objective and subjective factors in moral decision making, the institutional church will begin to foster wisdom and discernment among Catholics rather than insist on uniform obedience. For a generation now, catechetics in the United States has stressed the religious roots of morality. This approach makes sense in religious education grounded in the New Testament. The key question for the Christian is not, What is the law that I must follow here? Instead, it is the more personal question framed by James M. Gustafson, What is God enabling and requiring me to be and to do? Christian moral life is a response to the gift of God and the leading of the Spirit. Its requirements flow from the gift and empowering guidance of God. Because it mandates responsibility for addressing human suffering in ways that must be creatively fashioned, discernment is even more important than obedience. Finally, its normative foundation is not a set of objective moral laws but the narrative of the life, death, and resurrection of Jesus Christ.

Service Rather Than Perfection

The Christian is primarily called to serve the neighbor in need rather than to strive for individualistic moral perfection. Before Vatican II Catholic

spirituality focused on the pursuit of "perfection." The evangelical counsels were "counsels of perfection," religious life was "the state of perfection," and so forth. The notion is equally central to the moral theology of
the catechism.

From the beginning of the moral section, the catechism repeatedly
appeals to Mt 5:47: "Be perfect as the heavenly Father is perfect" (3006).
Here again it lapses into proof-texting by ignoring the context of the biblical citation. The injunction should be interpreted by the portion of the
Sermon on the Mount that it concludes. It follows the description of God
who "makes the sun rise on the evil and on the good" (Mt 5:45) and criticizes those who love only people who love them. The context shows that
Jesus commands his followers to imitate God by loving others without
distinction.

Taken in isolation, the command has often been read as mandating
Christians to become perfect paragons of virtue. Perfection takes prece-
dence over discipleship as the basic pattern of Christian life. To define
Christian holiness, the catechism translates the following of Christ into
the call to perfection. The "disciple of Christ . . . is bound to strive toward
it, whatever his situation or state in life" (3209–10).

It is unclear how the pursuit of perfection is related to either Christ
or the neighbor. Although traditionally the concept of perfection has
included the exercise of love toward the neighbor, the concept has contributed to an individualistic spirituality where the attainment of virtue
holds center stage. The catechism risks this same trap. The life that the New
Testament portrays as response to relationship with Jesus Christ is translated into a pursuit of individual excellence through perfect obedience.

Here again the dominant Christology of the document shapes the
moral agenda. Is sinless obedience and perfect practice of virtue the heart
of Christ's mission or is the pattern of his cross and resurrection? "In giving up his life for Christ, the martyr gives the highest witness to perfection. In accepting death for the faith he comes 'closest of all' to Christ in
the paschal mystery of his passion and death" (3217). However, since
Jesus endured the cross to free all his neighbors from the slavery of sin,
we conform our lives to the paschal mystery by laying them down *for the
neighbor in need*. The martyr does radical service by the witness of blood.

The overriding framework of law in the catechism interprets the new
commandment of Jesus. Christian love illumines and internalizes the law
but does not supplant it in any detail. Love supports the natural virtues
that "create in man a kind of sympathy with the calls and commands of
the moral law" (3067). Because God manifests all the virtues, the call to
imitate God becomes the mandate to practice all the virtues, as coordi-

nated by love (3023). The final impression is that the call to Christian holiness is primarily a mandate to personal perfection and moral spotlessness. (Despite some feeble attempts to resurrect "merit" and indulgences, the catechism does not dwell excessively on everlasting rewards and punishments, which too often encourage a self-interested practice of morality. Serving the neighbor then becomes a stepping stone to eternal reward.)

A radically different emphasis emerges when the life of Christ becomes the guiding norm of morality. Religious education materials in the United States have stressed discipleship as the heart of Christian morality; it appears that the catechism would discourage this approach. Although the following of Christ has been central to Christian liturgy and prayer since the beginning, moralists have only recently tried to integrate it into their theology. Following the lead of Bernard Haring, moral theologians prior to the council began to retrieve the biblically based morality that patristic and medieval writers advocated. From this perspective, Jesus lived a life of response to the Father and service to the neighbor in need. He lived as a servant among us and commanded us to do the same. Servants are effective when they pay attention to the needs of those they serve, not their own advancement.

The New Testament presents gratitude and compassion, not the drive for perfection, as the motives for Christian action. Note that the concrete actions Jesus uses to define the love command are always focused on the neighbor. He explains love of neighbor by telling the parable of the good Samaritan (Lk 10:25–37). In John 13 he washes the disciples' feet to symbolize the serving love that he mandates. This startling action sets the context for his "new commandment" that makes his love for them both the norm and the motivation for their love of each other and all people (Jn 13:34).

In the Last Discourse the paradigm for loving one another is not a set of virtues but the event of his laying down his life for them (Jn 15:12–13). Paul uses the cross and resurrection as the basic paradigm of Christian love (see Phil 2:1–11). These New Testament definitions of love refer to the historical actions of Jesus as the normative pattern for Christian love. Scripture, therefore, gives a more practical standard for love than the abstract definitions of the catechism. The life of Christ plays only a minor role in the catechism as a whole and almost no role in the moral section.

Virtues and commandments in Christian experience are shaped by the life of Christ and the actions of God. Behind the principles lies the history that discloses a personal God calling for response. The commandments—indispensable though they are for community life—are not the primary self-revelation of God to Israel. The saving events of God (Exodus, the creation of Israel, Exile) reveal the character of the Lord and shape the response: "Be holy as I am holy." Notice how often the prophets invoke the compassion and justice of the Lord that were shown in the Exodus. This history gives specific content to the commands to care for the widow, orphan, and migrant worker, "since you yourselves were once slaves in Egypt" (see Ex 22:20–22; Jer 34:8–14). The very term *commandment* implies a personal relationship that is more immediate than "universal objective moral laws."

Paul does not refer to divine law to settle moral questions in his unruly congregations; he takes the Decalogue for granted. He appeals to the cross of Christ as the lens through which they should view everything, especially their recalcitrant opponent. He is, after all, "the brother for whom Christ died" (1 Cor 8:11). He urges the members of Christ's body to discover their gifts and make their personal contributions to build up the community (1 Cor 12, Rom 12). It is sad that Paul appreciates "lay" participation in the church more than a catechism written twenty centuries later.

Christian catechesis, particularly in its moral dimension, should be grounded in the kerygmatic story of Jesus of Nazareth. Contemporary narrative theology roots personal identity in the fundamental stories we incorporate. The self relies on authoritative stories to guide its path. Since personal conversion involves changing the story of our lives by accepting the story of the Christian community as our own, the gospel story becomes basic to our new identity. Neither natural law nor its expression in the Decalogue can supplant the gospel as the basis for Christian ethics.

Principles and virtues may be sufficient norms for particular acts and specific dispositions, but they cannot provide the paradigm for the personal identity. Narrative theology argues that task requires a story. It is appropriate, therefore, that God address us in gospel, a form of story that aims at personal transformation. Once we see that morality is a matter of the agent's emerging identity, then the need for narrative in catechesis becomes clear. In the synoptic Gospels Jesus employs parables as the primary medium of moral teaching. He does not expound the Decalogue or Torah as a good rabbi. Instead, he addresses the imagination to shock the audience out of their set ways. While myths establish a world, parables subvert it, as John R. Donahue writes, "as religious language they present not simply a series of ethical paradigms or exhortations, though they are often so interpreted, but a vision of reality which becomes a presupposition to ethics."[10]

Narrative theologians describe all virtues as "narrative-dependent," that is, they are displayed through story. We need the interplay of character, plot, and time to see how virtuous dispositions should be enacted. Human values do not exist in generic fashion but are always specified by the stories and exemplars of a particular culture. The Gospels, for example, redefine fairness in the context of God's graciousness, as in the parable of the laborers of the vineyard (Mt 20:1–16). The story of Jesus and the woman caught in adultery (Jn 8:1–11) provides a concrete norm for compassion better than any abstract definition could.

The narrative of Jesus fits around a central core that is normative. All the parables, miracle accounts, and teachings of Jesus fit the master paradigm of the cross and resurrection; the words and deeds of the Master are interpreted through the climactic event of his life. That event captures the specific character of Christian love, as 1 John insists. Although it may be difficult for a rationalistic theology to conceive of a "norm" that is embedded in paradigmatic events and stories, a biblically grounded ethics must be more attentive to paradigms than to abstract principles.

Every generation must interpret the story of Jesus for its time and discern its own calling. Our era discovers the face of evil in the structures of oppression and the massive suffering of starving millions. Although the catechism makes a perfunctory nod to social evil, it reduces its roots to individual sinful choices (3085). Political oppression, economic domination, militarism, racism, poverty, and sexism constitute an environment of sin that holds the neighbor in bondage. A catechism for the nineties should start from these challenges rather than from the pursuit of personal perfection. It should focus on the community of believers as the agent of prophecy and healing if it hopes to engage the next generation. It also must respect the initiative and insights of the nonclerical majority in the church. The catechism speaks as though the official church has all answers and that docility is the main virtue of the faithful: "Ignorance, a refusal to accept the teaching authority of the Church, a wild appeal to the autonomy of conscience—these are what foster wrong judgments in moral conduct" (3039).

Conclusion

In sum, the moral section of the proposed catechism is one of its weakest portions. It is unthinkable that so inadequate a treatment would have emerged from a consultation of mainstream moral theologians. The document needs reformulation in its basic structure (the commandments), its Christology (which downplays the life of Christ), its moral vision (obedience to official laws), and its ecclesiology (a self-sufficient clerical "teaching church" instructing the masses of the "learning church"). It is difficult to imagine how national conferences of bishops could adapt this memento of pre-Vatican II moral theology to the church of the nineties. A massive shift in Catholic experience and practice has occurred since the council. For those who believe these developments have been the work of the Holy Spirit, this catechism represents either repudiation or retrenchment.

Hence, a final piece of advice to our Rip Van Winkle: A lot has happened during your hibernation. Try reading the Gospel of Luke to find out where the Spirit has been leading the people of God since the 1950s. This draft of the catechism is dominated by a narrow reading of Matthew: fulfillment of the Law, Jesus as the new Moses, judgment, setting boundaries, and spelling out obligations. While the church after Trent depended heavily on Matthew for its liturgical readings, that selection reflected an institution that concentrated on clear doctrine, clerical status, law, and accountability. Surely the whole canon remains normative, but Luke may be the most appropriate Gospel for Vatican II and beyond. Luke's Jesus is the prophet who heals outcasts and welcomes them to his table, the companion of women and spinner of parables, the servant whose victory over death launched the Spirit that reaches beyond boundaries, creates new forms of community, and brings the liberating gospel to the ends of the earth. Now that is Good News.

Social Morality
in the Catechism

David Hollenbach, S.J.
Weston School of Theology

"If the trumpet gives an uncertain sound, who will get ready for battle?"
(1 Cor 14:8)

The catechism in its present form will reinforce longstanding tendencies
toward a dualism of the sacred and secular, the spiritual and the social.

During the years since the Second Vatican Council, reflection on Christian responsibility for the quality of social life has been developing rapidly. These developments have been marked by both creativity and conflict.

The creativity is evident in numerous ways: the council's close linkage of the church's mission in society with its duty to proclaim the gospel; the initiatives taken by popes, bishops, and laity for the promotion of human rights; the rise of liberation theology; the pastoral letters of the bishops of the United States on peace, economic justice, and the concerns of women; and the increasing efforts by lay Christians to integrate their faith commitment with their work and public lives.

At the same time, these developments have generated strong resistance. This is often rooted in a fear that these new social initiatives can dilute the church's proper religious mission by falsely politicizing it, or that they risk reducing the gospel to a this-worldly humanism. Critics of liberation theology and of the United States bishops' pastoral letters have voiced such fears.

The provisional text of the *Catechism for the Universal Church* is marked by similar signs of both creative development and guarded hesitation when it addresses the social responsibility of Christians. The creative development of the past twenty-five years is most visible where the catechism schematically presents aspects of the conciliar and postconciliar teachings of the Roman magisterium on subjects such as religious freedom, family life, war, human rights, economic justice, global interdependence, and the need for new forms of solidarity among peoples.

The 1977 synod of bishops, which discussed catechetics in our time, noted that "one of the principal tasks of catechesis today is to encourage and sustain new forms of commitment, especially in the field of justice."[1] The drafters of the universal catechism have made a serious effort to carry out this task. Specific social-moral issues are dealt with chiefly in part 3, section 2 of the catechism, on the Ten Commandments. At the same time, hesitations about linking these matters too closely with the central mysteries of Christian faith and mission are more evident in the sections that deal with the creed, liturgy, sacraments, and the grace of Christ. This caution also appears in the discussion of a few of the more specific moral issues.

The attention given to the social dimensions of Christian life is a major historical breakthrough in the tradition of officially sponsored catechisms since the Council of Trent. For this we should be grateful. But the theological vision that frames the discussion of social-ethical matters severely reduces the likelihood that a strong sense of social responsibility will be integrated into the faith-life and spirituality of those whom the catechism aims to educate. The catechism, in other words, is a call to communicate the developments in church social teaching to all the faithful. But it is a hesitant call—an "uncertain trumpet" that is likely to produce a weak response.

Decalogue

The creative developments in the catechism's approach to social morality are contained chiefly in the exposition of the Decalogue. The discussion of the moral life follows the structure of the familiar biblical text. But it makes no pretense of being either a critical presentation of the literal meaning of Ex 20:1-17 or a theologically developed interpretation of this literal meaning.[2] Rather, the Decalogue serves as an occasion to present an overview of some major themes of recent church social teaching. This approach does not correspond to the council's desire that the "scientific exposition" of moral theology be "more thoroughly nourished by scriptural teaching" ("Decree on Priestly Formation," no. 16).

The catechism's justification for its somewhat fast and loose way of connecting the themes of recent social teaching of the church with Exodus 20 is its traditional insistence that the Decalogue "renews and confirms the natural law" (3244) and therefore implicitly contains all the moral guidance that the magisterium has proposed based on its insight into natural law. There are significant problems with this approach (to be noted below). But it is probably an inevitable consequence of the need to find a place for social ethics within the framework of the structure of the sixteenth-century *Roman Catechism*.

The exposition of the first three commandments concerning the lordship and holiness of God alludes in passing to a few important problems of contemporary social life. For example, the first commandment—"I am the Lord your God who brought you out of the house of bondage; you shall have no gods before me"—forbids placing any creature in the place of God. This stands in judgment on all forms of idolatry. The catechism identifies some distinctive contemporary temptations to this sin: single-minded pursuit of "wealth, honor, success, power, sex, drugs, nation, race" (3318).

At the same time, the glory of God is reflected in the created world, especially in the human person, who is created in God's image and who has responsibility for the advance of creation (3309). When these passages are read in light of the lengthier treatment of creation under the first article of the creed, one can discern the outlines of an environmental ethic that stresses the interdependence of all creatures while also affirming that human beings are the "crown" of creation. Thus human beings are "to govern the earth together as stewards of God . . . in order to lead [all of creation] to God" (1201). This is a minimal treatment of human responsibility for the environment. But its appearance in the catechism is noteworthy.

Fourth Commandment

Under the "Second Table" of the Decalogue most of the questions of social morality are treated explicitly. As one would expect, discussion of the fourth commandment ("Honor your father and your mother") stresses the importance of the family in the Christian moral life. The family is both a "natural community" that is the foundation of civil society and, for Christians, a covenantal communion that anticipates the full communion of the kingdom of God. Because families are oriented to these larger forms of social life and communion, "the bonds of family life though important are not absolute" (3502). This is a healthy counterbalance to the Catholic tradition's tendency to value family life in a way that is sometimes detrimental to a strong sense of social responsibility.

The catechism uses its discussion of the relation between the family and the larger society as the occasion for its most explicit discussion of politics and government. Ideally families are the communities where "the young, old, sick, and handicapped are cared for." But when families are unable to provide this care, it "is the duty of society to insure that adequate help is available" (3462–63). Implicit here, of course, is the "principle of subsidiarity" often enunciated in papal encyclicals. Society at large has a duty to come to the assistance of all those who are weak and vulnerable, including the poor, whenever other smaller communities such as the family are unable to do so. In contemporary circumstances where the extended family is giving way to the nuclear family in many cultures, this may call for greater support from society at large both for the family itself and for poor and vulnerable persons who lack the communal support once provided by extended families (3466).

This leads the catechism to set forward a list of "family rights" that also includes some of the rights of individual persons. These include the right to found a family, to have children, and to educate them in accord with the religious faith of the parents. More broadly, all people have a right to social security, housing, health care, and care for the elderly. The catechism states that "the State has a duty to protect and promote" these rights (3490).

This, of course, touches on important and controversial questions about the welfare state. The position of the catechism on this matter is clear but general. The state has the responsibility to promote the common good, which includes the securing of the above-mentioned rights. At the same time, government must be based on the freedom of its citizens, and it must not deny "individuals, families, and other social groups their proper rights and due role" (3491–97).

Thus, in a few short paragraphs the catechism outlines a theory in which government is both limited by basic human rights and also obligated to take positive action to secure these rights, especially for the weak, the vulnerable, and the poor. This is standard Catholic social theory, and it is succinctly stated. But one wonders whether it will be catechetically productive to discuss such large and controversial matters under the heading of the fourth commandment.

Even more remarkable is the way the catechism introduces a very brief discussion of "lawful opposition" to government and even a hint of the possibility of civil disobedience in the context of the morality of family life. When civil authority exceeds its proper power, "it is legitimate and indeed necessary to defend the rights which are being set aside." In such cases "opposition may be morally justified" and "the individual has the duty to resist its demands and authority whenever these violate his conscience." Such opposition is in accord with the teaching and example of Jesus (3497–3500, 3519).

The abuses of authoritarian and totalitarian regimes are clearly in the background here, though one can imagine situations where such opposition might be called for even in democratic societies. As general principles these statements are unexceptionable, and they are anticipated in a general way in what the *Roman Catechism* said about obedience to civil authorities. But the way they are treated in the draft catechism goes well beyond what was said about the responsibilities of citizens in much of the catechesis of the not-too-ancient past. Again, one can ask whether the context may not obscure this.

Fifth Commandment

The inclusion of several major issues of social morality in the discussion of the fifth commandment ("You shall not kill") is considerably less surprising. There are analogies between the *Roman Catechism*'s brief treatment of war and what is said here. But the importance of socially organized forms of killing is given much greater emphasis in the new text, and this is the focus here. (Biomedical questions such as euthanasia, genetic manipulation, and abortion are discussed in Lisa Sowle Cahill's essay in this volume.)

The exposition begins by stating that God is the "master of life." All life is a gift of God. Thus, "to love God is to love the life he has given us. To love our neighbors is to love the life they have received" (3522–28). Because of original sin, however, there are instincts of violence in the human heart that make us capable of destroying each other through "personal crime." These tendencies to violence are given new scope by the tools of contemporary technology. The socially organized threats to human life are evident: war, terrorism, hostage taking, torture, the dangers to which the environment is exposed by toxic wastes. A conversion of heart is especially needed today if we are to respect the gift of life in this context.

The catechism states that the fifth commandment "forbids every attack on life and anyone's physical integrity. *This principle is absolute*" (3532, emphasis added). There is reason, however, to question the adequacy of this formulation of the norm forbidding killing. Only a few paragraphs later we come upon a section entitled "When to take life is not forbidden," which says this absolute may be "set aside" for defensive wars, self-defense, or the defense of others (3540–41). Classically, moralists have drawn a distinction between killing and murder (unjustified killing). This distinction may be presupposed by the provisional text of the catechism. Yet there are problems with interpreting the text this way too quickly. These problems go to the heart of one of the most hotly debated questions in Catholic moral theology today, namely, the existence of absolute material norms of behavior.

The catechism outlines a direct but inadequate sketch of its response to this controversy. It states that "human acts are never morally neutral. Conformity with the 'objective norms of morality' places them in the category of good; non-conformity in the category of evil." It immediately adds that "circumstances" can increase or diminish the goodness of evil of human acts, but "cannot make an act that is bad into one that is good." Similarly, the intention that orders an action is "essential to its morality." But "a bad action done with a good intention cannot be justified . . . [though] a bad intention removes the moral worth of an action in itself good" (3050–52).

These categories echo the classic treatment of the considerations that determine the "species" of a human act as moral or immoral. These were: the *object* (the physical or material behavior in question—e.g., killing a human being, uttering a statement that is contrary to fact); the *circumstances* (e.g., killing a human being when he or she is attacking one's children versus killing a human being because the population is growing too rapidly); and *intention* (e.g., killing combatants in war to secure justice for oppressed people versus killing noncombatants to terrorize one's military adversary).

For Thomas Aquinas all three of these had to be considered before one could declare that a material act of killing should be specified as a moral act of murder. Some very careful reasoning is needed to reach such a conclusion in the complex questions of life taking we face today. A catechism is not the place for this sort of casuistry. But the provisional text begs the question by claiming that circumstances and intentions can mitigate but not change the essential morality or immorality of an action.

Following Thomas Aquinas, one should rather conclude that the morality of a human action cannot be determined at all apart from a consideration of circumstances and intentions. Physical or material behavior is not yet human action at all (i.e., behavior guided by freedom and reason) unless the circumstances and intention are included in its definition. That my behavior leads to the death of another person does not in itself say that my behavior is moral or immoral. This follows even from pacifist presuppositions, for clear-headed pacifists acknowledge that their refusal to use lethal violence against unjust aggressors can sometimes result in the death of innocent people.

This all-too-brief sketch of a very technical debate in moral theology is not introduced here for its own sake but to raise a very basic question about the catechism's approach to the fifth commandment and to the whole domain of moral norms. Total war, the use of nuclear or conventional weapons to destroy cities, terrorism, hostage taking, torture, and the manufacture and use of chemical weapons are all condemned, with no exceptions allowed. For example, the provisional text says that hostage taking is "absolutely proscribed," that torture is "utterly immoral," that total war "is utterly proscribed," and that "defense strategies that rely on weapons of indiscriminate destruction ('anti-city') are morally wrong" (3542, 3543, 3559, 3564).

These are crucial conclusions reached by the official teaching office of the church in its reflection on modern social and military realities ("circumstances") and the inadequacy of any alleged purposes that might justify these forms of social behavior ("intentions"). I fully agree with them. That these conclusions have appeared in the draft catechism is a sign of the great seriousness of the church's attention to some of the major social moral problems of contemporary society.

But the catechism risks undermining its own conclusions on these practical matters by its almost studied effort to blur the distinction between absolute proscriptions of total war or torture and the statement that the proscription of every attack on life is absolute. The former are crucial and defensible, the latter contradicts the provisional text's own conclusions. This confusion will not help the effort to present a clear picture of the essentials of Catholic doctrine in the domain of morality. It also risks bringing the very important contributions of the magisterium on questions about the morality of warfare into disrepute among those educated Catholics and other Christians who can recognize an inconsistency when they see one.

Sixth and Ninth Commandments

Before moving on, one social-ethical remark on the treatment of sexuality under the sixth and ninth commandments is called for. The provisional text lays down an absolute proscription regarding the role of government in population limitation: "The Church opposes *every intervention* of the State in this matter, whether for eugenic reasons or to limit the number of births; such action is an intolerable interference in the rights and responsibilities of married people" (3611, emphasis added).

This is very different, both in spirit and in letter, from what Pope Paul VI said in *Populorum Progressio*. Paul VI noted that demographic increase can lead to the temptation to limit population growth by "radical measures." He rejected all state actions that threaten the "freedom of married couples" or deny "the inalienable right to marriage and procreation." But in words that contrast strikingly with the catechism, Paul VI stated: "It is certain that public authorities *can intervene*, within the limits of their competence, by favouring the availability of appropriate information and by adopting suitable measures, provided these be in conformity with the moral law and that they respect the rightful freedom of married couples" (*Populorum Progressio*, no. 37, emphasis added).

Thus the catechism says that "every" state intervention for population reduction is "intolerable," while Paul VI says that such intervention is "certainly" legitimate within specified limits. It is not moral theologians who are "confusing the faithful" here. Nor is it surprising that such a dramatic divergence in magisterial teachings has emerged in the area where sexual morality and social morality intersect. For it is at this point of intersection that two fundamentally incompatible ways of thinking about the moral life become evident in the official teachings of the church. The catechism has not solved this problem; nor should it have been expected to do so. But it has certainly made matters worse by its attempt to gloss over the conflict by quick declarations of absolute conclusions.

Seventh and Tenth Commandments

One last word needs to be said on specific questions of social morality treated under the seventh and tenth commandments ("You shall not steal. You shall not covet your neighbor's house . . . or anything that is his"). This section is a clear example of how the Decalogue serves as a convenient hook on which to hang some of the more creative developments of recent church reflection. The provisional text explicitly states that it is going beyond "the literal meaning of the Decalogue" by applying what it says about justice and solidarity among individuals to the relationships that ought to exist among nations (3664).

However, the text is doing considerably more than this. The commandment "You shall not steal" is taken as emblematic of a much more encompassing obligation to avoid "all violence against another" and every "attack on the freedom and integrity of the person" (3665). Thus the prohibition of stealing is viewed as but one aspect of an entire ethic of human rights and social solidarity based on personalist foundations. The most basic obligation contained in these commandments is the duty to avoid "any kind of subjugation, whether by violence or domination" (3668).

Within this framework the catechism denounces several abuses that are frequently mentioned in recent church social teaching. These range from using the need for state security as a pretext for the denial of human rights, to the scandal of the disproportionate development of rich and poor nations, to the immorality of all forms of racial discrimination and apartheid. From a more positive point of view, the text emphasizes that economic activity is concerned with the creation of wealth and that all people have a duty to work responsibly as well as rights to economic initiative, access to employment, and a just wage. These duties and rights of individuals can be exercised only within the framework of larger social systems.

The catechism recalls the repeated insistence of church teaching that the goods of the earth are meant for all and that this sets limits to the rights of private property. The growing reality of global interdependence, however, often creates "perverse mechanisms" and "structures of sin" that operate as obstacles to the development of poor countries (3714, 3739). For these reasons, structural change in the global economy is necessary and the de facto interdependence of nations must become that form of moral interdependence that John Paul II calls "solidarity" (3727). This solidarity is the basis of a "preferential love for the poor" that must be translated into action both by individuals and through political decisions (3740–41).

Clearly, from this brief sketch, the provisional text of the catechism contains a rich and complex vision of the societal dimensions of the Christian moral life. Almost all of the magisterium's recent teaching about these questions is at least touched upon in the exposition of the Decalogue. There are questions that are inadequately handled, such as the prohibition of all killing as a moral absolute. But in general the text does a competent job of briefly discussing the social moral issues it addresses. Nevertheless, there remains a nagging sense that there is something fundamentally amiss. In part this is due to the way that the Decalogue serves as a procrustean bed for the discussion of social morality. Questions that should be treated together are treated separately and vice versa.

The Relation of Faith to Morals

More fundamentally, the structure of the catechism has the unfortunate effect of disconnecting the discussion of social morality from the central doctrinal questions treated under the creed and the sacraments. This leads to a lack of integration between spirituality and social responsibility, as Lawrence Cunningham's contribution to this volume points out. But the problem is more than one of editorial structure. I think it is rooted in the catechism's guiding theology.

Throughout parts 1 and 2 (on the creed and on liturgy and the sacraments) there are recurrent statements that distinguish the Christian life of faith from any sort of human achievement in society. The new trinitarian life made possible by the coming of Christ and the outpouring of the Holy Spirit is described in a way that stresses its discontinuity from social life in the public world. The discontinuity of the "religious" and the "social" is emphasized much more than their integral connection, both by what the catechism says and by what it does not say. This can be illustrated briefly.

First, in the catechism's ecclesiology. Vatican II described the church as "a sacrament or sign of intimate union with God, and of the unity of all humankind. It is also an instrument for the achievement of such union and unity" ("Dogmatic Constitution on the Church," *Lumen Gentium*, no. 1). This sacramental model of the church is given primacy of place in the ecclesiology of the catechism. The catechism rightly interprets this model in a way that emphasizes the communion of believers with God and with each other within the church. But it questionably downplays the societal implications of the church's vocation to be sign and instrument of the "unity of all humankind."

The council taught that the sacramentality of the church is directly linked with social mission. According to *Lumen Gentium*, communion with God and other Christians in the church helps us "learn through faith the meaning, too, of our temporal life as we perform, with hope of good things to come, the task committed to us in this world by the Father" (no. 48). There is, in other words, a much stronger and more intrinsic connection in Vatican II than in the catechism between communion achieved sacramentally within the worshiping community and the solidarity and interdependence of persons to be sought in social life.

For example, the council states that the church's mission of bringing all people to union with Christ has special urgency today because of growing "social, technical, and cultural bonds" of global society (*Lumen Gentium*, no. 1). The church's mission is religious to be sure; but from this religious mission come a "function, a light, and an energy that can serve to structure and consolidate the human community" ("Pastoral Constitution on the Church in the Modern World," *Gaudium et Spes*, no. 42). This intrinsic linkage between communion within the church and the church's social mission is almost entirely lacking in the ecclesiology of the catechism.

Those instructed by the catechism will have difficulty seeing why all the questions of social morality it discusses are integral to the Christian faith itself. The catechism in its present form will reinforce long-standing tendencies toward a dualism of the sacred and secular, the spiritual and the social. This dualism has been a major obstacle to sustained social engagement by Christians throughout the modern era. Religious education guided by the underlying theology of the draft text would undo much of the council's contribution to a spirituality in which faith and social mission are intrinsically linked.

A second illustration of the problem is the catechism's eschatology. Here the text emphasizes the discontinuity of the religious and the social even more than in its ecclesiological sections. Its comments on the article of the Apostles' Creed that proclaims that Jesus Christ "will come again in glory to judge the living and the dead" have a strongly apocalyptic ring. Before the return of Christ, the church will pass through a period of tribulation and temptation. Pseudo-messiahs will appear, offering the human race apparent but false solutions to its problems. This pseudo-salvation is a religious imposture, the work of the Anti-Christ. It appears in the world "every time the claim is made that the messianic hope is being established in history, a hope that cannot be fulfilled except by passing through the eschatological judgement" (1524–25). At the time of this judgment, the church and all things human will follow Christ through death to new life. Thus the fulfillment of eschatological hope is sharply distinguished from the triumph of the church in history and from rising historical progress. It will come only on the other side of "the eventual cosmic dissolution of this passing world" (1526).

No doubt there are strong biblical warrants for this apocalyptic vision. Nor should that hope for the promised kingdom of God be identified with hope in human progress. Also, despite this stress on the discontinuity between the kingdom and history, the catechism does at one point affirm that belief in eternal life includes a hope that the "entire universe," including matter, animals, and humanity, will be transformed and glorified in a state of happiness, peace, and communion at the end of time (1861–69).

Nevertheless, the catechism's exposition of these eschatological themes is notably different in emphasis from that of *Gaudium et Spes*. The target of this emphasis is clearly liberation theology and all those influenced by liberation theology. The claim that "messianic hope is being established in history" is clearly wrong if it implies that movement toward greater justice is the same thing as the reign of God in its fullness. But to suggest that messianic hope has nothing to do with hope for justice in history is contrary to a central emphasis of the Second Vatican Council.

Like the catechism, the council clearly distinguished the coming of the kingdom of God from historical progress. But the council saw a more intrinsic link between the enhancement of justice and peace among nations on the one hand and ultimate eschatological hope on the other. *Gaudium et Spes*, in a passage cited but not quoted by the catechism, stated that

> while we are warned that it profits a man nothing if he gain the whole world and lose himself, the expectation of a new earth must not weaken but rather stimulate our concern for cultivating this one. For here grows the body of a new family, a body that even now is able to give some kind of foreshadowing of the new age.
> Earthly progress must be carefully distinguished from the growth of Christ's kingdom. Nevertheless, to the extent that the former can contribute to the better ordering of human society, it is of *vital concern to the kingdom of God*. (*Gaudium et Spes*, no. 39, emphasis added)

There are few hints in the provisional text of the catechism of why efforts to cultivate justice and peace in the world are of vital religious concern to those whose final hope is in the eschatological kingdom of Christ.

The theological questions of how to interpret the apocalyptic aspects of the Bible and how to understand the relation of the eschatological end-time to historical existence are complex ones. A catechism is not the appropriate place to develop a systematic response to these questions. But neither is it the place to lay down a single theology as a "point of reference" in light of which bishops "in different regions" should judge the adequacy or inadequacy of "national and/or diocesan catechisms" (0016–19).

Here, as elsewhere, the catechism fails to distinguish theology from doctrine. The adoption of a particular theological exposition of doctrines concerning the nature of the church and the relation between eschatology and history should be regarded with particular suspicion when it departs from important emphases of the Second Vatican Council.

The catechism's theology of the relation between the life of faith and social existence is not universal but particular. Not surprisingly, it contains echoes of the recent writings of Cardinal Joseph Ratzinger on church involvement in the social sphere. Ratzinger has been very critical of what he calls the "messianism," "enthusiasm," and "fanaticism" that result whenever Christians attempt to "elevate the kingdom of God into a political program."[3] Ratzinger's targets here are clearly Latin American liberation theologies, German political theologies, and perhaps some aspects of what the U.S. bishops have tried to do in their recent pastoral letters. He writes that "the New Testament is aware of political ethics but not of political theology." By this he means that "politics is not the sphere of theology but of ethics." And ethics is a domain governed by reason, not an effort to translate eschatological hope in the kingdom of God into a social or political program.[4]

I have no desire to reject the importance of reason and natural law in Christian ethics, especially Christian social ethics. Both are indispensable. However, recent epistemological and hermeneutical discussions of the nature of morality have increasingly shown that it is impossible to separate a working understanding of reason from the traditions in which reason is embedded. Put another way, this means not only a Christian social ethic *ought not* to choose between reason and the tradition that puts us in touch with God's revelation. It means that we *cannot choose* between these two sources for the interpretation of our responsibility in society, at least if we wish to remain both Christian and reasonable.[5]

We need both the explicitly theological sources of Scripture and Christian tradition and the sources of human reason and experience to formulate an adequate Christian social ethic. A political ethic that is genuinely Christian also must be a political theology, just as a political theology that is genuinely reasonable must make full use of philosophical reflection on social experience. Ratzinger's portrayal of an either/or opposition between these alternatives is a false one. It is also based on a serious oversimplification of the theologies it criticizes.

This theoretical point has practical implications. It means, for example, that it is illegitimate to distinguish a natural morality based on reason from a perspective on morality based on revelation and faith. This dualistic approach is evident in the catechism's claim that the Decalogue "renews and confirms the precepts of the natural law" that are rooted in creation. This completely neglects the fact that the Decalogue was proclaimed to the people of Israel at the central moment in their exodus from slavery to a new life in the promised land.

The theme of liberation from bondage into community is integral to the meaning of the Decalogue itself. The Decalogue is at least as much a theological statement of what it means to live as persons who have been liberated from bondage and who have entered into covenant with God and each other as it is a restatement of the natural law. This theme of liberation and covenant is correlative with the philosophical argument that the dignity of the human person is essentially social and achieved only in solidarity with other persons.

An adequate Christian social ethic cannot separate key religious ideas such as liberation and covenant from ethical ideas such as human dignity and solidarity. The provisional text of the catechism betrays its desire to compartmentalize faith and social existence by avoiding all consideration of these connections between liberation, covenant, and law in the Bible. The same desire is evident when the catechism asserts that the New Law is interior and written on the heart while the Old Law is simply an external code (3122, 3135). In ancient Israel, as well as in Christianity, spiritual interiority and life in society are inseparable. Or so, I think, the Second Vatican Council said.

This dichotomy of the spiritual and the social is equally evident in the catechism's stereotypical characterization of Judaism as a religion of the external law and of justice, while Christianity is a religion of the inner heart and of love. In the history of Christian theology such stereotypes of Judaism have always been a prelude to a strongly dualist understanding of the relation between faith in the gospel and life in society. These stereotypes have also had truly vicious consequences in the way Christians have treated Jews throughout much of Western history.

Conclusion

In short, there is much to admire in the way the provisional text of the catechism seeks to incorporate many dimensions of social morality into its presentation of "the whole of Catholic doctrine, both of faith and of morals" (0016). But with a certain sadness, I am led to conclude that it does not succeed in accomplishing what it has tried to do in this area. Major revisions are called for, both in the structure of the text and even more in its governing theology. Such revisions will be much easier to achieve if the present text is treated much the way the initial draft documents prepared by the Roman curia were treated by the bishops at Vatican II. The bishops voted *non placet* (it does not please) – and the drafting was begun again from scratch. A similar new beginning is needed if a catechism suited to the real needs of the universal church is to be produced today.

The procedures established in Rome for consulting the bishops on the draft seem designed to prevent precisely this. But the bishops' collegial responsibility for the life of the universal church should lead them to insist on a change in these procedures. The religious education of hundreds of millions of believers – now and in generations to come – is at stake. The bishops carry no responsibility more weighty than that of deciding how they will deal with the provisional text of this catechism.

Sex, Gender,
and Bioethics
in the Catechism

Lisa Sowle Cahill
Boston College

Does this teaching really arise from experience, or is it merely superimposed on it?

The catechism's basic frame of reference for understanding sexuality's meaning is heterosexual, permanent, procreative marriage.

A catechism is scarcely the place to find new ventures in moral theology. Above all in the realm of sexual morality, the positions taken by the *Catechism for the Universal Church* come as no surprise. At the same time, such factors as context, phrasing, and choice of emphasis in presentation can be crucial in giving standard magisterial teaching a distinctive tone, or even a fresh spirit. For example, the U.S. bishops' draft pastoral on women's concerns, "Partners in the Mystery of Redemption," stayed within officially prescribed limits on sexual behavior, ordination, and women's roles, but it managed at least to raise the episcopacy's profile regarding receptivity to criticism, concern for the economic and social disadvantages faced by women, and consciousness of sexism as a serious sin.

The catechism's authors try to uphold high ideals of sex and marriage, as part of a total communion of persons. Unfortunately, from my perspective, Rome has again missed an opportunity to highlight the essential, the positive, and the hopeful elements in the Roman Catholic vision of sexuality and family and to manifest a real interest in dialogue about its value with the church as a whole. One suspects that the authors' sensitivity to and interpretation of Christian moral experience in those realms is still governed above all by a precommitment to shore up the familiar negative norms about contraception, divorce, homosexuality, and so on. Some of the positive dimensions of sexuality seem worked out primarily to serve as foundations for those norms, while the laity are warned that their sexual and marital experiences will conform to the magisterial framework.

Recent Catholic Thought

But the concerns and conclusions of the catechism cannot be understood out of context. It is important, first, to place its teachings on sex, marriage, family, and gender roles in the context of other recent Catholic thought, noting general lines of controversy and development that are particularly relevant to church teaching on sexuality. At least five such movements, gaining strength especially since Vatican II, are important to understanding the catechism's presentation of sex and gender. These concern natural law, Scripture, personalist philosophy, sex and personality, and women's roles.

One may surmise that the catechism's teachings are at least to some extent meant to acknowledge the basic legitimacy of such developments while foreclosing the possibility that they might result in any substantive change in these very sensitive and even politicized areas of morals. The five movements, with a few comments on the relation of each to the catechism, follow. After reviewing this background, I will look at the catechism's positions in five specific areas of sex and gender ethics. Finally, three bioethical topics will be noted briefly.

The Evolution of Natural Law Thinking

An essential characteristic of "Catholic" ethics is its commitment to an objective moral order, which reasonable, well-intentioned persons can generally discern even without religious guidance. This objective moral order provides a basis for ethical discussion and general agreement among persons from different cultures, religions, places, and times. This commitment to a reasonable and potentially universal ethics has in the past been captured by the term *natural law.*

In recent decades, however, there has been a renewed appreciation of the fact that human reason operates not abstractly and with absolute certainty but out of particular histories and experiences, through which the possibly universal is glimpsed. Consequently—and as Aquinas himself noted[1]—it is in questions of applied ethics, that the most diversity, uncertainty, and need for revision of formulations will arise.

Although the catechism tries to set aside the issue of inculturation, human institutions like marriage and family are always culturally shaped, and any formulation of what is normative in such areas is always induced from particular cultural experiences. The catechism would benefit by a clearer statement of the importance of natural law to the Roman Catholic tradition of ethics and of the relevance of culture and history to the formulation and reformulation of specific moral norms.

The catechism does provide a discussion of natural law in an overview of types of law that introduces the Ten Commandments. It states that the moral law belongs to "man's" divinely created nature, is internal rather than imposed, fulfills the person and brings happiness, and is "accessible to all" but needs clarification by the magisterium, which has a mission to interpret it (3098). But the origin of natural law ethics in Aquinas, its overriding importance in giving shape to Catholic moral theology, the historical evolution of the Christian concept of natural law, and the relatively recent biblical renewal of it are not explained adequately.

Thus, the reader of the catechism may lack a sense of just what it is that makes Roman Catholic ethics or sexual teaching distinctively different from that of other Christian denominations, and of how the notion of natural law itself has been reinterpreted in the last few decades so that it can respond more effectively to the historical consciousness of the modern world. What has taken place in these decades is the evolution of the traditional Thomistic natural law approach from an intellectualist and deductive method to a more experiential and inductive method.

Joining Scripture to Natural Law

Another trend has been to reappropriate Scripture in Catholic theology and gradually to modify natural law thinking by joining it to biblical perspectives. Catholic theology and ethics since the council, and in ecumenical dialogue with Protestant communities, have tried to recover Christianity's biblical base. This renewal is in principle embraced by the catechism. It holds the potential to revitalize Catholic ethics by imbuing the moral life with the inspiration of discipleship, thereby destroying the grip of the obsessive legalism so long a treacherous tendency, particularly in sexual morality.

Yet in the catechism and in Roman Catholic moral theology generally, Scripture is not always fully and successfully integrated with other, more traditional sources, such as natural law and church teaching. Do Scripture and reason always arrive at the same conclusions or enjoin the same behavior? And in the realm of sexual ethics, long dominated by the notion that reproductive function provides certain "natural" behavioral norms, can the conclusions already authoritatively taught find a ready and congenial grounding in the Bible?

When they reach the sections on sex-related ethics (fourth, sixth, and ninth commandments), the catechism's authors seem more concerned with trying to pull together scriptural supports for conclusions traditionally derived within a natural law framework than in addressing the significant historical and theological differences in the two approaches and in clarifying on what basis they might be thought to be complementary. But this will leave many readers confused about exactly where these proposals come from and about what kinds of evidence actually can and do back current teachings about marriage's purposes, contraception, abortion, homosexuality, and so on. Granting that a catechism is not a systematic theology, some of these basic connections need to be tightened and strengthened in service of a more persuasive pedagogy.

Personalist Philosophy

A third trend in moral theology has been the introduction of "personalist" philosophy into sexual and marital morality. With it has come an emphasis on the lived experience of persons as providing the genuine foundations and substance of their moral obligations. The "personalist" transformation of Catholic ethics is part of the general movement to take an inductive rather than an abstract approach to human nature.

Personalism became an important influence in Roman Catholic sexual ethics in the 1930s, through the work of Herbert Doms and Dietrich von Hildebrand, theologians influenced by phenomenological philosophy.[2] Their efforts to accord love the primacy traditionally assigned to procreation in defining the meaning of marriage were rejected by the Vatican. But their basic insistence on grounding normative morality in the experience of couples eventually became incorporated by thinkers as influential as John Paul II.

The pope's thought, influenced more directly by the German phenomenologist and social philosopher Max Scheler, does not draw explicitly on Doms and von Hildebrand. Nonetheless, it reflects the sort of approach to sex and marriage that they represented to the theological world. In his Wednesday audience talks on the "Theology of the Body" (1979-81),[3] the pope uses the metaphor "language of the body" to interpret sexual experience as an "intersubjective" union of persons.

And since *Gaudium et Spes* (1965) and *Humanae Vitae* (1968), the ranking of ends of marriage has been abandoned in favor of an equality and harmony of conjugal love and the transmission of life. Incorporating this shift in the official understanding of the purposes of marriage, the catechism calls spouses to realize the "double end" of marriage (love and life) and speaks of the marriage relation itself as a communion of persons in mutual self-giving. The attempt by the magisterium to confirm its sexual teaching by saying it reflects actual experience is a significant development and furthers the evolution of the Catholic understanding of natural law.

Yet questions about the rationale behind church teaching remain, since this new approach is again joined to standard conclusions. Does this teaching really arise from experience, or is it merely superimposed on it? In what way does the church hear and appropriate the testimony of sexually and maritally experienced persons? For instance, does the experience of spouses support the demand that there be a procreative meaning in each and every act of intercourse, or that artificial means of exercising "responsible parenthood" are decisively worse than natural ones? If so, on what ground does the magisterium know this, if its claim is not simply a priori—not accountable to experience in any but the most superficial way? The church's newly discovered personalist and experiential approach will not come across as genuine, sincere, or helpful until some of these questions receive more satisfactory answers.

Sexuality as an Aspect of Personality

Recent Catholic thought has also had a greater tendency to see sexuality as an aspect of the personality rather than just in terms of sexual acts. There is also a greater tendency to see sexuality as a positive reality and force shaping the lives of the vowed celibate, the single heterosexual, and the homosexual person, as well as married couples.

For instance, recent statements on homosexuality, such as the Congregation for the Doctrine of the Faith letter "On the Pastoral Care of Homosexual Persons" (1986), recognize that homosexuality is a fundamental sexual orientation and that evaluation of it should be distinguished from that of homosexual acts. The catechism tells us that "sexuality colors everyone's affective life. It contributes to the formation of the human personality" (3596). But the church has still to get much mileage out of this insight. The clear agenda to back magisterial conclusions about genital and procreative acts usually informs the preliminaries about the nature of sexuality. Sexuality itself is still understood almost exclusively at the practical level in terms of the spousal relationship. The catechism is no exception.

Women's Roles

A fifth trend in moral theology has been attention in a much more explicit and self-conscious manner to women's roles in family, church, and society, and to the consequences of women's roles for sexual ethics generally. This is part of a tendency to recognize the "social" implications of traditionally "personal" ethical matters.

Ambivalently, the present magisterium seems to affirm men's and women's equal dignity and access to both public and domestic roles, while simultaneously insisting that woman's maternal role is her most important one. It affirms that she has innate characteristics—both physical and psychological—that equip her for this maternal role and set her off from man (*Familiaris Consortio* and *Mulieris Dignitatem*).

The catechism follows in this path. Again, one detects a larger agenda not far below the surface: arguments for reliable family planning for all women and for women's ordination will become stronger if the church concedes that women have no innate traits that reduce their capacity to participate in those nondomestic roles traditionally reserved only for males. On the one hand, the teaching church wants to give some attention to injustice and oppression toward women. On the other, its investments in social and ecclesial institutions that tend to assign women second-class citizenship, as well as in certain specific propositions about sexual behavior, predictably preclude any radical challenge to the patriarchal institutionalization of women's roles.

Specific Teachings

The catechism's positions on the moral aspects of sexuality and of gender can be sorted into five categories: gender relationships, family, the basic meanings of sexuality and of sexual status, sexual sins, and abortion.

Gender Relationships

A paradigm mentioned several times in the catechism is the creation of Adam and Eve, both made in the image of God, and "equal as persons" (1197; 3594: "equal personal dignity"). The authors are to be commended for their appropriation of recent biblical scholarship that challenges traditional subordinationist interpretations of the creation stories, that is, that the woman is secondary because she was taken from the man's rib, or that as "helpmate" she is his subordinate.

Instead, notes the catechism, the rib signifies that the two share the same humanity (1196). Also, the two are to be helpers to one another, with the word "helper" creating not a hierarchy but a parallel with the Hebrew understanding of the divinity as the "God who helps" (1197, 2804). The two are also to share in common rather than gender-separated tasks: to transmit life and to be together the stewards of creation (1199–1201).

Yet despite this encouraging beginning, the catechism reflects the ambivalence about women's full entry into social and political life that has characterized writings of John Paul II (*Familiaris Consortio, Mulieris Dignitatem*). Perhaps the possibility that basic male and female reproductive differences have some psychological and affective ramifications should not be absolutely dismissed. However, no scientific evidence to date indicates that such differences are significant enough to destine men and women for different social roles rather than simply influencing at some level the ways in which the sexes carry out common roles.

The catechism insists on a vocabulary of "complementarity." This term is a red flag to many feminists because of its typical function in stressing gender differences that are in large part culturally created and in assigning women to less socially influential and prestigious domestic roles. According to the text, Adam and Eve are "complementary as masculine and feminine" (1197; 2853: marriage is based on "natural complementarity"). Feminist qualms about social consequences will not be allayed by the assertion that "the harmony of a group or of a society depends greatly on the manner in which it demonstrates the complementarity of the sexes" (3598). Certainly a more helpful word, such as *mutuality,* could be found to avoid the danger of sexism in speaking of the relationship between the sexes.

The catechism does approve the "movement" aiming "to free women from a state of subjugation." But citing *Familiaris Consortio,* it still protects maternity as a female role with an importance to women's identity in no way paralleled by the significance of paternity for men. The "distinctiveness of women" must not be denied, nor should "'the value of their maternal and family role, by comparison with all other public roles and all other professions'" be "eclipsed" (3600).

The authors also seem to see the relationship between man and woman as "especially" poisoned by sin in a "universal" way: "by disorder, the spirit of domination, of infidelity, of jealousy and every kind of conflict which can go as far as hatred and separation" (2806). The intention behind and consequences of such a statement are ambiguous. On the one hand, theologians from the early church on have laid the blame for much of human suffering on the pride, sensuality, or insubordination of women. On the other, modern feminists often claim that male domination is the most pervasive form of human evil. Perhaps it finally remains a question whether it is wise or true to take the line that male-female relationships are more radically sinful than other human relationships.

Family

The normative definition of the family is "a communion of persons showing mutual love, respect and care for each other" (3452). The family is a natural institution, but the Christian family is analogous to the communion of the Godhead (3458). Within the family, parents should provide for the growth, self-knowledge, and self-confidence of their children (3484); adult children should care for their elderly parents out of love and gratitude for past care (3472). The family is also the basis of society, contributing to the common good (3487). Civil authority should protect and support the family (3489), especially since the extended family is in many cases being superseded by the nuclear family.

Unfortunately, something of a "raise the barricades" mentality emerges when the idea of the family as a "domestic church" (*Lumen Gentium*, no. 11) is taken to mean that families are "little islands of christian life in an unbelieving world" (2868). The home should radiate faith "in a world which is often alien to the faith" (2869). Missing is a sense of a positive, integral mission of the Christian family to and fully in the world, in the spirit of Vatican II.

Although the catechism is on the right track in providing a basically appreciative rather than a critical model of family life, it might have given more recognition to the potential for domination and violence within the family, to the economic and social pressures faced by the family, and to nontraditional family groups, especially those that are responses to various forms of social duress.

Further, the catechism calls the family to live by the love characteristic of the kingdom of God, "a sacrificial love, a love to the end, a fruitful love. It is the characteristic of the Kingdom" (3507). The phrases "to the end" and "fruitful"—not terms the New Testament commonly employs to characterize love of neighbor—lend the impression primarily of preemptive strikes against divorce and contraception. Moreover, this call deserves a practical feminist critique. While love should characterize family life and sacrifice is a part of Christian love, the call for "self-sacrifice" has rarely been applied equally to men and to women, especially in the family. This has been most true when the marriage relationship is in trouble, or when the family is burdened by unanticipated or excessive births.

One also notes that the catechism's ideal of (nuclear) family life is both modern and Western, stressing free interpersonal communion to the almost total neglect of the kinship bonds so important to family both in the Hebrew Scriptures and in non-Western cultures today. Although it is right to highlight personalist values in morality, and to avoid "physicalist" interpretations of sex and gender, Christian ethics also should avoid voluntarist and contractualist understandings of the family. The interpersonal commitment that ideally forms a marriage and sustains family relationships needs to be integrated explicitly at some level with the kinship networks of blood, genes, and lineage in which the notion of "family" is cross-culturally grounded.

The practical import of maintaining the integration of these two dimensions of family can be seen in controversies over nontraditional forms of procreation, in which a third party donates sperm, ovum, embryo, or child (as in surrogacy) to a married couple. Such arrangements are problematic in that they treat genetic relationships as dispensable or important only to the extent that they are voluntarily recognized to be so. While it is sometimes right to forgo the interpersonal family relation implied by the blood kin relation (as in adoption), it is still necessary to retain kinship as in general (not absolutely) a normative meaning of family, a meaning that connects the married couple and the nuclear family with a broader social, economic, and political network.

The Catholic tradition of ethics, with its strong roots in history and nature, should seek an effective contemporary rearticulation of the insight that sexuality and the relationships it creates are both embodied and intersubjective realities. What is the most true and effective mediation of the physical/procreational and personal/committed aspects of human sexuality? How do these aspects contribute to the formation of families? The recognition that the physical yields moral meanings should go beyond merely reiterating that physical acts of sexual intercourse should not be artificially foreclosed from their physical reproductive outcome. But neither current magisterial teaching nor this catechism move in any fresh, creative, or convincing way toward the fulfillment of this task.

The Meanings of Sexuality and Sexual Relationship

As in the overall Christian tradition, the catechism's basic frame of reference for understanding sexuality's meaning is heterosexual, permanent, procreative marriage. Along with the sacrament of order, marriage serves "communion," and is "directed toward the salvation of others" (2702). This positive description helps to remove the older, limited, and derogatory view that marriage is directed outward primarily through its function in perpetuating the species, and that it is really a moral compromise allowed for those who would otherwise yield to concupiscence.

States the catechism, the "covenant of man and woman" reflects the covenant of God with the Chosen People and the union of the incarnate Son of God with "all humanity" (2812). What is necessary to constitute a marriage is consent, and that consent is given to unity or conjugal love, fruitfulness or openness to procreation, and fidelity or indissolubility (2852). The personal communion of spouses "encompasses their whole life" (2853). They have a duty to nurture and educate children, although the marriage of a couple without children "can radiate with a fruitfulness of charity, welcome and sacrifice" (2858). Regarding the responsibility to regulate their number of children, couples are referred to *Humanae Vitae* and the magisterium, to which they are told conscience "submits" (2859). (It is this sort of resolution of genuine moral dilemmas and conflicts that lends the magisterium's personalist rhetoric a disingenuous tone.)

Even in cases where there has been a "breakdown" of marriage, and cohabitation is "impossible," the marriage is said to continue to exist and to forbid remarriage (2864). The assertion that the church cannot "compromise with the divine law of indissolubility" and should take "in a literal sense the words of the Lord: 'What God has joined together, let no man put asunder' (Mt 19.6)" could stand critical scrutiny. In the first place, as noted earlier in the document (0273–76), Roman Catholicism does not follow a literalist or fundamentalist biblical hermeneutics on other issues. In the second, Matthew and Paul both seem to allow for an exception of some sort to Jesus' original prohibition (Mt 5:32, 19:9; 1 Cor 7:10). It also strains credulity and places an inappropriate burden of guilt on the shoulders of the divorced to claim that, compared to adultery, divorce "is an even greater offence against the law of the sixth commandment" (3620).

Some wrestling with the human realities of divorce have influenced the catechism's demand that the whole community should continue to show divorced and even remarried persons "attentive care" (2866). Indeed, the catechism calls for a "just balance" to "appreciate the situation of . . . civilly remarried, divorced people." It recognizes that there is "a difference" between persons who have by "grave fault" destroyed a marriage and those who have been "unjustly abandoned by their partner." It even acknowledges that when new unions are created, children and families result that also "need protection" (2865). Even in situations in which it is "not easy" to maintain the equilibrium between truth and charity, such persons deserve the "particular attention" of pastors and of the community in endeavoring to raise their children in the Christian faith.

Although this treatment holds on to the purely juridical stipulation of canon law that even a marriage with no experiential characteristics of a marriage is still a marriage, and even though it under no circumstances admits the divorced and remarried to the Eucharist, it is still fair to say that it emphasizes equally with these prohibitions the duty of the Christian community to "show an attitude of compassion and welcome" to divorced Catholics and their new families (3625).

Besides the married state, sexuality also may be channeled into a life of consecrated virginity or celibacy, "for the Kingdom" (2820, 3504–5). This vocation is "a special gift from God" (3504) and "a powerful sign of the preeminence of the bond with Christ," but "implies no depreciation of marriage" (2824; 3505: "To lead a life of celibacy for the sake of the Kingdom is in no way to deny the importance or value of the vocation of marriage"). The virtue of chastity is commended both to the married and to the consecrated celibate (3649–50).

Unfortunately, a large gap in the treatment of sexuality is the calling of the single, nonconsecrated person. The programmatic statement that sexuality deeply colors personality needs to be elaborated with ministry to the single adult Catholic in mind. But the catechism only adds, as a lame afterthought to vocational celibacy, that those who are unmarried "because of particular circumstances" should also be continent (3651).

Sexual Sins

Both "trial marriages" and "premarital relations" are rejected as "grave" error and sin because they "offend God and . . . are contrary to Christian morality" (2840). The only specific reason developed is that the former "often indicates a lack of confidence in self and in the other" (3630). Polygamy is rejected as contrary to the "unity" of marriage and as relegating women to "the state of dependence and inferiority" (3628, 2855).

In the background here are the ongoing "inculturation" battles, especially in Africa, where the argument has sometimes been made that the sacramental system should be more adaptive to indigenous marriage customs, and that it is equally unjust to women to force a converting polygamist to renounce all but one of his wives. Left unaddressed here is the problem of how to make a just, practical transition to the Christian ideal of monogamy in cultures in which kinship, women's status, and even economics are organized around the practice of multiple marriage.

As has been noted, contraception is condemned as a violation of the procreative meaning of the marital union (3573, 3610), and sterilization receives the same judgment (3544). Rape is rather vaguely and inadequately attributed to "a lack of mastery over self" (3634), and pederasty and incest are briefly but vehemently condemned as degrading to human dignity (3636). Masturbation is still classified as in itself "a grave moral disorder," but it alone is described explicitly as a sexual offense for which guilt should be measured against the age and emotional stability of the sinner. One wonders why compassion has (as in the past) flowered at this particular spot. We may be reminded that experience is key to moral sensitivity when we consider that this may be the one sin to which the traditional clerical moralist, once himself an adolescent, may have suffered any serious or prolonged temptation.

It also should be noted that, while the catechism distinguishes between "grave" and "venial" sins and singles out some sexual sins as "grave," it refrains from repeating the familiar formula that in the area of sexuality all sins are by definition mortal.

In the discussion of homosexuality we see a distinct advance over the much-criticized 1986 offering of the Congregation for the Doctrine of the Faith, "On the Pastoral Care of Homosexual Persons." Homosexuality is handled in a separate category, apart from "deviations, abnormalities, and perversions." And while homosexual acts are condemned, the brief section concludes, "Those who have a homosexual tendency should be welcomed with delicacy and understanding, and should not be subjected to discrimination" (3633). The earlier document had not only implied that homosexuals were to blame for violence against them but had also seemed to some to shift the moral condemnation of genital acts onto the orientation itself by calling it "a more or less strong tendency ordered toward an intrinsic moral evil" and an "objective disorder" (no. 3).

In the background of the catechism's rejection of all sexual expression outside marriage, and of nonprocreative sexuality and nonsexual procreation within marriage, are some statements issued in an earlier section on human responsibility ("Man Responsible for His Actions," 3049–56). The authors want to counteract the recent probing by some moral theologians of the meaning of the term *intrinsically evil act* as applied, for example to contraception, in vitro fertilization, and all sexual acts outside marriage.

The revisionist position is essentially that the morally good or sinful quality of such acts cannot be determined in the abstract (in traditional terms, from the "object" alone), apart from any consideration of circumstances. This is not to say that such acts are "neutral," but that their negative dimensions might be outweighed in situations in which they become the greater good or lesser evil. The catechism's authors, seeming not fully to grasp this point, counter, "Human acts are never morally neutral." They either do or do not conform to "'objective norms of morality.'" Circumstances and intention "cannot make an act which is bad into one which is good" (3051). But the issue here, which almost always seems to arise in relation to sexuality, is whether a "bad act" can be meaningfully defined and absolutely prohibited with no reference at all to the situation (and other options) of which it is a part.

Abortion

Falling under "personal sins" against the fifth commandment, abortion, handled in four sentences, receives a properly limited share of attention. Even so, the treatment might benefit from greater nuance and especially from more sensitivity to the social dimensions of unwanted pregnancy. The catechism speaks against "pressures" to legalize abortion and asserts that "the Church has always maintained the inalienable right to life of the child in the mother's womb" (3547). Similarly, the embryo must be "recognised" as "a personal being whose first right is that of physical life" (3548).

These formulations are misleading, since the church has not in fact always taught that there is a "child" or "person" from the moment of conception,[4] and since "rights" language is a modern phenomenon. It would be more accurate to say that the church has always taught that abortion is wrong, though sometimes for reasons less than homicide, for instance, because abortion short-circuits the natural outcome of sexual intercourse. Donum Vitae stated more circumspectly, "The Magisterium has not expressly committed itself to an affirmation of a philosophical nature [about the "personhood" of the embryo], but it constantly reaffirms the moral condemnation of any kind of procured abortion" (I.1).

The catechism also repeats the oft-recited judgment of Gaudium et Spes, "'Abortion and infanticide are abominable crimes'" (3547). However irresistible its rhetorical impact, this is one quotable quote that, especially when taken alone or as a sort of irrefutable conversation-stopper, does little more than impugn the motives of those with whom one disagrees and hardly furthers our understanding of the complexity of abortion.

Would that the drafters had instead taken their lead here from Mulieris Dignitatem. There the pope introduces his rejection of abortion by using the New Testament example of the woman caught in adultery to illustrate men's complicity in women's sins, via what he calls "habitual discrimination against women in favor of men" (no. 14). He sees the "unwed mother" as a modern example of such complicity. She is often abandoned, with the father unwilling to take responsibility. Hence she acts "as a result of various pressures" to "'get rid of' the child before it is born" (no. 14). (It also should be noted that the pope at the same time reinforces gender stereotypes by mentioning that a woman has an "innate readiness to accept life" that will cause her to feel a special guilt should she seek an abortion [no. 14].)

The church's witness against abortion will not gain credibility until it develops some effective practical response to the argument of the pro-choice movement that abortion is the only available means to provide some women relief from destitution or domination. This means putting financial support not only behind women during pregnancy but also behind the creation of more educational and economic opportunities for teenagers and women with children. The catechism should start the process by sensitizing its readers to the plight of women who seek abortions in the first place. And particularly in addressing the young, it should foster a realistic and not overly idealized approach to sex education, to the woman's control of her own sexuality, and to reliable and consistent means of avoiding unwanted pregnancies.

Some Conclusions

On the positive side, one can appreciate the effort to integrate Roman Catholic moral teaching with biblical foundations, and particularly to search the creation stories for a paradigm of human male and female relationship. One also commends the centrality given to the interpersonal dimensions of committed sexual relationships. There is also the clear indication that since virginity "for the Lord" and marriage are both callings and graced opportunities for service to the community, they should not be hierarchically ranked. Here we see evidence of another clear change in magisterial presentations of sexuality, following on the shift in the 1960s to an equality of love and procreation as purposes of marriage. Finally, the catechism should help clarify the church's stand that a homosexual orientation is not in itself a moral evil, and that unfair and intolerant social practices toward persons with this orientation are unchristian.

There are negatives also. The natural law and biblical bases of Roman Catholic moral thought need better integration, particularly since traditional teachings on sex—substantively still in place—have been grounded almost exclusively in the natural law.

A major disappointment was the energetic resuscitation of the "complementarity" and "masculine-feminine difference" language, following upon consistently sexist language throughout the catechism. This flies in the face of other magisterial statements to the effect that women should enjoy access to all public roles and functions (*Familiaris Consortio*, no. 23). An existing ambiguity in church teaching has been deepened rather than resolved. Required here is a clear critique of sexism, a development, for instance, of the papal view that "machismo" is clearly wrong (*Familiaris Consortio*, no. 25). No current church document should be allowed to back away from this stand.

Another continuing deficiency in church teaching is a theology, spirituality, and ethics of "singlehood"—grounded in the experience of those in this state. We are slowly moving toward the incorporation of married persons' experience in Catholic sexual ethics, although we are still living with what seems to many a mismatch between references to that experience and traditional conclusions about such problems as contraception and divorce. Now we need to move beyond marriage to consider more profoundly the sexual identities and experiences of persons in other ways of life. In sexuality as in other areas, a convincing "catechesis to" will be informed by an authentic "learning from."

Some Bioethical Questions

Gathered under the heading "Personal sins" against the fifth commandment are some further matters pertaining to bioethics: termination of medical treatment, euthanasia, and human experimentation. (Abortion, sterilization, and infertility therapies, already discussed, are also mentioned here.) It is dismaying to encounter such a perpetuation of the division of social and personal morals, since all these matters arise in a social context, have immense social repercussions, and become questions for practical decision making by individuals only within social institutions of health care, funding, and research. The analysis offered on each is brief.

Euthanasia, the direct killing of "the incurably sick and dying," even with the aim of giving a "painless death," is, of course, condemned (3539). Those who are sick or handicapped deserve special protection (3549). The treatment of removal of life-prolonging measures is somewhat more extended and is in keeping with the Congregation for the Doctrine of the Faith's 1980 "Declaration on Euthanasia," which favored "a due proportion in the use of remedies." Thus, there is no obligation to use means that are risky, burdensome, disproportionate to the expected results, or that impose "excessive expense on the family or community." Refusal of such means "is not the equivalent of suicide" but rather "an acceptance of the human condition."[5]

The catechism affirms likewise that although physical life should be respected, it "is not an overriding [absolute] value." Not only is the "neo-pagan . . . cult of the body" to be opposed, but the "integrity of human life" does not reside in physical health alone. "It also demands prudence and discretion in the medical treatment of those whose incurable sickness has brought them to the threshold of death. The necessary and lawful care which such illness calls for does not require the use of extraordinary measures to ensure survival. It is necessary always to take into account both the costs involved and the needs of others" (3553).

The draft takes no explicit position on the question of artificial nutrition and hydration, now hotly debated in the United States, with some pro-life activists arguing that the removal of such artificial means is the equivalent of murder. But the draft does reaffirm the Catholic tradition that life need not be preserved at all costs and in every condition. Legitimate moral consideration should be given to the usefulness of such treatment beyond a mere prolongation of life, its expense, and the effects on others of providing it.

The commentary on "modern experiments" seems focused on "genetic manipulation" and is guided by a concern about overconfidence in the promise of human interventions that could have "disastrous" consequences for "the very future of humanity." Though expressed with the rather extravagant claim that through such research "man" seeks to be "master of life and death," the warning that "ethical criteria" should guide and that some limits ought to be contemplated should be well taken. Rather than prescribing the specific nature of such criteria and limits, the document calls for a "consensus" among politicians and those who work in the life sciences.

Conclusion

In summary, one would have to conclude that while the vast social dimensions of such questions continue to be forced into the old framework of the individual doctor-patient decision, the catechism manifests the greater flexibility the tradition has generally shown toward medical-moral problems in contrast to sexual ones. Of particular value is the insight that "extraordinary" or "disproportionate" treatments are not morally necessary, and that the specific meanings of those terms must be evaluated in each case with regard to the circumstances of the patient.

While the catechism displays concern for the welfare of each handicapped, ill, or dying person, it does not equate respect with indefinite prolongation of life. Using genetic engineering as a point of entry (3545–46), it expresses concern and even alarm about modern (Western) tendencies to place naive trust in science and technology but leaves the formulation of specific programs of control to those who have the requisite scientific and political expertise.

One is left wishing once again that the magisterium's approach to sex, marriage, and family could be characterized similarly. On reproductive technologies, for instance, why not express concern about naive trust in expensive and not remarkably successful technologies, which place immense stress on the marital and sexual relationships of those who have resort to them—and leave millions of children worldwide in need of adoptive homes? At the same time, a real nuancing of the moral understanding of such techniques should be heavily dependent on the contributions of those who are married, are parents, or have experienced infertility.

Similar comments could be made about contraception, divorce, homosexuality, singleness, and so on. While the church has an important witness to make on each of these issues, that witness should be articulated fundamentally in terms of the values of sexuality and the body, of interpersonal commitment, of parenthood and its relation to love and sex, and of the cooperative potential of men and women in the sexual, parental, domestic, and social spheres of life. Conversely, church teaching needs to be more broad, creative, and experiential in delineating what is sinful in sexual, familial, and gender relationships. The old focus on "venereal pleasure" outside a procreative context has not been adequate for some time. Even within the "indissoluble" procreative marriage, sexuality can be repressed, can be used manipulatively or oppressively, or can simply fail to be genuinely nurtured within a total relationship that is both physically and psychologically intimate. Required now is a prophetic voice against such evils as sexism; sexual violence and domination; emotional, verbal, and physical abuse; and even emotional distance in sexual relationships and in families.

Roman Catholic ethics has always been characterized by its commitment to take particular moral decisions and acts seriously and to offer relatively detailed guidance to church members. This commitment should not be abandoned. However, concrete norms must not only be more flexible, more culturally specific, and more frequently revised than basic moral values and principles. The concrete norms also depend for their truth and adequacy on the honest engagement of inherited wisdom with current practice.

The authoring of a catechism does not provide the appropriate occasion for the fundamental reexamination of church teaching. Yet it might have lent itself at least to a more pronounced shift of emphasis away from specific negative norms and toward the potential contributions of the groups with which it ostensibly wants to communicate, as the whole church works toward a renewed moral appreciation of sexuality, family, and gender.

PART 5

PRACTITIONERS
LOOK AT THE
CATECHISM

Children
and the
Catechism

Francis J. Buckley, S.J.
University of San Francisco

The division into creed, sacraments, commandments, and the Lord's Prayer assumes and prolongs a false split between faith and life, between doctrine and liturgy, between morality and spirituality.

The catechism makes little attempt to present its content as a message of liberation, connecting Christ and the church to existing cultural values, human needs, and hopes.

In the catechism one finds no dialogue, no listening. There is only a monologue.

The prologue to the *Catechism for the Universal Church*, citing Cardinal Joseph Ratzinger's address to the 1987 synod of bishops, makes it clear that the catechism is not written to be read by children, much less to be memorized by them: "This catechism is intended for those whose responsibility it is to compose and/or to approve national and/or diocesan catechisms. It is therefore intended first of all for Bishops, as teachers of the Faith" (0018).

Children will be affected by this work only indirectly, through their teachers and graded texts. "Through the bishops, doctors of the faith, this catechism is intended for those who draw up catechisms, for catechists and so for the whole People of God" (0019).

Since the catechism is intended to reach the whole people of God only through the mediation of experts (bishops and writers of texts first, then the catechists), it would not seem fair to compare this book with the far more readable catechisms of Luther, Canisius, and Bellarmine or the more modern Dutch and German catechisms, which were intended to be read by ordinary people.

The Catechism as a Reference Work

The catechism will surely be consulted by writers of religion texts as a checklist to be sure that all essential matters relevant to children are adequately covered in any graded series that provides materials from kindergarten through grade eight.

In such a religious reference work the attention given to a topic should be proportioned to its importance, its centrality to the Christian message and Christian life. But the catechism unduly neglects the history of salvation as recounted in the Scripture: everything between the fall of Adam and Eve and the incarnation is omitted except a brief reference to the Old Law (3104–12); it treats minimally the public ministry of Jesus (1379–1400). The catechism can, however, be a useful source for some citations from Scripture, liturgy, theologians, and saints (almost all of them male).

The catechism's use of technical language, even ecclesiastical jargon (anaphora, epiclesis, anamnesis, parrhesia, doxology, catechumens, neophytes), as well as its use of Latin and other languages both in the text and in the summaries, certainly puts it beyond the reading level of children and beyond most catechists and parents as well. This will not be remedied by the proposed glossary.

The catechism might be used as a supplemental reference tool in graduate courses in religious education, in seminaries, and in training programs for catechists, with proper care to explain special terms and answer questions. Most parents and teachers, however, will not have the time, energy, background, or motivation to slog through 434 pages of mostly turgid prose. They will have to rely on popular articles or books that single out sections of the catechism for development, and so they will have no direct contact with the catechism itself.

The *Catechism for the Universal Church* is in effect a part, a very lengthy part, of a catechetical directory: the equivalent of part 3, chapter 2, of the *General Catechetical Directory* and chapters 5, 6, and 7 of *Sharing the Light of Faith: The National Catechetical Directory for Catholics of the United States*. The catechism candidly calls attention to its limits: "It is not its function to supply the adaptations demanded by the 'enculturation' of the christian faith. It is not a substitute for diocesan or regional catechisms; on the contrary, it seeks to encourage their realization. Its aim is not to propose catechetical methods, which could not be identical for all the differences of age and culture that are to be found in the Church" (0020).

Structure of the Catechism

The authors of the catechism do not seem to be aware that their very choice and arrangement and treatment of materials already involve a catechetical method that causes serious damage. The division into creed, sacraments, commandments, and the Lord's Prayer assumes and prolongs a false split between faith and life, between doctrine and liturgy, between morality and spirituality. The author of the section on the sacraments was aware of this danger and tried to overcome it by rooting sacramental life in a profound theology of the Holy Spirit. But even that section did not integrate liturgy with moral behavior. Liturgical spirituality did not clearly lead into collaboration with God in creating and redeeming the world.

The section on the creed does teach in a holistic, integral way the content of the Christian message in order to develop knowledge and understanding, and it cites (as proof texts) Scripture, the fathers, and the liturgy, but it does not evoke a sense of mystery or adoration, nor commitment to collaborate with God's ongoing work. For example, the entire section on the creation of the earth and of humanity (1165–1201) is inadequate in its mention of ecology.

The section on the sacraments does go beyond providing information. It deepens appreciation of God's presence and action, leading to more prayerful celebration of the liturgy, but not to social action.

The section on the commandments helps readers become aware of the conflict between Christian values and those of contemporary culture. It calls attention to some cultural obstacles to Christianity (economic systems, political systems, greed, superstition, fatalism). It mentions that Christianity should liberate from all that is sinful in and around us. Its treatment of the social teaching of the church invites cooperation with God in transforming the world. But these many good elements do not flow out of prayerful contemplation or celebration of the God who acts in history but from consideration of natural law.

The section on the Lord's Prayer is an appendage. Beautiful in itself, it does not show how it recapitulates the entire creed, worship, and action of the church. It could have. It did not.

This compartmentalizing of head, hands, and heart—or knowledge, feeling, and action—can have dire results in the catechesis of children if new programs of religious education revert to the old system of the *Baltimore Catechism:* one year on the creed, the next year on the commandments, the next year on the church and sacraments. The cycle was then repeated with more details, then repeated again. The very structure of treatment made it difficult for children—and their parents and teachers—to see the proper connection between the materials treated years apart.

The result was horrendous: the creed listed what we had to believe to get to heaven; the commandments listed what we had to do to get to heaven; the sacraments were helps we needed to believe the creed and observe the commandments. Christianity was presented as a burden. No wonder that so many trained in that system dropped out of the church once the Second Vatican Council removed the pressure!

After the Second Vatican Council the most popular catechetical programs in the United States have tried a different approach. This approach is "kerygmatic," insofar as it presents salvation history and the story of Christ as good news (*kerygma*) and "experiential," insofar as it integrates the Christian message with the life experience of the children. Its intention is to root the children more deeply and personally in the Christian community by making religion lessons explorations of the Christian doctrinal and liturgical mysteries that spontaneously lead to joyous faith, expressed in prayer and action.

In the kerygmatic and experiential approach, the creed recalls all that God has done and is doing for us out of love. The sacraments celebrate his loving presence and action and our prayerful response. The commandments guide us in expressing our grateful love to God and neighbor. Scripture and liturgy are not dragged in to illustrate theological or moral themes; they form the central part of the lessons. The resulting catechesis takes much more account of the liturgical year than does this catechism. The history of salvation as recounted in the Bible is at the heart of the good news; the public life of Jesus gets the same proportion of attention in catechesis as it had in the Gospels. This healthy development has been strikingly reversed in the catechism.

This catechism aims at being a "compendium of the whole of catholic doctrine, both of faith and of morals . . . a point of reference for the Catechisms or compendia that are drawn up in different regions" (0016). As an "organic and synthetic exposition of the essential and fundamental topics of catholic doctrine concerning faith and morals, in the light of the Second Vatican Council and in continuity with the preceding Tradition of the Church" (0017), the catechism has the strengths and weaknesses of all syntheses.

Fidelity to the Second Vatican Council

If the documents of the Second Vatican Council are truly "the great catechism of modern times," as Pope John Paul II declared (0010), this catechism should be compared to those documents. Although some sections of the catechism, notably on the church (1610–1769), consist virtually of citations from the conciliar documents, other sections, especially the section on Scripture, are notably weaker.

The catechism makes little attempt to present its content as a message of liberation, connecting Christ and the church to existing cultural values, human needs, and hopes. It does not interpret or explain the active presence of God in current events and why this is good news today, translating Christianity into cultural words and symbols that will not be misinterpreted.

Indeed, the entire catechism seems uncomfortable with liberation, which Pope Paul VI in *Evangelii Nuntiandi* (9, 30–38) identified as the heart of the gospel. Section 3048 on freedom is clearly an afterthought, as the numbering reveals. The catechism states, "In the evolution of modern society there emerge new sensitivities (concerning, for example, solidarity, social justice, the absolute rejection of war), new demands and hopes (for example, equality of rights, liberation movements, feminism, mastery over life), which sometimes make the perception of values and moral obligations less easy to arrive at" (3041). That statement as it stands is unfairly slanted. Sometimes those new movements make perceptions of Christian values and moral obligations much more easy to arrive at.

What is worse, the entire dialogic structure of Vatican II's "Pastoral Constitution on the Church in the Modern World" is lacking. There the church listened to the deepest longings of human hearts, the joys and hopes, fears and sorrows of people in all cultures and asked what the church could learn from them as well as say to them, what help it could receive as well as proffer. In the catechism one finds no dialogue, no listening. There is only a monologue.

The authors of the catechism may reply that this was not their task, that this is not the function of a catechism. But the great strength of the *Dutch Catechism* lay in its addressing those very human questions. The task of addressing them cannot be shunted off to local or regional catechisms: they are universal questions to be heard and responded to in a catechism intended for the universal church. The catechism should provide a model that local and regional catechisms can follow.

Matters of Faith and Theological Speculation

The church today sorely needs some way of distinguishing infallible from noninfallible teaching. This is notably absent from the universal catechism. Failure to make this distinction has been leading to great confusion among catechists and the children they teach. If all teachings bear the same weight, when some are changed—as happened with various reforms after the Second Vatican Council (vernacular language, altar facing the people, no abstinence on Fridays, more frequent annulments)—then all appear arbitrary. The catechism must make clear what teachings cannot ever be changed because they are matters of Christian faith.

For example, the sections on the fall of the bad angels and original sin (1215–38) confuse theological speculation with matters of faith, presenting everything on the same level of certitude. This is also true of preternatural gifts (1204); the denial of ignorance in Jesus (1280, 1311); the substitution theory of atonement instead of Jesus' solidarity with each human being (1457, 1462); Christ resting in the tomb on Holy Saturday as "the sign of God's great rest after his work" (1463); the denial of any possibility of intercommunion (2477); the imposition of an obligation to receive the anointing of the sick (2630); reading a rejection of all competition into the Beatitudes (3141); the pious practice of assigning patrons' names at baptism (3405). Such mixing of faith with speculation is the very problem that led to the withdrawal of the imprimatur from Anthony Wilhelm's *Christ Among Us!*

Bishops and priests in the past were helped by the "theological notes" that were attached to statements: to statements "solemnly defined" or "infallible from the ordinary magisterium" an assent of faith was due.[1]

But the catechism fails to make clear that to give the assent of faith, the highest form of certitude, to what is not taught infallibly is imprudent and sinful, extending the conclusions beyond the premises, giving an assent of absolute certitude to what may not be true and may indeed be false.[2]

Nevertheless, the church demands a certain assent, a "religious assent" (*obsequium religiosum*), to official teachings that are not taught infallibly.[3] What is the nature of this assent? Authors differ.[4]

The church rightly demands an assent of prudence, a prudential judgment, a certain decision that the teaching of the church was prudently and reasonably arrived at and that it is certainly prudent to follow this guidance in practice.

Note that two contradictory propositions cannot both be true. But two contradictory, even contrary, propositions may both be prudent: "Look before you leap," but "He who hesitates is lost."

Even if one proposition is certainly prudent, the opposite may be more prudent. It is certainly prudent for a five-year-old child to hold onto its mother's hand while crossing the street. But holding back is certainly more prudent if the child sees that mother is stepping in front of a speeding truck!

Catholics must give the magisterium the benefit of the doubt that they have done their homework, weighed carefully the arguments on all sides, and reached a wise and prudent decision, guided by the assistance of the Holy Spirit—unless one is aware that the process was seriously and fatally flawed.[5]

Even when the process of reaching the decision is honest and open, the most that can be claimed for a noninfallible teaching is that it is "morally certain," not that it is absolutely certain. Otherwise it would be infallible.

It is possible that not only learned theologians who have probed the reasoning behind the decisions but also mature laity who have prayerfully reflected on their experience, consulted others, and weighed carefully the consequences of their decisions may make a responsible prudential decision at variance with official church teaching that is not infallible, especially in the area of morals.

Use of Scripture

The section of the catechism dealing with the creed makes extensive use of Scripture. This could have been very helpful to catechists, especially in cultures like those of the United States, where Protestants love the Bible. Its use of Scripture, however, is uncritical and fundamentalist. For example, in various places the catechism mixes citations of a Gospel, the book of Acts, and a pastoral epistle (0001); mixes literal and applied senses (0003); interprets Acts 2:38 in a historically inaccurate manner (1063); interprets the Genesis 2–3 account of the creation and fall with no sensitivity to the literary form used by the sacred author (1202–32); gives biblical references to angels drawn from a variety of literary forms that are all treated as historical in the same sense (1156–58). Such use of Scripture can reinforce an uncritical approach and play into the hands of fundamentalists.

It is not acceptable exegesis simply to juxtapose seemingly opposed texts with no attempt to resolve the difficulty, as is done with 1 Jn 3:9, 5:18, and 1:8 in 2506–7. The principles given for interpreting Scripture (0275–83) are inadequate and esoteric (literal, allegorical, moral, and anagogical senses are mentioned without any explanation or development). They do not satisfactorily reflect the teaching of the church in the "Constitution on Divine Revelation" of the Second Vatican Council nor more recent documents, which encourage the use of modern critical methods.

This entire section should be expanded in the light of the official church teaching on Scripture and then used throughout the catechism to insure that it practices what it preaches. It does not do so now.

It is astonishing to see the commandments treated with no advertence to the pervading covenant context of Exodus 20. Though Ex 20:1–3 is cited, the words "who brought you out of the house of bondage" are totally nonfunctional to the catechism's presentation of the first commandment or anything else.

This cavalier dismissal of biblical scholarship can have dire consequences for the catechesis of children if the authors of religion programs imitate the catechism's distorted use of Scripture to shape their treatment of faith, morality, and the spiritual life.

Summaries

The use of larger type for the doctrinal exposition, smaller type for quotations from patristic, liturgical, and magisterial sources, and italic type for brief summaries is an excellent idea and makes the text much easier to read. However, some statements now in large type should be in small type; some in small type should be in large.

Some authors of catechetical materials may be tempted to put questions before the summaries and so produce a "catechism." This would be a great mistake. The material contained in the summaries varies in style and orientation: throughout most of the introduction and creed (0101–1530) it is exclusively cognitive; the chapter on the Holy Spirit (1535–1602) has only one set of summaries (1603–9) rather than summaries after each article; the summaries for the treatment of the Spirit until the end of the creed (1603–1879) are more biblical in orientation and even prayerful, as are the summaries for the first section on the liturgy and sacraments (2001–2163). Some statements in the summaries contain material not even mentioned in the text itself (2335, 2570, 2630, 2767, 3016).

Since the intention of the catechism is to provide in these summaries "comprehensive, memorable formulae" (0025), it would be wise to have the author of the sections at the end of the creed (1603–1879) rewrite the other summaries, so that they all can have a biblical and prayerful quality. Some summaries in the sections devoted to creed and sacraments should point to consequences for Christian life also.

Most of the summary statements, apart from biblical citations and quotations from council documents, are instantly forgettable. But some are excellent and could well be memorized by adults and older children: for instance, the meaning of the names "Jesus, Christ, Son of God, Lord" (1290-93); the meaning of the incarnation (1314-19); the mission of the Holy Spirit (1603-9). Fewer than one tenth of the summary statements are truly memorable. These should be clearly marked, either by asterisks or boldface type. But they would not suffice to make a catechism; indeed, that would simply compound the compartmentalization that already characterizes this catechism, isolating doctrine from prayer and action.

The authors of this catechism should be commended for resisting the temptation to define God. The *Baltimore Catechism* fell into that trap and produced "God is the Supreme Being, infinitely perfect, who made all things and keeps them in existence"—a formula that could have been written if there had been no Bible and no incarnation. This present catechism wisely states, "In revealing himself, God remains ineffable mystery." It then cites St. Thomas Aquinas: "Of God we know rather what he is not than what he is" (1048). More positively, it proclaims, "The God of our faith is at the same time he who is—who subsists by himself—and who has made himself known as love. His being itself is love" (1047).

Style

The sexist language characteristic of curial documents really should be avoided in English. It is no longer tolerable in our culture, especially when English is one of the official languages of the text.

The general style of writing is difficult for bishops, theologians, and catechetical writers to follow. Most of it is dry and uninteresting. This is a pity. The church really needs a comprehensive presentation of the authentic teaching of the magisterium in an organized way. But the catechism could be much more.

The section on the Holy Spirit (1531-1609) is a model of what the catechism could be: warm, even poetic, with a fine eye for patterns that pull the material together and intensify the response of faith. The section on the Holy Spirit is a masterful work of theology, enriched by splendid contributions from the Eastern fathers.

The introductory section on the "Celebration of the Christian Mystery" (2001-2163) is another gem, sparkling with beauty. It moves well beyond the "Constitution on the Sacred Liturgy" of the Second Vatican Council in its use of the liturgical traditions of the Eastern churches. For example, it substitutes "the time of 'Theosis' or deification, in which the Holy Spirit conforms us to his glorious Body (time after Pentecost)"

(2073) for the colorless Western term "ordinary time." This is a major advance. Sacramentals and popular devotions are very well presented (2094–2104). If the wealth of those other traditions had been applied to the earlier sections on the creed (0101–1530) and the later sections on the spiritual life and commandments (3001–3816), the catechism would have been much more attractive!

Warmth and joy are particularly important in catechesis for children. Whether for children or adults, God's self-revelation is not intended simply to provide information to satisfy curiosity or even simply to provide necessary information to reach the goal of life. Rather, it is an invitation to enter into a deep personal relationship with our Father, the source of our life who tenderly watches over us at every moment and longs for our response of love. The God who acts and speaks calls us to listen, to respond with our whole being, and to share in his loving action. The entire catechism, not just the section on liturgy, should serve this catechetical purpose.

The Spiritual Life

Despite the condemnation of rationalism by the First Vatican Council, a subtle rationalism has infiltrated and corrupted the treatment of faith and prayer. For example, "To deepen faith, one must deepen the reasons for believing" (0329). In reality we all know that faith is deepened in other ways also: by prayer, by action in union with the Spirit, sometimes even by sharing the sufferings of Jesus for the sake of his body, the church (Col 1:24).

Another example: "We only touch these realities [of God] with the aid of the formulations of the faith which enable us to express and communicate the common faith" (0331). Not so. The experience of God in faith can sometimes be too deep for words. This section of the catechism seems very uncomfortable with religious experience.

Another example: "Communion in the faith is not possible without a common language of faith" (1001). Quite the contrary. Communion in the faith often precedes a common language, which may emerge from discussions. This regularly happens at church councils, where all share a common faith but struggle to find the right words to express it. Furthermore, some formulations or technical terms drawn from philosophy may prove to be obstacles to faith for those from another culture. And some terms, like *salvation*, have become so familiar that people do not listen to the reality behind the words. The discussion of "salvation" (1259–63) assumes that everyone is fully aware of the root metaphors of healing, rescue, liberation.

Language is a serious catechetical problem for catechists and children that is not well addressed by the catechism. The glossary is a good idea, but it does not get at the more fundamental issue of language as a barrier to the perception of the good news. We are moving beyond the five centuries dominated by printing into an age in which images projected by the media will be the major means of communication. This catechism does a disservice to the church by not facing this.

Unfortunately, the sections on the theological virtues (3194–3201) and the way of perfection (3215–30) take material that is fascinating to our contemporaries (workshops on spirituality are sellouts at catechetical congresses) and makes it tedious and boring.

The section on the Beatitudes (3124–31), by contrast, is good. Though the paradoxical quality of the Beatitudes puts them beyond the grasp of younger children, catechists who work with older children, adolescents, and adults will find this section helpful.

It is surprising to see the Decalogue treated with so few references to the covenant, to the common good, or to human rights. Despite the section on the spiritual life that precedes, the commandments are treated with little sense that our behavior as the people of God should be a response of gratitude, love, and imitation of God's own intervention in history. Natural law seems in practice to displace revelation and grace as the primary norm for the formation of conscience. Such a treatment hardly reflects the developments in moral theology or catechetics during the last fifty years. This entire section should be reworked lest catechists feel torn between the utterly outdated approach of this catechism and the approach of the texts of the religious education programs being used – an approach that more faithfully reflects the Second Vatican Council.

The treatment of the second commandment (3366–3409) is a jumbled mess: after introducing the name of God (3367–73), the name of Jesus is discussed (3374); mention of baptism leads to a digression on Christian names and patron saints (3375–77); then the text returns to God's name (3379–82), then to names in general (3383), then to Jesus' name again (3384); then care and concern for animals is treated here rather than under the fifth or seventh commandments (3388).

Since parents are the primary religious educators of their children,[6] both by what they say and what they do, the catechesis of children can be powerfully affected by the images of marriage and family life projected by the catechism. The treatment of marriage, both in the section on the sacraments (2801–83) and the commandments (3450–3520, 3592–3663), properly reflects changing cultural situations and an improved theology of marriage. There is notable sensitivity to preparation for marriage and mixed marriages (2839–45), a valuable section on "the domestic church" (2868–71), a helpful expansion of the notion of care in the family (3462–66), a fine list of family rights (3490).

One would have expected to see some mention of pornography, sexism, and sexual discrimination under the sixth and ninth commandments.

One of the best features of this catechism is that it includes the social teaching of the church. If this is reflected in religion programs for children, awareness of social sin and collective responsibility to counteract it will grow. People will no longer be able to say, "Church teaching on politics and economics cannot be important. The catechism never mentioned it."

Most of the section on the seventh and tenth commandments is quite specific, but parts are so vague as to be useless, making references to "squalid traffic" (slavery? prostitution?) and unspecified "disorders in the social and economic life" (3674 and 3676).

The development of the eighth commandment is generally good, but no mention is made of advertising, not even in relation to the mass media.

Refusal to Accept the Teaching of Vatican II

Although the mandate of the writers of the catechism was to integrate the teaching of the Second Vatican Council with tradition (0017), there are some flagrant failures to do so. These would surely give aid and comfort to archconservative groups who have never accepted the liturgical reforms or ecumenism of the council documents.

For example, "Instituted in the context of a meal, the eucharist is not itself a meal" (2413). As it stands, this sentence contradicts the "Constitution on the Sacred Liturgy" (no. 47) and the "Pastoral Constitution on the Church in the Modern World" (no. 35), to say nothing of sacred Scripture and the tradition of the church. It is even contradicted in the catechism (2464 and 2469). Many people who oppose the reform of the eucharistic liturgy have said that the Mass is not a meal but a sacrifice. The catechism should not lend any credibility to their position. In fact, the Eucharist is both a sacrifice and a meal; it is a sacrificial meal. This sentence should be reworded to say, "The Eucharist is not just a meal or not an ordinary meal." This particular error would have serious repercussions on catechesis for children, especially their preparation for First Communion and their ongoing catechesis about the Eucharist.

Another example: "The ecclesial communities separated from the Catholic Church, 'have not preserved the proper substance of the eucharistic mystery in its fullness, especially because of the absence of the sacrament of Order' (UR 22). It is for this reason that eucharistic communion with these communities is not possible for the Catholic Church" (2477). Quite the contrary, the very same document of the council explicitly states that it is possible and sometimes desirable:

> As for common worship, however, it may not be regarded as a means to be used indiscriminately for the restoration of unity among Christians. Such worship depends chiefly on two principles: it should signify the unity of the Church; it should provide a sharing in the means of grace. The fact that it should signify unity generally rules out common worship. Yet the gaining of a needed grace sometimes commends it.[7]

A major development of the Second Vatican Council was the shift of attention in the liturgy from canonical validity to spiritual fruitfulness, from the proper observance of the ritual by the celebrant to the effects produced in the hearts of the faithful ("Constitution on the Sacred Liturgy," nos. 10–11, 14, 19, 21). This concern for a full human response to God's revelatory self-gift or self-communication lies behind the renewed emphasis on the Liturgy of the Word in the vernacular, the lengthened preparation for the sacraments reflected in the Rite of Christian Initiation of Adults, and the central role of the community. This shift and these new emphases do not receive due attention in this catechism, whose treatment of the sacraments reflects manuals of theology written long before the council.

Conclusion

Although there is a real need for a compendium of faith and morals that could serve as a reference tool for bishops and writers of catechetical materials, this catechism is not what is needed:

It confuses matters of faith with theological opinions, soliciting an objectively sinful act of faith based on insufficient evidence.

It does not faithfully reflect the dialogic structure or openness to pluralism of the Second Vatican Council.

It fails to integrate doctrine with liturgy and the spiritual and moral life.

Its style is alienating, not faithful to the gospel.

It does not use Scripture as the church officially states it should.

It does not reflect the advances in biblical, dogmatic, liturgical, and moral theology of the last fifty years.

It gives encouragement to those who have persistently refused to accept the teachings of the Second Vatican Council.

Though some parts are quite good, as a whole it is positively harmful and should be thoroughly rewritten to be of service in catechesis.

Adolescents and the Catechism

William J. O'Malley, S.J.
Fordham Preparatory School

Quotations from Iraeneus of Lyons and Nicholas of Flüe—or even from Vatican II—carry little clout with the audience the church has missioned me to serve.

If the overall thrust of the catechism were successful, our schools would turn out many loyal conformists but not a single apostle.

I find it not just unhelpful for its ultimately intended audience, but a positive obstacle.

I write as a religious educator, the intended beneficiaries of the *Catechism for the Universal Church*. According to its prologue, it offers itself as "a point of reference for the Catechisms or compendia that are drawn up in different regions" (0016). There is much in the catechism no genuine Christian could cavil with (Jesus' divinity, the resurrection, the obligation to worship and serve), and much that is admirable (some of part 3, "The Law of Christ," the epilogue on the Our Father). But I would not serve the church if I were to say the catechism is a helpful document. If I were set the task of translating it into a useful tool for catechizing the young, I would find it more hindrance than help.

In honesty, I was not "disappointed" in the catechism, since much of it was just what I feared: the mind-vising prose, the suffocating proliferation of supporting quotations from Scripture and tradition (each with its parenthetical references), its consistently sexist language ("man inevitably asks himself questions" [0120]). Far more important, however, is its resolute legalism, its overemphasis on the transcendence of Jesus at the expense of his humanity, and its painful concern for sin. What is more, it resolutely avoids even supportive evidence from other disciplines—psychology, physics, biology—as if nothing had been discovered about humanity since the closing of the Deposit of Faith. Similarly, until three quarters of the way into the book, the catechism does not concern itself in any way with the problems of the world in which we presently find ourselves. Worst of all, the catechism completely avoids any consideration of the majority of the audience it intends to serve: not the relatively few adult, educated catechumens, but the young who are baptized but not yet converted.

For a start, the catechism's sheer compendiousness acts against its purposes, with arcana such as the fall of the angels and "the third hell" given equal or more space than such crucial tasks as a meaningful explanation of what faith and conscience mean. Similarly, its development along the framework of the Apostles' Creed, as if each element were as important and accessible to its audience as every other, dooms the document to being doctrinally thorough and as intriguing to its potential audience as celestial calculus.

The prologue quotes John Paul II from *Catechesi Tradendae* (0006): "Very soon the name of *catechesis* was given to the whole of the efforts within the Church to make disciples, to help people to believe that Jesus is the Son of God." Thus, one assumes the mandate to the authors was to design an instrument "to help people to believe": an instrument of conversion. Yet the document approaches its task without the slightest consideration of the need for persuasion in that task or of the psychology of conversion. It ignores also the major obstacles any catechist in the world faces today—the very obstacles the first apostles faced: materialism and skepticism. The book was not written with an eye to young men and women in developed countries who have peeked into *Playboy* and watched MTV. Even in the Third World, the hunger in young bellies echoes more loudly than the call to holiness, and it is difficult to give credence to any God who could allow such a callous world.

Like a teacher who has logically developed lesson plans and refuses to acknowledge students' questions when the matter provokes them, the catechism lets the subject matter dominate the audience. In short, it is a document written not for those responding to the needs and receptivities of potential converts (which include almost all our baptized young) but for those dealing with the already convinced and committed. It sows without plowing and does not serve as an instrument "to help people to believe." "Know" does not mean "believe."

Core Problems

Like the well-meaning parent trying to project an image of an all-wise protector, the catechism undermines its own credibility by its very claims to certitude: "only with this certain knowledge" (0012); "arrive at true certainties" (0126). Since Heisenberg won the Nobel Prize in 1932, we know that even physics, the hardest of the "hard" sciences, does not claim anything more certain than a high degree of probability.

Surely if the word *faith* has any meaning at all, it is in direct confrontation with certitude. Faith is a calculated risk based on evidence. Whether it is the faith one pledges in God or the faith two people pledge in marriage, they are not sure it is going to work out; they are *betting* it will work out. The catechism itself recognizes this, late and briefly: "To believe means to accept and to recognize as true and corresponding to reality the content of that which is said, because of the credibility of the one who says it. 'Believe' has a double reference: to the person and to the truth; to the truth in consideration of the person who possesses credibility" (0346).

It seems to deny that one can discover the truth *without* a direct human intermediary, simply by studying the evidence. Had the catechism used that as its governing principle in its all-too-brief study of the meaning of faith, it would have changed the whole unfortunate thrust of the document.

In its seven short paragraphs on faith, the catechism never gives an explanation of the development of faith nor of what supports it: experience of God. It says nothing of how imagination (which the document constantly downplays) helps in that effort, nor even what role reasoning plays in conversion. "By faith," the catechism says (0304), "Sarah conceived the Son of the promise." In fact, Abraham and Sarah originally shared a skeptical laugh at the Lord's proposal that Sarah would conceive. The catechism seems to ignore the fact that Abraham and Sarah did "what they had to do" to have Isaac despite their skepticism because of the evidence of their longtime personal relationship with the One who promised.

The catechism equates faith not with trust based on evidence and experience but with passive obedience: "the Magisterium of the Church fulfills an essential part of its prophetic role, which is to tell men what they are and what they must be before God" (3148). That could strike some as a direct denial that God gave human beings intelligence and invited them to use it. It might remind readers of Dostoevsky's Grand Inquisitor, who removed the awesome burden of freedom from his servile subjects by also removing their need—and even their ability—to do the one thing that separates us from apes: think. Yet elsewhere, speaking of the filial respect of children for their parents, the document says, insightfully, "Unquestioning obedience is not necessarily a sign of filial respect, and may be nothing more than an act done out of servile fear" (3469).

From the beginning the catechism presumes an audience that is not there because, I assume, the document was written not by teachers but by academicians. "Man inevitably asks himself questions" (0120). True enough, but the catechism fails to distinguish between being befuddled and the ability to reason to an answer. Nor does it seem to acknowledge that one can desire the end without being willing to make the considerable effort to undertake the means to the end. As the catechism says itself: "Man does not carry within himself in vain that capacity for truth." The crucial word is *capacity*. Like the potential for having children, that capacity does not necessarily guarantee its actualization. To suppose that is to deny the very original sin the document holds so important—and is the only Christian doctrine one can prove conclusively from the daily newspapers. Whoever wrote this document never taught grammar school or even high school, the very audience for which it was ultimately destined.

Further, the catechism seems to presume that both faith and conscience are somehow inborn: "Faith is a supernatural gift which implants revelation in the human intelligence" (0350); "the natural law written in his heart" (3091); "the natural law is written in man's heart" (3094). Yet if conscience were effortlessly accessible in one's heart and faith were given in baptism, it is difficult to explain Voltaire, James Joyce, and Fidel Castro, all of whom had hearts and were baptized. If the faith were so easily accessible, there would be no need for religious education or for the catechism. There is nothing said about gathering the evidence, sifting it, coming to a personally validated conclusion, and testing it out. That, to me, is the basis for any decision whatever, including the decision to trust in the Lord Jesus and to choose moral good over moral evil. It is true that most students come to me believing that conscience is inborn and requires no effort whatever to forge. I never knew before where they had gotten that ludicrous idea.

The catechism also continues the oversimplification of sin into "mortal" and "venial," which seems—at least to the young—to say that unless a sin utterly sunders the relationship with God it is by that very fact trivial. Rather, there is a spectrum of sins from the trivial through the increasingly more serious to the ultimate negation of a relationship with God. Retaining this simplistic "two-bin" description of sin gives rise again to the old self-serving games like "how far can I go?" Only in one place (3056), three quarters through the catechism, is any mention made of "moral ambiguities of social life." The certitude the rest of the catechism claims is just too smug for skeptical young people to swallow.

In ignoring other approaches to understanding humanity, the catechism not only dodges problems, it also impoverishes itself of enriching,
supportive insights and continues the suspicion that somehow Catholicism is entrenched against "the World" and its ways, as if true psychology
or true science could possibly be at odds with true religion. What is more,
it undercuts its credibility by trying to prove itself by itself. It supports its
arguments with Scripture, quotations from the magisterium and the
church fathers, even from saints like Joan of Arc and Thérèse of Lisieux.
But other than one quotation from Newman, I found nothing of Teilhard,
Rahner, Maritain—much less authors far closer to the ultimate audience
than the catechism is: G. K. Chesterton and C. S. Lewis. Quotations from
Iraeneus of Lyons and Nicholas of Flüe—or even from Vatican II—carry
little clout with the audience the church has missioned me to serve.

Further, in ignoring the legitimate insights, questions, and problems
raised by the natural sciences, the document not only ignores their supportive insights but abandons the task of harmonizing the unchallenge-
able truths of natural science with what appears to the young to be
contradictory religious truth. Your everyday school teacher, who often
does not have the skill for this task of reconciliation, would look to a
document such as the catechism for help, but does not receive any. Worst
of all, this evasion gives the appearance of denying that God revealed
himself in the laws of physics long before he revealed himself in the Law
of Moses.

The catechism says (0137), quoting Pius XII, "the truths concerning
God and man are completely beyond the order of things that are accessible to the senses," and "the human mind, to attain to such truths,
encounters obstacles from the senses and from the imagination." What of
the sense of the numinous, which most often causes the very first suspicion of the immanent presence of God? What of the imagination, which
such giants at prayer as Ignatius Loyola propounded as a way of gaining
insight into the gospel? Surely it was not a speculative thinker to whom
God presented himself in the burning bush, nor was it speculative thinkers to whom Jesus presented his message in parables. Can one gain no
insight into God from Donne, or Dostoevsky, or Bernanos, or Greene, or
Updike?

In the end, one of the deepest influences on the catechism is the attitude quoted from St. Augustine that the natural sciences are "a branch of
knowledge of no use for salvation" (1168) and in the heading "*There will
be no further Revelation*" (0221). Brazen of me to take on Pius XII,
Augustine, and the catechism on one page, but I cannot elude the sus-

picion that such a position is not only self-impoverishing and repugnant to intelligent people but also a denial of the immanent presence and movement of God in his creation and creatures.

Even when the catechism uses the scriptural evidence to which it restricts itself, it avoids precisely the problems that make religious education so tricky (and intriguing!) since Vatican II: the historicity of the Gospels is merely asserted (0289); the document quotes all the sources—from Qoheleth to Augustine to Joan of Arc—as if they were univocal; nothing is said of the influence of postresurrection faith on the wording of the Gospels (e.g., Peter, a resolute monotheist without the benefit of the trinitarian controversies in the later church, calling Jesus "Lord" [1272, 1286]). And most damaging of all, it merely declares that scriptural truths are often couched "in the language of imagery," without any explanation of how symbols and stories can reveal truth—whether it be in Aesop, Genesis, Luke, or Shakespeare. Thus, it seems that the catechism is taking the dove at Jesus' baptism as a literal event, finessing the obstacles and leaving them to the ordinary teacher who might not be as learned and surely is not as powerful as the writers of the catechism.

Nowhere is this apparent literalism more damaging than in the treatment of original sin. Relying on the too-facile economic metaphor, it makes God a grudge-bearing Scrooge. The simplicity of a catechesis on human nature couched solely in the terms of Genesis and the insights available in the first centuries of the church councils is pretty tough for the pseudo-sophisticated young people I teach. Not merely the very bright ones but even more so the not-so-bright ones usually grasp the evidence just enough to misunderstand it entirely. It is far better to show young people that even though the story of the fall is almost certainly not literally true, it does impart an unavoidable truth whose results are undeniable: of all the species on earth, only human beings are free not to live up to the nature that is programmed into them. No lion refuses to act leonine, but the daily papers give irrefutable evidence that human beings refuse to act human. Why?

Because love requires freedom, God chose to give intelligence and freedom to an as yet imperfectly evolved tribe of apes. As a result, narcissism and inertia are nearly inevitable. The self-absorption and sluggishness inherited from our animal ancestors, mixed with the canniness and freedom of the human mind, made sin nearly inevitable. Rather than threatening true religion, true psychology can enrich it.

So, too, can natural science. Why should a present-day catechist be shackled only to the heavy metaphors available twenty centuries ago, like big-shouldered angels with wings to fly from "all the way out there where heaven is"? There are much more intriguing analogies, like "intelligent neutrinos" whizzing in our very midst—if indeed the God who has direct access to our hearts needs messengers at all. Why not enrich the message by saying that Jesus was "the last step in human evolution," from human to divine? At the very least, it would avoid the painful near-literalism of the catechism: "The dogmatic definition of Benedict XII in 1355 . . . affirms that the souls of those who damn themselves go after death straight down to hell" (1838). I do not deny that they go to hell, but I sure know they do not go "down." In 1355 Benedict XII did not know that in the heliocentric solar system "up" and "down" have meaning only relative to where the speaker happens to be standing. If Jesus ascended "up" to heaven, an old lady in Australia would ascend "up" in precisely the opposite direction. I teach high school seniors, and every time I tell them that, they are surprised. The church has done a good job in training them to keep religion in one lobe of the brain and science in the other and, like Jesus and the old lady from Australia, never the twain shall meet.

But it is precisely that separation that makes it such an easy task for atheist college professors to convince youngsters to shed religion as simplistic. We bring it on ourselves. Our very pretense at certitude makes it all the simpler to find our clay feet.

To say, as the catechism does, that "death is a consequence of sin" and "death was therefore contrary to the intentions of God the creator" (1808) and "death makes its entry into human history" (1231) because of the fall may get God off the hook. But it forces the reader to deny several other truths, among them God's ultimate wisdom and foreknowledge. Perhaps death did make its entry into human history at the fall, but death had existed for millennia before human history began. Objective fact. We have the bones to prove it.

Death and suffering—the problem of physical and moral evil—are most profound arguments against the existence of a good and provident God. It is the substance of all great literature from the book of Job through *Candide* to *Waiting for Godot*, and it is thus the greatest obstacle any teacher has to "helping people to believe that Jesus is the Son of God."

"The witness of Scripture is unanimous: [God's] providential care is *concrete* and *immediate*, attentive to the smallest details" (1131, emphasis in original). But what, a skeptical reader might ask, of the witness of experience? What about the question of Job? The question of Ivan Karamazov? On that profoundest of questions, the catechism is either unhelpfully assertive or silent.

As for moral evil, it states: "God is in no way, either directly or indirectly, the cause of moral evil" (1137). This, too, is unhelpful to the unconvinced and uncommitted. Someone could make a pretty unsettling argument that in giving us freedom without the certitude so ardently desired by Adam and Eve (the inborn knowledge of good and evil: equality with God, certitude), an all-knowing God was at least an indirect contributor to the existence of moral evil. The genuine Catholic believes a good God must have a reason for that, however inscrutable from our vantage point, but it hardly solves the problem to evade it with unsubstantiated assertions to the contrary.

A great deal of what is in the catechism surely is of interest only to perfectionists and theoretical theologians. Why on earth, I asked myself, start with the Trinity in "helping people to believe that Jesus is the Son of God"? Is there any reason a prospective convert—or even a lifelong Catholic—should know the various creeds the church has promulgated in two thousand years? Or know the technical meaning of "consubstantial," or the manner in which the Father, Son, and Spirit are related? Or the meaning of *hypostasis*? Or about angels, concerning whom there are nine paragraphs and of their sin five more? Why would anyone but an expert want to clutter the substantials of Catholicism with "matter and form," the two wills and two operations in the personality of Jesus, with an "ardent desire for the Second Coming," with what occurred when Jesus descended into hell? To the not-yet-convinced "the temporal punishment due to sin whose guilt has already been forgiven" (2552) seems to picture a God who is more reluctant to let go of a grudge than his Son asks us to be.

Such overabundance is all the more puzzling when one considers what is omitted or glossed over, such as Jesus' ringing inaugural speech in the synagogue, pledging himself to serve the needy, and the mandate at the Last Supper to wash each other's feet. There is little or nothing of the very core of the gospel: healing and forgiveness. There is nothing of Jesus as a model of our own apostleship, only Jesus as obedient sacrificial victim, not Jesus the challenger. We are enjoined consistently "to become a child," "one must humble himself" (1369), "Jesus was 'obedient'" (1376), "by this submission, [Jesus] can grow in wisdom and in grace" (1376). Nothing about being "busy about my Father's affairs." Nothing about standing up and being counted, making a difference, healing. If the overall thrust of the catechism were successful, our schools would turn out many loyal conformists but not a single apostle. The catechism thus can be read as a call not to shepherds but to sheep.

Along that same submissive line, there is one number (1417) that puzzled me: "In the eyes of many, Jesus seems to act against the essential institutions of the chosen people." The catechism then spends three pages doing real logical gymnastics to show that Jesus was four-square for the Law. Later (3132) it says, "Jesus speaks of loving God and loving our neighbor as 'the first and greatest commandment' (Mt 22.38). Its priority does not lessen the importance of the other commandments for the law stands in its entirety." On the contrary, Mt 22:38 says that loving God is the first commandment and loving the neighbor is the second commandment. "On these two commandments hang the whole Law, and the Prophets also." Such statements of the catechism about "the Law" give rise to suspicions that it is claiming that the full Hebrew Law is incorporated into the Christian Law—or that the present laws of the church have taken its place. This contrasts with Paul's lengthy struggle to convince the Judaizers that one did not have to become a Jew before becoming a Christian and with his description of the Law (Gal 3:10) as a "curse," and with Peter's description of it as "the useless way of life your ancestors handed down" (1 Pt 1:19).

More to the point, it denies that if Jesus had just kept quiet, if he had kept away from Jerusalem, he never would have been executed. Worse, it engenders in the Catholic the belief that following Christ is precisely the opposite of what Jesus did: to bow your head before legitimate authority and be submissive.

I was not disappointed in the catechism; I was saddened by it because it could have helped so many, all over the world. I doubt that many even zealously committed religious educators will be tempted to struggle very far into it, if at all. It is saddening because it was such a prodigious effort, doubtless at considerable expense and with the best of intentions. But I find it not just unhelpful for its ultimately intended audience, but a positive obstacle.

Bishops and the Catechism

Raymond A. Lucker
Diocese of New Ulm, Minnesota

Unity can be achieved, indeed is enhanced, by a pluralism of expressions.

"Slow down; consult broadly; give us more time to consult pastors and lay people."

The *Catechism for the Universal Church* released by the Holy See is written *"ad episcopos,"* for bishops. The provisional text has been sent to individual bishops for consultation. As Pope John Paul II pointed out to the Commission on the Catechism in 1986, it is intended to be "an important help in guaranteeing the unity of the faith." Three years later he declared that there is a need, indeed an urgency, for "a concise and clear exposition of the essential and fundamental contents of the faith and of Catholic morality."

The 1985 synod of bishops called for the preparation of a catechism "of the whole of Catholic doctrine, both of faith and of morals." Thus, the catechism is to be a compendium of the faith of the church.

As a summary of the essential doctrine, the catechism will serve as a reference point for bishops in the presentation of the content of the message of the faith in the development of diocesan, regional, and national catechisms, textbooks, and instructional materials. Bishops are to use it as a guide for the renewal of religious education, or "catechesis," to see that the Christian message is heard everywhere in the most effective way.

I will focus on some issues that bishops need to face as they respond to the provisional text of the catechism and as they prepare for its eventual use.

A Catechism for Our Time

Bishops have been writing catechisms for centuries. One thing is sure about them: there will never be a definitive catechism. They always admit of change. While essential doctrines do not change, the expression of doctrine does change. Catechesis is an important and serious task for bishops. Handing on the faith is at the heart of the church's mission. It involves three steps: (1) evangelization, the result of which is initial faith; (2) catechesis, which is aimed at strengthening faith and making it mature; and (3) theology, which is concerned with understanding the faith.

The ministry of the word is centered on faith, that total human response given under the impetus of grace to the living word of God. The ministry of the word is also concerned with the content of faith. Bishops have been so interested in catechisms over the ages precisely because they are charged with the responsibility of handing on the faith "that comes to us from the Apostles."

In the early days of the church the Latin word *catechismus* meant the same as the Greek *catechesis*, the content of the teaching given by the church and the way in which it was presented. It was centered on a family, a faith-filled community, and the celebration of the feasts and seasons of the liturgical year.

Through a whole series of historical circumstances, the English word *catechism* came to refer only to a book, often in question-and-answer form, which contains the doctrine to be taught, usually to children. But for fifteen hundred years there was no such thing as a catechism book as we know it.

Martin Luther was the first to call a book a catechism and more than anyone else popularized the catechism as a question-and-answer book. Catholics followed with similar manuals containing clear, concise, accurate statements of Christian doctrine. Examples of these were the ones written for children and the uninstructed by St. Peter Canisius and St. Robert Bellarmine.

These early catechisms became models for similar manuals published throughout the world, many of them written by bishops. All of them reflected a particular need to express the truths of faith simply and accurately according to the needs and concerns of the time.

The *Roman Catechism* was prepared at the order of the Council of Trent (1545–63). It was not a manual for children or for ordinary folk, and it was not used as a model for subsequent catechisms. It was written as a guide *for pastors* in preaching and teaching both adults and children. It was a remarkable book, wonderfully unified, and a beautiful expression of the early tradition in catechesis. Divided into four parts—the Apostles' Creed, the sacraments, the Ten Commandments, and the Lord's Prayer—it described the circle of love coming from God to every person and from all of us back to God with Christ as its center. It narrated what

God did and does for us in Christ and how we are to respond to God in Christ. Popes and bishops continued to encourage its use even until recent memory.

At the First Vatican Council three hundred years later, there was a call for a uniform catechism, one that would be used for religious instruction throughout the world. There were several abortive attempts, including an effort by Pope Pius X to produce such a manual. But the project was never completed.

The Second Vatican Council opted not for a uniform catechism but called for the renewal of catechetics and for a catechetical directory to assist in this renewal. The *General Catechetical Directory*, published in 1971, was to be a guide for bishops and others in the development of catechetical programs and in the production of religion textbooks. It called for the development of similar catechetical directories in each country. The National Conference of Catholic Bishops approved a national catechetical directory in 1977 under the title *Sharing the Light of Faith*. This document was a remarkable achievement coming after several years of consultation involving hundreds of thousands of people across the United States.

In every age people need catechetical guides in handing on the message of Jesus. Bishops will always be involved in stating the unchanging truths of faith in ever-new ways. No catechism will be the last word.

Renewal of Catechetics

The *Catechism for the Universal Church* can be an important project. It may have an impact on the church for a long time. But bishops can fall into the trap of thinking that if they can come up with the perfect book, the catechetical problems of the church will be over.

Bishops should use the catechism project, and the consultation involved, as a blessed moment for the renewal of catechesis. Bishops need to be convinced that the greatest need in religious education is the catechesis and evangelization of adults.

In the *National Catechetical Directory* the American bishops said that catechesis for adults is the chief form of catechesis. The church has not been able to put that into practice. Religious education in the United States is so centered on the handing on of truths to children in classrooms, using approved textbooks, that people neglect using the resources necessary to foster the conversion and growth in faith of adults.

The challenge is to help create conditions where people can come to conversion and renewal.

Catechesis best takes place within the community of believers. The classroom is an important aspect of this community effort. Yet for fifteen hundred years Christians handed on their faith without having classrooms as we understand them. St. Jean-Baptiste de la Salle (1651–1719) was the first to popularize classroom teaching. Thereafter, schools and classrooms became the ordinary means for handing on Catholic teaching. This practice removed parents from seeing themselves as the primary evangelists and catechists of their children. Classroom instruction builds on and strengthens what is done in the home and community.

Bishops need to believe that catechesis is a lifelong process. All followers of Christ go through stages in their lives when they grow weak in their faith, when they need to be converted anew. All need continually to grow in their relationship with the Lord and in their understanding of the truths of faith. Many of our people have drifted away and are alienated. Huge numbers of young people are not receiving adequate catechetical formation. The Rite of Christian Initiation of Adults is just beginning in many parts of the country. Many children, youth, and adults have only a minimal understanding of our Catholic tradition and history. We have a long way to go if a catechetical renewal is to touch most Catholics.

A textbook is not the center and the focus of catechesis. Still, the *Catechism for the Universal Church* is to be a guide for bishops in the development of national and regional catechisms. In the United States the catechisms in common use are graded religion textbooks. These catechisms have been developed by textbook companies following guidelines prepared by bishops. Bishops are grateful to textbook writers and publishers for their enormous contribution to religious education in the last seventy years. Some people have made textbooks the central problem in catechetics, but what is called for is a renewed people of God, a people converted to Jesus and committed to living the message he taught.

Faith and Theology

It is axiomatic to say that there is one faith and there are many ways of expressing that faith theologically. This is a central issue, if not the issue, for the committee writing the catechism. Theologians use science, philosophy, linguistics, and other areas of human knowledge, for example, to organize, clarify, and understand the data of faith and apply them to new circumstances. Each area and age has its own cultural expressions and applications. Over the centuries the church has not only tolerated variety in theological expression, it has encouraged it.

Is it possible to write a summary of the truths of faith that will have the same meaning throughout a world church? That is the major challenge. By the very fact that it is set in writing, the catechism is conditioned by language, culture, and history. That simple fact needs to be kept in mind. Language changes. People of every culture need the gospel proclaimed to them. The principles of morality need to be applied to new and changing situations.

The catechism is to contain the traditional dogmas of the church for people today. It is said to be a summary of the truths of faith. But the present draft does more than that. It also contains theological positions subject to change.

For example, the catechism shows a genuine ambivalence about the real human knowledge of Christ (1311). It declares that Jesus had a real human knowledge and then denies almost any possibility that it could really be limited.

And it surely must have been a slip to declare, "the eucharist is not itself a meal" (2413). Certainly it is a sacred meal. It is also a sacrifice, a communion, and a sacred presence of Jesus.

Again, the statement "revelation makes known to us the state of original justice in which man and woman lived before they sinned" (1213) needs to be interpreted in the light of biblical criticism.

The deliberate change of the word *subsists* to *exists* in the passage from Vatican II's "Dogmatic Constitution on the Church" is bound to cause consternation among ecumenists (1736). This is especially true since only after lengthy and serious discussion did the council declare: "This church [of Christ], constituted and organized in the world as a society, subsists in the Catholic Church" (no. 8).

Classical theology distinguishes two aspects of faith: faith as a relationship with an all-loving God and faith as an assent to truths revealed by God. In most of the stories in the New Testament, Jesus stresses faith in the one God and faith in him. He also calls for an assent to the truths that he reveals. Central to catechesis is the response. There is a body of doctrine, of course. Catechesis especially aims at response of faith in God—Father, Son, and Spirit—faith that is mature and comes from the depths of one's being. We must never give the impression that catechesis is simply a matter of handing on a body of information, or that it tends only to the assent of the truths revealed.

There is some confusion in the provisional text on this point. If it is to be a compendium of truths, declared by the church as doctrines of the faith, a much simpler document is called for, something like the section of the *National Catechetical Directory* called "Principal Elements of the Christian Message." If it includes theological positions that are open to change, which the provisional text clearly does, it needs to allow for other legitimate theological expressions.

Unity or Uniformity

Bishops are teachers and guardians of the faith. There is confusion among many Catholics, even among priests, about what we believe as Catholics. "So much has changed," I hear them say. "What has not changed?" The *Catechism for the Universal Church,* in emphasizing the creed, sacraments, commandments, and the Our Father, reminds us of the central content of our faith. It is meant to be a means toward greater unity.

There is a danger, however, that we confuse unity with uniformity. As one, holy, catholic, and apostolic church throughout the world, we are united in our faith with our Holy Father, the pope. At the same time, there is room in the church for cultural expressions of the one faith and the application of our faith to different human circumstances. The provisional text of the catechism does not fully appreciate the role culture plays in the expression of the one faith. Unity can be achieved, indeed is enhanced, by a pluralism of expressions.

One obvious example of this is the use of language. The present draft is oppressively sexist in its language. Such language is not of faith; rather, it arises from a prevailing culture. There is no excuse for sentences like "The single end of the practice of the moral life is to lead each man to become what he is," or "Moral responsibility constitutes the greatness of man" (3803–4). Surely we could come up with something better than "Faith is man's response to the God who reveals himself and gives himself to him" (0101). One could site hundreds of similar examples.

Religious education materials in this country could not include statements framed in such language. Consultation with knowledgeable persons on this issue would greatly improve the text without in any way compromising the unity of the faith.

One other time the bishops of the United States expressed a desire to have a uniform manual for the whole country rather than use the different ones brought here by various immigrant groups. The project was discussed at the Third Plenary Council of Baltimore in 1884. After the council, the catechism was prepared in a few weeks by one person who compiled it from existing texts. It was approved by Archbishop James Gibbons as the *Baltimore Catechism*.

Considerable criticism of the catechism arose immediately after its appearance. A committee of bishops was appointed in 1895 to revise it, but no action was taken. Imperfect as the *Baltimore Catechism* was, an attitude prevailed for a long time that it was important to have a uniform text for the whole country. That attitude was so strong that the little catechism was not revised until the 1940s.

This *Catechism for the Universal Church* is to be a guide for the composition of instructional materials all over the world. We do disservice to the unity of the faith if we give the impression that one theological expression of the truths of faith is sufficient or that all theological issues are now solved.

Consultation

Individual bishops were given until May 31, 1990, to recommend any changes in the provisional text. The most important contribution that American bishops can make to the writing of the *Catechism for the Universal Church* is to share their experience with consultation. Bishops of this country know how important it is to consult with others in developing church documents. Consultation does not diminish the truths of faith. Greater clarity of expression can result from consultation. Other people, including theologians, Scripture scholars, liturgists, social justice activists, and regular parish members see implications that we as bishops just do not have the experience or background to see. Wide consultation also prepares people to receive and own the final document.

In the development of the 1972 pastoral letter "To Teach as Jesus Did," in the enormous project of compiling the *National Catechetical Directory*, and in the writing of the pastorals on peace and economics, the American bishops found that such documents are more effective if people participate in their development.

The *National Catechetical Directory* took six years to complete and involved several drafts. There were national, regional, and diocesan consultations that generated hundreds of thousands of written interventions. After a dozen years, it continues to be a practical guide for religious educators and a sourcebook for textbook writers.

Five short months does not give enough time for individual bishops to conduct even a minimal consultation on the catechism. A preliminary reading of the provisional text indicates that major changes are needed.

Any real consultation within the National Conference of Catholic Bishops should take a year or more. Without the involvement of the whole conference, bishops will feel isolated and alone in their individual efforts. The short consultation time allowed only the minimal involvement of an ad hoc committee of bishops and no discussion by the full body of bishops. This gives the appearance of collegiality without the reality.

The catechism project has to be taken seriously by every bishop. Bishops need to find ways to listen to catechists, parents, priests, teachers, a broad range of professionals, and people in the pew.

Each bishop needs to say to the Commission for the Catechism, "Slow down; consult broadly; give us more time to consult pastors and lay people. The *Catechism for the Universal Church* can then be expressed in language that people can understand, mistakes can be avoided, and people will be prepared to receive it when it is finally published." Otherwise, the whole project can surely fail.

Notes

Introduction

1. *Catechism for the Universal Church* (Vatican City: Libreria Editrice Vaticana, 1989). All references to the catechism in this book are by paragraph numbers.
2. *General Catechetical Directory* (Washington, D.C.: U.S. Catholic Conference, 1971).
3. *Sharing the Light of Faith: The National Catechetical Directory for Catholics of the United States* (Washington, D.C.: U.S. Catholic Conference, 1977).
4. Synod of Bishops, "The Final Report," *Origins* 15 (December 19, 1985): 448. See also Thomas J. Reese, "Extraordinary Synod," *America* 153 (December 14, 1985): 415–16, and "Synod Relaunches Vatican II," *America* 153 (December 21, 1985): 437–38; Berard Marthaler, "The Synod and the Catechism," in *Synod 1985: An Evaluation*, ed. Giuseppe Alberigo and James Provost, *Concilium* 188: 91–98.
5. The other members of the commission are Cardinal Antonio Innocenti, prefect of the Congregation for the Clergy; Cardinal Jozef Tomko, prefect of the Congregation for the Evangelization of Peoples; Cardinal D. Simon Lourdusamy, prefect of the Congregation for Eastern Churches; Archbishop Jan Schotte, secretary general of the synod of bishops; Archbishop Jerzy Stroba of Poznan, Poland; Greek Melkite Archbishop Neophytos Edelby of Alep, Syria; Archbishop Henry Sebastian D'Souza of Calcutta, India; Coadjutor Archbishop Isidore de Souza of Cotonou, Benin; Bishop Felipe Benitez Avalos of Villarrica, Paraguay.
6. The editorial or drafting committee was composed of Bishop José M. Estepa Llaurens, military ordinary for Spain; Bishop Jean Honore of Tours, France; Bishop Alessandro Maggiolini of Carpi, Italy; Bishop Jorge Medina Estevez of Rancagua, Chile; Bishop David Konstant of Leeds, England; Archbishop William J. Levada of Portland, Ore.; Archbishop Estanislao Esteban Karlich of Paraná, Argentina. Rev. Christophorous von Schönborn, O.P., was named secretary of the drafting commission. The names of the forty consultors have not been made public.
7. Secretariat for the Catechism for the Universal Church, "Explanatory Note to the Provisional Text" (Vatican City, [November 1989]), 2.
8. Joseph Ratzinger, "Toward a Universal Catechism or Compendium of Doctrine," *Origins* 17 (November 5, 1987): 382.
9. "Report of the Ad Hoc Committee on the Catechism for the Universal Church," (Washington, D.C.: National Conference of Catholic Bishops, March 1990); reprinted as "Ad Hoc Committee Report on the Universal Catechism," *Origins* 19 (April 26, 1990): 773–84.
10. Early versions of some of these papers were published in *America*, March 3, 1990, and *Commonweal*, March 9, 1990. Copies of these articles were sent to all the U.S. bishops and to episcopal conferences around the world. For news accounts of this symposium, see the *Tablet* of London, February 28, 1990; the *Boston Globe*, January 30, 1990; the *National Catholic Reporter*, February 9, 1990; Catholic News Service, January 29, 1990; Religious News Service, January 29, 1990; and an Associated Press story in the *Los Angeles Times*, January 27, 1990.

11. Russell Shaw, "How Not to Write a Catechism," *National Catholic Register,* April 29, 1990. Also see Russell Shaw, "Look at Universal Catchism Reveals Shortcomings," *Our Sunday Visitor,* March 18, 1990.
12. Michael D. Schaffer, "Vatican Document is a Draft of Division," *The Philidelphia Inquirer,* March 25, 1990.
13. Nicholas Lash, "Concerning the Catechism," *The Tablet* 244 (March 24, 1990): 406.
14. Shaw, "How Not to Write a Catechism."
15. For a defense of the catechism by Christophe Von Schönborn, O. P., the secretary to the drafting commission, see Hans Rahm, "The Defense Replies," *30 Days,* May 1990, 13–15.

The Catechism Seen as a Whole

1. John XXIII, "Pope John's Opening Speech to the Council," in *The Documents of Vatican II,* ed. Walter M. Abbott, S.J., and trans. Joseph Gallagher (New York: America Press, 1966), 715.
2. Berard L. Marthaler, *Catechetics in Context: Notes and Commentary on the General Catechetical Directory* (Huntington, Ind.: Our Sunday Visitor, 1973), xvi–xxx.
3. *Nicene and Post Nicene Fathers,* vol. 2 (Grand Rapids: Eerdmans, 1957), 473.
4. *Nicene and Post Nicene Fathers,* vol. 1 (Grand Rapids: Eerdmans, 1966), 238.
5. Thomas Aquinas, *In duo praecepta caritatis et in decem legis praecepta, expositio,* prol. 1, ed. Raimondo M. Spiazzi, nos. 860–61, p. 193. Quoted in A. Etchegaray, *Storia della catechesei* (Ancona: Edizioni Paoline, 1965), 199.
6. Another anomaly is exemplified in paragraphs 2306–8 explaining differences between East and West regarding sacramental practice. Although one is led to believe by the fact that these are in small type that they are of lesser doctrinal importance (0023), the differences are highlighted in the summary (2334).
7. "It would involve a dangerous deviation for the faith if the meaning of the word *catechism* came to be reduced to a summary (or compendium) of the formulae which it is necessary to know, say and believe, and if the essence of the task of catechisation consisted of the universal imposition of these formulae." Jean Joncheray, "What 'Catechism' for What 'World,'" in *World Catechism or Inculturation?* ed. Johan-Baptist Metz and Edward Schillebeeckx, *Concilium* 204 (1989): 21.
8. See articles by Jean Joncheray, David Tracy, Johan-Baptist Metz, Emilio Alberich, Peter Schineller, and Peter Rottlander in *Concilium* 204 (1989).
9. *L'Osservatore Romano,* June 28, 1982, 1–8. Reprinted with other texts of John Paul II in Aylward Shorter, *Toward a Theology of Inculturation* (Maryknoll, N.Y.: Orbis Books, 1988), 222–38. For a summary of all his statements on culture through 1984, see *The Church and Culture since Vatican II,* ed. Joseph Gremillion (Notre Dame, Ind.: University of Notre Dame Press, 1985), 223–34.
10. See *Origins* 17 (September 24, 1987): 251–52; (October 8, 1987): 295–98; (October 15, 1987): 305–9, 335–36.
11. Shorter, *Toward a Theology of Inculturation,* 222–38.

The Structure of the Catechism

1. Joseph Ratzinger, "Toward a Universal Catechism or Compendium of Doctrine," *Origins* 17 (November 5, 1987): 381.
2. See J. N. D. Kelly, *Early Christian Creeds,* rev. ed. (New York: McKay, 1972); Henri DeLubac, *The Christian Faith: An Essay on the Structure of the Apostles' Creed* (San Francisco: Ignatius Press, 1986); Catherine Mowry LaCugna, "The First Presentation: The Creed," *Catechumenate* (July 1989): 2–9. For another, less liturgical, tradition of catechesis, see Berard Marthaler's essay in this volume.

3. St. Cyril of Jerusalem, *The Works of Saint Cyril of Jerusalem*, trans. Leo P. McCauley, vols. 61 and 62 of *The Fathers of the Church* (Washington, D.C.: Catholic University of America, 1969-70), or *St. Cyril of Jerusalem's Lectures on the Christian Sacraments*, trans. F. L. Cross (London: SPCK, 1951).
4. *Egeria's Travels to the Holy Land*, trans. John Wilkinson (Jerusalem: Ariel, 1981), 144.
5. See Gerard S. Sloyan, "Religious Education: From Early Christianity to Medieval Times," in *Shaping the Christian Message*, ed. Gerard S. Sloyan (New York: Macmillan, 1958), 3-37.
6. Milton McGatch, "Basic Christian Education from the Decline of Catechesis to the Rise of the Catechism," in *A Faithful Church: Issues in the History of Catechesis*, ed. John Westerhoff and O. C. Edwards, Jr. (Wilton, Conn.: Morehouse-Barlow, 1981), 79-108.
7. Thomas Aquinas, *The Sermon-Conference of Saint Thomas Aquinas on the Apostles' Creed*, trans. Nicholas Ayo (Notre Dame, Ind.: Univeresity of Notre Dame Press, 1989).
8. *The Church's Confession of Faith: A Catholic Catechism for Adults*, trans. Stephen Wentworth Arndt (San Francisco: Ignatius Press, 1987).
9. Marianne Sawicki, *The Gospel in History: Portrait of a Teaching Church/The Origins of Christian Education* (New York: Paulist, 1988), 138.
10. Franz Jozef van Beeck, *God Encountered: A Contemporary Catholic Systematic Theology*, vol. 1 (San Francisco: Harper & Row, 1989), 267. Emphasis in original.
11. *The Living God: A Catechism*, 2 vols. (Crestwood, N.Y.: St. Vladimir's Seminary Press, 1989).

Scripture in the Catechism

1. Enzo Bianchi, "The Centrality of the Word of God," in *The Reception of Vatican II*, ed. Giuseppe Alberigo, Jean-Pierre Jossua, and Joseph A. Komonchak (Washington, D.C.: Catholic University of America, 1987), 117.
2. Ibid., 116.
3. Daniel J. Harrington, "The Jewishness of Jesus: Facing Some Problems," *Catholic Biblical Quarterly* 49 (1987): 7.
4. The catechism distinguishes between quotations from Scripture and references to it (0022). In a rough count of the document's 4,126 paragraphs, there are 1,831 quotations and 1,704 references. So Scripture is used some 3,535 times. Of the 1,831 quotations 284 (or 15.5 percent) are from the Hebrew Bible, many of which are from Genesis or Isaiah; 318 of the 1,704 references (or 18 percent) are from the Hebrew Bible.
5. See Joseph Fitzmyer, *Scripture and Christology: A Statement of the Biblical Commission with a Commentary* (New York: Paulist, 1986), 19. For a fine survey of pertinent ecclesial texts, see Raymond E. Brown and Thomas Aquinas Collins, "Church Pronouncements," in *The New Jerome Biblical Commentary*, ed. Raymond E. Brown, S. S., Joseph A. Fitzmyer, S. J., and Roland E. Murphy, O.Carm. (Englewood Cliffs, N.J.: Prentice-Hall, 1990), no. 72:1-41.
6. See Paul Ricoeur, *Interpretation Theory: Discourse and the Surplus of Meaning* (Fort Worth: Texas Christian University Press, 1976).
7. See James J. Megivern, ed., *Official Catholic Teachings: Bible Interpretation* (Wilmington, N.C.: McGrath, 1978), no. 744.
8. See Helga Croner, ed., *More Stepping Stones to Jewish-Christian Relations: An Unabridged Collection of Christian Documents 1975–1983* (New York: Paulist, 1985), 224.
9. Gerard Sloyan, "The Lectionary as a Context for Interpretation," *Interpretation* 31 (1977): 133.
10. *God's Mercy Endures Forever: Guidelines on the Presentation of Jews and Judaism in Catholic Preaching* (Washington, D.C.: United States Catholic Conference, 1988), no. 19-20. See also Bishops' Committee for Ecumenical and Interreligious Affairs, National

Conference of Catholic Bishops, *Criteria for the Evaluation of the Dramatizations of the Passion* (Washington, D.C.: U.S. Catholic Conference, 1988).

11. See Brown and Collins, "Church Pronouncements," in *The New Jerome Biblical Commentary,* no. 38.

12. National Conference of Catholic Bishops, *To Teach as Jesus Did: A Pastoral Message on Catholic Education* (Washington, D.C.: U.S. Catholic Conference, 1973), no. 44.

13. See J. P. M. Walsh, "Contemporary English Translations of Scripture," *Theological Studies* 50 (1989): 336–58.

God in the Catechism

1. *L'Osservatore Romano,* September 21, 1978, 2.
2. Karl Rahner, "Christology," *Theological Investigations,* vol. 11 (New York: Crossroad, 1982), 218.
3. John Paul II, *Dominum et Vivificantem,* no. 7, *Origins* 16 (June 12, 1986): 80.
4. John L. McKenzie, *Dictionary of the Bible* (Milwaukee: Bruce, 1965), 841–42.
5. John Paul II, *Dominum et Vivificantem,* no. 15, *Origins* 16 (June 12, 1986): 82.

Jesus Christ in the Catechism

1. Pontifical Biblical Commission, "On the Historical Truth of the Gospels," trans. and commentary by Joseph Fitzmyter, S.J., *Theological Studies* 25 (1964): 386–408.
2. Pontifical Biblical Commission, "Scripture and Christology," trans. and commentary by Joseph Fitzmyer, S.J., *Theological Studies* 46 (1985): 407–79.
3. John Paul II, *Redemptor Hominis* (Washington, D.C.: U.S. Catholic Conference, 1979), no. 7.
4. Karl Rahner, "Current Problems in Christology," *Theological Investigations,* vol. 1 (Baltimore: Helicon Press, 1961), 149–200.
5. Saint Cyril of Jerusalem, *Patrologia Graeca* 75, ed. Jacques-Paul Migne (Paris: Minge, 1857–94), 369.
6. "Pastoral Constitution on the Church in the Modern World," in *The Documents of Vatican II,* ed. Walter M. Abbott, S.J., and trans. Joseph Gallagher (New York: America Press, 1966), 221.

The Church in the Catechism

1. Avery Dulles, S.J., *Models of the Church* (Garden City, N.Y.: Doubleday, 1974; expanded ed., 1987).

The Liturgy and Eucharist in the Catechism

1. Vatican Council II, *The Conciliar and Post-Conciliar Documents,* ed. Austin Flannery (Collegeville, Minn.: Liturgical Press, 1975), 569.

The Sacraments in the Catechism

1. Sacred Congregation of Rites, *"Instructio de Cultu Mysterii Eucharistici,"* Enchiridion Documentorum Instaurationis Liturgicae, vol. 1, ed. Reiner Kacyznski (Rome: Marietti, 1976), 904. See *Presbyterorum Ordinis,* nos. 5–7.
2. "Christian Initiation: General Introduction," par. 1, in *Rite of Christian Initiation of Adults* (Chicago: Liturgy Training Publications, 1988).
3. See Enrico Mazza, *Mystagogy: A Theology of Liturgy in the Patristic Age,* trans. Matthew O'Connell (New York: Pueblo, 1989).

4. For some thoughts pertinent to a contemporary mystagogy, see Aidan Kavanagh, "Theological Principles for Sacramental Catechesis," *The Living Light* 23 (1987): 316–32.
5. "General Introduction," in *Pastoral Care of the Sick: Rites of Anointing and Viaticum* (Collegeville, Minn.: Liturgical Press, 1983), nos. 1–7.
6. *Pastoral Care of the Sick,* pp. 5–9.
7. *In persona Christi capitis* is from *Presbyterorum Ordinis,* no. 2, though the reference is not given. *In persona Christi* is cited with reference to *Lumen Gentium,* nos. 10 and 28, and *Sacrosanctum Concilium,* no. 33. *Nomine totius ecclesiae* is cited with reference to *Lumen Gentium,* no. 10, and *Sacrosanctum Concilium,* no. 33.
8. "Although closely linked with the human condition, sickness cannot as a general rule be regarded as a punishment inflicted on each individual for personal sins." "General Introduction," in *Pastoral Care of the Sick,* no. 2.

Prayer in the Catechism

1. *A New Catechism: Catholic Faith for Adult,* trans. Kevin Smyth (New York: Crossroad, 1984). The original edition, *De Nieuwe Katechismus* (1966) was commissioned by the hierarchy of the Netherlands and produced by the Higher Catechetical Institute at Nijmegen.

The Moral Vision of the Catechism

1. The term *root metaphor* has been a commonplace in Christian ethics since H. Richard Niebuhr's *The Responsible Self: An Essay in Christian Moral Philosophy* (New York: Harper & Row, 1963). See especially "Appendix A: Metaphors and Morals," 149–60. He shows how three different "root metaphors" lie behind the three basic conceptions of the moral life: the agent as "maker" (teleological ethics of values and goals), the agent as "obedient citizen" (deontological ethics of rules and principles), and the agent as "responder" or "answerer" (the ethics of responsibility that Niebhur sees as encompassing the other two and being a more adequate model for our time).
2. For a more accurate account of Jesus' complex relation to the Law, see Wolfgang Schrage, *The Ethics of the New Testament,* trans. David E. Green (Philadelphia: Fortress, 1988), 46–68.
3. See Joseph A. Fitzmyer, S.J., "Pauline Theology," in *The New Jerome Biblical Commentary,* ed. Raymond E. Brown, S.S., Joseph A. Fitzmyer, S.J., and Roland E. Murphy, O.Carm (Englewood Cliffs, N.J.: Prentice-Hall, 1990), 1407.
4. Joseph Ratzinger with Vittorio Messori, *The Ratzinger Report* (San Francisco: Ignatius Press, 1985), excerpt in Roland P. Hamel and Kenneth R. Himes, O.F.M., *Introduction to Christian Ethics: A Reader* (New York: Paulist, 1989), 372.
5. Karl Rahner, *The Shape of the Church to Come,* trans. Edward Quinn (London: SPCK, 1974), 68.
6. Richard A. McCormick, *The Critical Calling: Reflections on Moral Dilemmas since Vatican II* (Washington, D.C.: Georgetown University Press, 1989), 202.
7. Thomas Aquinas, *Summa contra Gentiles* 3, 122.
8. *Schema constitutionis pastoralis de ecclesia in mundo huius temporis: Expensio modorum partis secundae* (Vatican City: Vatican Press, 1965), 37–39. Discussed admirably in McCormick, *Critical Calling,* 14–23.
9. John Mahoney, S.J., *The Making of Moral Theology: A Study of the Roman Catholic Tradition* (Oxford: Clarendon, 1987), 330.
10. John R. Donahue, S.J., *The Gospel in Parable* (Philadelphia: Fortress, 1988), 17.

Social Morality in the Catechism

1. Synod of Bishops, "Message to the People of God," *Origins* 7 (November 10, 1977), no. 10.
2. For a fuller treatment of the use of Scripture in the catechism, see the essays of Mary C. Boys and William C. Spohn earlier in this volume.
3. Joseph Ratzinger, *Church, Ecumenism and Politics: New Essays in Ecclesiology,* trans. Robert Nowell (New York: Crossroad 1988), 216.
4. Ibid.
5. For a fuller discussion of this point, see my "Fundamental Theology and the Christian Moral Life," in Leo J. O'Donovan and T. Howland Sanks, eds., *Faithful Witness: Foundations of Theology for Today's Church* (New York: Crossroad, 1989), 167–84.

Sex, Gender, and Bioethics in the Catechism

1. "The practical reason . . . is busied with contingent matters, about which human actions are concerned; and consequently, although there is necessity in the general principles, the more we descend to matters of detail, the more frequently we encounter defects." Thomas Aquinas, *Summa Theologiae,* 1-2, q. 94, a. 4; see also 1-2, q. 91, a. 3.
2. Herbert Doms, *The Meaning of Marriage* (New York: Sheed and Ward, 1939; originally published in German in 1935); and Dietrich von Hildebrand, *Marriage* (New York: Longmans, 1942; originally published in German in 1929).
3. The series was published in three volumes: John Paul II, *Original Unity of Man and Woman: Catechesis on the Book of Genesis* (Boston: Daughters of St. Paul, 1981); *Blessed Are the Pure of Heart: Catechesis on the Sermon on the Mount and Writings of St. Paul* (Boston: Daughters of St. Paul, 1983); *Reflections on Humanae vitae: Conjugal Morality and Spirituality* (Boston: Daughters of St. Paul, 1984).
4. The theological debates about when in the process of gestation "ensoulment" occurs continued into the twentieth century. Clear statements about the full protectability of the embryo from conception were finally made by Pius XI, Pius XII, and *Gaudium et Spes.* See John T. Noonan, Jr., "An Almost Absolute Value in History," in John T. Noonan, ed., *The Morality of Abortion: Legal and Historical Perspectives* (Cambridge, Mass.: Harvard University Press, 1970), 39, 44–46.
5. Congregation for the Doctrine of the Faith, *Declaration on Euthanasia* (Boston: St. Paul Editions, 1980), 11–12.

Children and the Catechism

1. "Dogmatic Constitution on the Church," in *The Documents of Vatican II,* ed. Walter M. Abbott, S.J., trans. Joseph Gallagher (New York: America Press, 1966), 47–50 (no. 25).
2. "Error manifeste habet rationem peccati," St. Thomas Aquinas, *De malo,* 3, 7, c. See also *De veritate,* 17, 4–5.
3. "Dogmatic Constitution on the Church," in *The Documents of Vatican II,* 48.
4. Charles Curran, "Public Dissent in the Church," *Origins* 16 (1986–87): 178–84; "Authority and Dissent in the Church," *Origins* 16 (1986–87): 375–76; Avery Dulles, S.J., *A Church to Believe In* (New York: Crossroad, 1982), 118–32; "Authority and Conscience," *Church* (Fall 1986): 8–15; David Fitch, S.J., "Curran and Dissent: The Case for the Holy See," *America* 156 (1987): 341–43, 349–50; Archbishop William J. Levada, "Dissent and the Catholic Religion Teacher," *Origins* 16 (1986–87): 195–200; Archbishop Roger Mahony, "The Magisterium and Theological Dissent," *Origins* 16

(1986–87): 372–75; Richard A. McCormick, S.J., "L'Affaire Curran," *America* 154 (1986): 261–67; "The Search for Truth in the Catholic Context," *America* 155 (1986): 276–81; "Notes on Moral Theology: 1986," *Theological Studies* 48 (1987): 87–105; Ladislas Orsy, S.J., "Reflections on the Text of a Canon," *America* 154 (1986): 396–99; "Magisterium: Assent and Dissent," *Theological Studies* 48 (1987): 473–97; Archbishop Daniel Pilarczyk, "Dissent in the Church," *Origins* 16 (1986–87): 175–78; Francis A. Sullivan, S.J., *Magisterium* (New York: Paulist, 1983), 153–73.

Dulles brings out the complexity of the assent; Orsy and Sullivan mention prudential judgments but do not pursue the point. Levada admits more latitude for dissent from prudential judgments of the hierarchy but distinguishes them from magisterial teaching.

5. See Richard A. McCormick, S.J., "The Search for Truth in the Catholic Context," *America* 155 (1986): 278.
6. "Decree on the Apostolate of the Laity," nos. 11, 30; "Pastoral Constitution on the Church in the Modern World," no. 48; "Declaration on Christian Education," nos. 3, 6–8; "Dogmatic Constitution on the Church," nos. 11, 35, in *The Documents of Vatican II.*
7. "Decree on Ecumenism," in *The Documents of Vatican II,* 352.

Subject and Name Index

Index by References to the Catechism for the Universal Church*

---

* Numbers in parentheses are paragraph numbers in the Catechism. All other numbers refer to page numbers in the Reader.